## Garden Template

I love springtime because it's like a clean slate. Everything around you is coming back to life (myself included). My favorite way to enjoy spring is to garden, so I decided to use spring gardening as my template theme to inspire you to create great...

Daisy

Grass

Tomatoes

Plant marker

Sun

alpha
books

## Template Tips

➤ Trace and cut out of your favorite cardstock/layer with other colors.

➤ For dimension, cut design out of pattern paper.

➤ Trace and color in.

➤ Sponge in for a softer look.

➤ Trace and cut and then layer with different papers.

➤ Add hand-drawn doodles.

## Template Tidbits

➤ Store a piece of cardstock in between templates to keep them from getting tangled.

➤ Store templates in categories according to season.

➤ Store letter templates according to size.

➤ Store a pencil where you store your templates so you won't be scrambling to find one when you're ready to trace.

➤ Use cut-out shapes and trace.

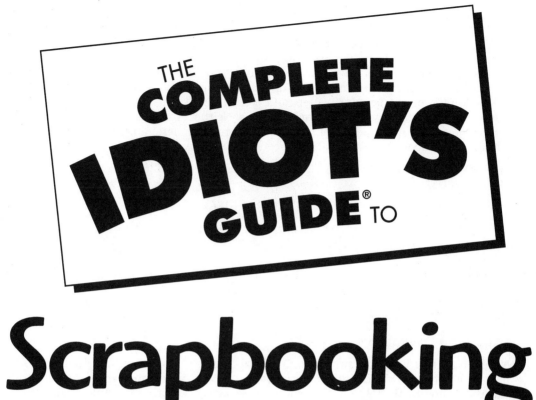

# THE COMPLETE IDIOT'S GUIDE® TO

# Scrapbooking

*by Wendy Smedley*

## alpha books

Macmillan USA, Inc.
201 West 103rd Street
Indianapolis, IN 46290

A Pearson Education Company

# Contents at a Glance

# Contents

# Foreword

I still remember the first time I walked into a scrapbooking store. I wasn't a complete beginner—I'd created scrapbooks as a teenager—but what I saw both astounded and scared me. I loved the piles of paper, rolls of stickers, shelves of albums, and machines for die cutting. What I didn't love was the instant anxiety attack. "Oh no," I moaned. "Where do I begin? I don't want to look stupid." I timidly approached a clerk, who guided me to just the supplies I needed. I felt so grateful, but also like a complete idiot.

I signed up for a couple of scrapbooking classes, where I copied every technique and used only the supplies demonstrated by the instructors. Soon I was ready to see what I could do on my own, and before long I was addicted to scrapbooking. Today it's not only my favorite hobby but my business as well. Still, I'll never forget the anxiety I suffered when starting, and hundreds of scrapbookers have told me they've felt the same way. Just hearing words and phrases like "lignin-free," "acid-free," and "journaling" can scare away even the most enthusiastic novice.

If you're a beginner, you could be saying, "This whole scrapbooking thing is a lot more involved than I expected. I thought it was supposed to be fun." It is! Scrapbooking is one of the most enjoyable, worthwhile hobbies out there. You're making memories for yourself and your family that will last for years. Imagine how delighted someone in the future will be that you took the time and made the effort.

But making these memories takes motivation, preparation, and information. You've already got the motivation or you wouldn't be reading this book. Next comes the planning. The problem lies in not knowing which archival products to buy, how to use them, and how to make them last. That's where this reference guide comes in handy. You'll find everything you need to get you started and keep you going—especially if you're struggling.

If you're beyond the beginning stage, you know it's tough to keep up on all the new techniques and products. Or, maybe you've hit a creative block—we all do—and just need something to give you a jump-start or jolt to help you create a masterpiece. If that's where you find yourself, this reference guide can help you review not only products, but themes, tips, and ideas as well. If you're like me, you can never get enough!

Scrapbooking today is about more than construction paper and edible paste. It's about using the right products to create long-lasting pages your family will treasure. It's about taking memorable photos. It's about writing down your memories—even if you think you have the worst handwriting in the world.

*The Complete Idiot's Guide to Scrapbooking* offers guidance for scrappers on any level. Use it to look up products, terms, or themes. You'll be able to walk into any scrapbook store with confidence. Better yet, you'll be able to create scrapbook pages that will stand the test of time. You can also help loved ones around you preserve their own memories. I've found this as rewarding as preserving my own. Here's to smart scrapbooking!

—Lisa Bearnson

Lisa Bearnson is the editor of *Creating Keepsakes* magazine.

# Introduction

Are you embarrassed by all the photos you have crammed into shoeboxes over the years? Do you cringe when your children ask what their first word was? This is a common experience, so many of us are scrapbooking, recording our lives as we go. Preserving history for the future, creating family unity, and giving ourselves that much-needed creative outlet is what this craft is all about.

It is enjoyed by thousands of people and spans age, race, culture, and taste. You will find something that works for you, and you will be thrilled with the results. So begin this journey with open eyes and remember that something recorded is better than nothing recorded. Set aside some time once a week, a month, or even a year to record your history.

We all have a story to tell. Some choose to tell their story using pictures and only a few words. Others like to write a lot—about the photographs and mementos and how they felt about the images depicted. Some like to focus on family, while others love to make interesting books about special events, travel, or pets. Something most scrappers have in common is that we love to browse in our books and remember back to days gone by. It is important that you tell your story not only for your family, but for yourself.

As you read, make notes in the margins on projects and pages you want to do. If stories or inspiration suddenly hit while you're reading, make a note so you won't forget, and you can include it in your next scrapbook.

## How to Use This Book

To teach the art of scrapbooking in an easy and organized fashion, the book is divided into six parts. **Part 1, "Putting All the Puzzle Pieces Together,"** covers scrapbooking for the newcomer. Maybe you are totally new at this and have no idea what scrapbooking is, or you have an idea or a few pairs of decorative scissors, and you want to know more. Start here to get a taste of the beginnings of this hobby, learn what items you really must have, and how to shop.

**Part 2, "Setting Up Shop,"** is a guide to the vast array of products available to you, not only products that are for general crafting, but also archival supplies that are made specifically for scrapbooking. I'll tell you my favorite ways to use these products, such as decorative paper, pens, cutting tools, and embellishments, and give you numerous ideas to get you excited. After reading this necessary part, you will gain the confidence you need to wander into a scrapbook store, virtual or real.

**Part 3, "Getting Started,"** will help you to begin organizing your materials. This part includes information on creating a workspace that is compatible with your scrapper needs. It also has sections on organizing the treasures you have unearthed on your hunt for old photos and memorabilia and learning about photography, improving your photo taking, and selecting the best film speed for your needs. You'll also see how you can tell your story to be preserved in history and read about ways to incorporate your stories into your scrapbooks.

**Part 4, "Scrap It, Stick It, Store It,"** will help you to move beyond the basics to become a creative scrapper. Although you can make nice books if you only read Part 3, Part 4 helps move you ahead. In this part, you will take a style quiz to define your scrapbooking style, discover ways to create terrific layouts using basic design guidelines, decipher the secret combinations to scrapbooking color success, and get the kids involved. This last part is important because it is one of the things that scrapping is all about—getting close with your loved ones.

**Part 5, "Theme Books and Great Pages,"** is full of ideas for photos, embellishments, and layouts on a variety of themes, like school days, baby's first year, weddings, anniversaries, travel, and capturing the seasons, as well as books that focus on sports and your great pets. Also look here for some alphabets to inspire the creative letterer in you.

Finally, there is **Part 6, "Post-Grad Scrapping."** This part is full of projects for the post-grad scrapper, including gift albums, family cookbooks, and more. Discover some of the great freebies around your house you can use to add zest to your pages. Foolproof border placement ideas, decorative ideas, and terrific projects you can make using all those fun scrapbooking supplies.

# Helpful Hints

This book contains four types of sidebars that offer information about scrapbooking.

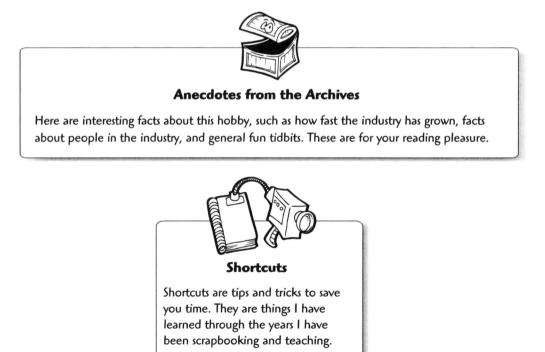

### Anecdotes from the Archives

Here are interesting facts about this hobby, such as how fast the industry has grown, facts about people in the industry, and general fun tidbits. These are for your reading pleasure.

### Shortcuts

Shortcuts are tips and tricks to save you time. They are things I have learned through the years I have been scrapbooking and teaching.

### Sticky Points

These are warnings and places where you could get stuck and stop. Read these points to keep you moving ahead. Learn from the mistakes I have made and have seen others make—I want to save you grief.

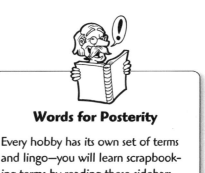

### Words for Posterity

Every hobby has its own set of terms and lingo—you will learn scrapbooking terms by reading these sidebars. With these words under your belt, you'll be able to walk into the scrapbooking world with confidence.

# Acknowledgments

The summer of 1996 found me searching for a small break from my challenging life, and I started out as a part-time cashier at a scrapbook store. Three years later, I am completing this book, and I have many people to thank. First, thanks to those who gave me a chance and saw in me a scrapbooker: Bridget Server, Brenda Birrell, Kim Cook, and Sandy Tippetts, all of my employers. Thanks to Barbara Tanner, Kim McCrary, Susan Nelson, and many others in the business who supported me (and put up with my attempts at humor). A special thanks to Heartland Paper Co. for letting me use their facilities to photograph products and scrapbooks, and all of my friends there who have encouraged me.

Behind the scenes my husband has been spurring me on, encouraging me, and listening to my scrapbook anecdotes; thank you, Kent, for your faith in me and in this project—I love you.

To my sister, Laurie, who discovered my voice and whose talents are unmatched in writing as she worked endless hours with me on this project.

My four beautiful children inspire me every day to see the good parts of life and to be more creative. I started out scrapbooking because I wanted to capture the fleeting moments of their childhood—I look back a few years when they were babies, and I can't believe how much they have grown. I am so proud of you, and I love you, Taylor, Justin, Jacob, and Nathan.

Thanks to my family and friends who have seen my potential even when I haven't been able to. To my mother and father who taught me the joy of work and the love of family, thank you for all of your encouragement and support. Thanks to my sisters, who are my best friends and accept me for who I am and still want to hang out with me. I am so proud of my younger brother, Shawn, who has become a self-made man; your efforts inspire me. To my older brother, whose untimely death changed me forever and gave me the ability to be more compassionate and loving. You are the writer, and your writing has always inspired me—I miss you. To Frank and Kay—thank you for always asking me how it is going and for the endless hours you spend caring for and loving my children.

Thanks to my dear friend Jill who has always been there for me: encouraging me, supporting me, and making me laugh.

Thanks to my other dear friend, Phil Jacobsen. His dedication to writing has always encouraged me. Of course, thank you Phil for the digital photography you did for this book; this project would not be nearly as interesting without your talent and eye.

Special thanks to Stacy Julian, the technical editor, for having faith in me; she has spurred me on through this project more than she knows. Thank you, Stacy.

And a big thank you to artist Yvette Dyer for the beautiful graphic design work on this book (and for getting stuff to me so quickly!). The work wouldn't have been completed on time without the last-minute efforts of Nikki and Roxanne Maw—thanks for your lettering and creative help. Also, a thank you to Sandy Tyson and Sharesse Russon, and to Laura Layton for help with the lettering.

To Jessica Faust, my Acquisitions Editor at the beginning of this project, thank you for the chance.

Much thanks to Tamar Smith, the Development Editor, for her inspiration and hard work on this project. Thank you for your patience and helping to make this a reality.

Special thanks go to Laurie Dyer, who assisted me with rewrites, fact-finding, and editing. Laurie is a freelance writer living in Bountiful, Utah, with her husband, Eric, and their two children. She writes regular columns for *PaperKuts* magazine and several regular newsletters as well.

I contacted countless manufacturers, industry experts, and retailers—thanks for your time answering questions and sharing information about this fascinating world of scrapbooking. Thanks to the following companies for so generously sharing their products with me:

| | |
|---|---|
| Cock-a-Doodle Designs | In My Mind's Eye |
| Creating Keepsakes | Paper Adventures |
| Crop In Style | Provo Craft |
| Fiskars | Quick Cuts |
| Handmade Scraps | Sticker Planet |
| Hot Off The Press | Tie Me To The Moon |

# Trademarks

# Part 1
# Putting All the Puzzle Pieces Together

*It's a common misconception that you have to be an artist to scrapbook. "I love scrapbooks," my friend Teri told me, "but they never turn out the way I want them to. I guess I'm just not artistic enough." The truth is, anyone with the right tools can create a beautiful, one-of-a-kind scrapbook!*

*In this section I'll introduce you to the trend of scrapbooking, and explain why it's so popular. Why do people do it? How did it begin? What do you have to have to start? Let's begin this journey together.*

# Chapter 1

# What Is Scrapbooking, Anyway?

## In This Chapter

➤ Tap your creative juices by scrapbooking (and you don't have to be an artist)

➤ Scrapbooks help us remember the past, keep us connected with family—and lead to cleaner closets!

➤ Kids and family members will have fun making scrapbooks together

The urge to collect and display mementos is something people love to do, and people have been making scrapbooks for ages. With items such as scotch tape, rubber cement, and even flour paste, they compiled books and books of photographs to pass on to their families.

In the last ten years, scrapbooking has become even more popular. Some crafting experts predicted that scrapbooking would soon fizzle out, but they were wrong! In fact, the Hobby Industries Association recently estimated that in 1998, $250 million dollars were spent on scrapbooking supplies. Scrapbook stores are cropping up all over the country. Scrapbookers (the majority of them women) are taking classes, attending workshops, and going on scrapbooking retreats. So many new products have been created for use in scrapbooks—such as acid-free paper, pens, and adhesives—that it is easier than ever to do.

This chapter is all about scrapbooks; what they are and the reasons people enjoy this hobby. Whether you are a stay-at-home parent with a house full of kids, a single person living with roommates, or a newlywed with pets, read on to find out why scrapbooking is for you.

# What's Your Story? Tell It with Scrapbooking

"What exactly is scrapbooking?" my neighbor asked me when I told her I was a scrapbook teacher. "Why would I have to take a class or go to a special store? I've been making scrapbooks since I was in grade school." I explained that modern scrapbooking is similar to the scrapbooking we grew up with but now uses better materials and new techniques. I convinced her to come to one of my classes, and after that, she was hooked. She is so excited about it that she keeps all her scrapbooks up to date, devotes one day a week to scrapbooking, and has a special table set up in her laundry room.

### Words for Posterity

Modern scrapbooks are much more than photos and clippings. A **scrapbook** is an artfully arranged collection of photographs, memorabilia, and journaling that's fun to look at.

### Words for Posterity

**Journaling** is just a fancy word for writing. Journaling is used to describe any words you write in your book, from titles and captions to long descriptions, poems, or stories.

When guests visit my home, I love to show my latest scrapbooking pages. "Your books are so cute, but that's too much work," one of these visitors told me. It can be time-consuming if you let it, but frankly, if scrapbooking feels like work, you probably aren't using the right products. Scrapbooking is supposed to be a fun way to preserve photos, certificates, and other memorabilia.

One of my favorite things about teaching scrapbooking is getting a chance to look at other people's scrapbooks. I've learned that scrapbooking appeals to a wide variety of people and that scrapbooks are as individual as those people. I've seen a variety of scrapbooks, ranging from scrapbooks with more journaling than photos, scrapbooks with no extras other than clip art, even scrapbooks with no photos—just certificates, newspaper articles, and journaling. All of these were appealing, informative, and told a story. And while the books differed greatly in style and format, they were created with archival products to ensure that they will be around for many generations to come.

Most people who start scrapbooking quickly become passionate about it, filling more and more pages. As a scrapbooking teacher, I have taught many beginners and seen their enthusiasm grow. When I ask my students why they like to scrapbook, I get the same answers over and over: "Scrapbooking is my creative outlet. It's the one thing I do that is artistic." Or, "I want to preserve my history." Or, "I'm concerned about the erosion of the family unit. Scrapbooking is a way to keep my family connected."

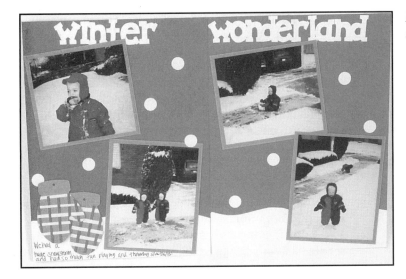

*Here is an example of a scrapbook page.*

### Anecdotes from the Archives

Hobby Industry Association is a New Jersey–based, international trade association. The association was founded in 1940 and now has over 4,000 member companies. Because all employees of a member company are members of HIA, the association is the world's largest in the craft and hobby industry, representing hundreds of thousands of industry members.

# Preserving the Past

Until now, long-term storage methods weren't available for the average person. With all the recent technological advances, it's now possible for anyone to take up scrapbooking with a minimal investment of time and money. You can make a scrapbook as simple or elaborate as you like. But regardless of how much or how little you do, you are preserving a portion of history.

My sister is a pack rat. Among many other artifacts from her childhood she has her baby blanket, three sets of miniature toy animal families, seventy-three notes from her high school friends, the gift wrap that enclosed the first Christmas present she got from her first boyfriend, and the dead roses from her first corsage. When asked why she has so many things like this, she replied, "I just want to remember what it was like when I was growing up."

**Shortcuts**

Do you own your mother's wedding dress, your grandmother's quilt, or your great uncle's cello? Try photographing it and writing the history behind it in your scrapbook. That way, even if the item is in storage, you can still display it.

**Words for Posterity**

**Genealogy** is the study of the descent of a person, family, or group from an ancestor. Some people are interested simply in creating a family tree, and others delve deeply into the history and characters in their family's past. Either way, researching your family's history can be a fun and exciting project.

Like my sister, most people want to hold on to some cherished objects from their past. Early American immigrants often lugged china, jewelry, and other heirlooms to the United States from their homelands. I have a great grandmother who insisted on bringing a piano across the plains in a covered wagon. We all want to keep tangible reminders of our lives, and scrapbooking is an extension of that. We preserve the pictures we have in order to preserve our past. Even though I have never met my ancestors, the stories I have about them give them life and give me a place in that life.

I think all of us need to feel connected. I know that I like to read information about my ancestors. My children, too, enjoy hearing stories of my childhood, as well as stories of their grandparents. For example, my accident-prone son, Taylor, never tires of hearing Grandpa Larry tell the story of when, as a young boy, he broke his leg. Somehow this story comforts Taylor and teaches him that bad things happen sometimes.

# Up a Tree—Researching Your Family History

If you aren't lucky enough to have information on your ancestors, help is out there. Many people have taken up genealogy, the study of the history of a family, and love it.

Why do we want to discover our ancestors? For some people, an interest in genealogy satisfies a desire to solve a mystery, and other people are interested in the medical history of their family, but most people who begin researching their roots simply want to know where they came from—the names of their ancestors, where they immigrated from, and what their lives were like. Most avid genealogists say that there is an excitement in learning about their heritage. Genealogy is the most researched topic on the Internet, and it is a task that consumes hundreds of thousands of people all over the world—you never know what you are going to find out when you start researching.

## Begin the Climb

If you are interested in researching the history of your family, I suggest starting with your family tree (known technically as your pedigree chart.) Take some time to jot down what you already know about your family. Start with the names of your siblings, parents, aunts, uncles, grandparents and, if you know them, your great-grandparents.

After doing this, you may discover that you already know quite a bit about your family's history from stories that you've heard over the years and family heirlooms and keepsakes. Or you may find that there is a great deal to learn. Either way, discovering your roots can be a lot of fun. Remember to enjoy the journey and don't get too frustrated when you can't find that important record or name—learn what you can about your ancestors and record what you discover for others to enjoy someday. Who knows, maybe you'll discover you have some famous, or infamous, relatives from long ago!

### Anecdotes from the Archives

Before people kept written records, the history of a family's genealogy was passed down orally. Without writing, communities and families relied on memory and, the Encyclopedia Britannica notes, they may have used mnemonic systems with knots or beads that indicated who people were, what position they held, and important events.

## Branching Out

Here are some resources for those who are interested in looking into their family histories (for more, see the resource guide at the back of this book).

Try going to the library or bookstore and browsing through their books on the subject—bring some books home to learn the terms and lingo. You will find many books and online sites to get you started researching your family tree:

➤ A great Internet site with over 47,000 links is http://www.cyndislinks.com.

➤ Another very good site is http://www.familysearch.org—this one is so popular that within its first week, the providers had to upgrade it so more people could get access.

In addition, here are two agencies that can supply you with vital genealogical information. For state records, send your written request to:

Superintendent of Documents
Government Printing Office
Washington, D.C. 20402-9325

For federal records, send your written request to:

United States Department of Commerce
Bureau of the Census
Pittsburgh, Kansas 66762

### Anecdotes from the Archives

Coats of arms—symbols on shields depicting the wearer's identity in battle—were used dating back to twelfth-century Europe. They later served as a family's emblem and were often ornamented with helmets, wreaths, crests, and a motto.

## *Families DO Grow on Trees*

People have become so interested in genealogy that some have family trees on display in their homes. I've seen family trees made with fabric, wood, and watercolor. For those of us with humbler talents, several companies sell family trees complete with blanks on which to write the names of your family members. These can even be matted and framed to hang on your wall. They make for a beautiful reminder of your family and where you fit in.

Of course, a family tree that you make or a pre-made one that you fill in can be a wonderful addition to a scrapbook about your family's history. (For more about researching family history, see Chapter 12, "Tell Your Story: Journaling in Your Scrapbook.")

*Here is an example of a simplified family tree chart that is perfect to use in a scrapbook.*

# All in the Family

We are living in an era of technology. It seems as though everyone has a personal computer, one or two cell phones, and a fax machine. Although technology has made our life easier in many ways, it has also taken us away from our families. Keeping up with all this technology takes time, time that we used to spend as families. I think that scrapbooking's popularity is a response to that.

Scrapbooking forces me to slow down and think about the things most important to me. The whole time I am working on my pages, I think about the photos and the stories behind them. The layout I did of my newborn twins brings to mind the jubilation, fear, and love that I felt on the day I brought them home from the hospital. The layout of my mom with my son Justin causes me to think about how much my relationship with my mom has grown since my children were born. My students have similar reactions to their photos. One student came to class with photos of a beloved pet. While putting the pages together, she said, "My cat, Sasha, is like a child to me. Only now she's getting old, and I don't know what I'll do without her." By making a scrapbook of her cat, she can enjoy the memories of her furry family member.

Of course, "family" means different things to different people. I have a husband and four sons, two cats, and a dog (not to mention some goldfish and my boys' latest bug collections). I also have parents and siblings, as well as in-laws, aunts, uncles, and cousins. But a family unit can consist of a single parent and child, a grandparent and grandchild, roommates, a single person and a pet, or any other combination. It's important to maintain family unity in any circumstance. Scrapbooking is a great way to do this. Your scrapbook will reflect the things most important to you, and family is probably high on this list.

## *Sharing Family Memories*

Scrapbooking is something I do that brings me closer to my children. I think it's important for their self-esteem for us to record their accomplishments. My kids love to look at their baby books and tell me who came to see them in the hospital. They take turns looking at their books and love to tell me all about who is in the photo (as if I wasn't there taking the pictures!). Kids gain a great deal of self-confidence when they see that their accomplishments are important enough to be documented in the family album.

I know that even as an adult, I enjoy pulling out my baby books and going through them. It brings back all my childhood memories—good and bad.

**Sticky Points**

Don't overlook the hard times in your scrapbook. Though they may be painful to document, they are still an important part of your life. Be discerning in selecting photos for your pages, though, and try to leave out photos that are disturbing or distasteful.

My favorite childhood photograph is the one of my brothers, sisters, and me in front of the Christmas tree. It was Christmas Eve, and we all had new pajamas. Everyone had

### Words for Posterity

**Memorabilia** is certificates, documents, and other three-dimensional items that tell a story. Memorabilia can include souvenirs from trips, or mementos from special occasions or historical events.

big excited grins on their faces—except my older brother (ten years old at the time). It seems like he was a little embarrassed about the teddy bear jammies my mom gave him. So instead of a smile, he wore a smirk—and never wore those pajamas again! We teased him for years about that photo, and looking at it now, it brings back all my childhood memories.

As adults, we need to remember our roots from time to time. Since I had a happy childhood, I like to go through my albums. It reminds me of what it was like to be a child and teaches me how to treat my own kids. If your childhood was not a happy one, remembering can be a healing process and a way to remind you how far you've come. Whatever the case, creating a scrapbook at any point in your life will give you a surprising perspective.

## Commemorating Family Events

Another reason I enjoy scrapbooking is that it helps me deal with the sad events in my life. When my brother Paul died three years ago, I was bereft and lonely. I turned to scrapbooking as a way to deal with my sadness. Because Paul left behind a five-year-old son, I decided to make a scrapbook for him documenting my brother's life. I included photos of Paul during his childhood all the way up to photos of the two of them together. Although this was the most challenging scrapbook I have made, it brought me great satisfaction. And I know that his son will always have this physical connection to his daddy.

### Shortcuts

Is your bulletin board or refrigerator covered with announcements, drawings, and awards? Instead of tossing everything into the garbage, go through it once a month and save the best drawings. Even things like soccer schedules and party invitations give detail and personality to your scrapbook.

I know that other people who have experienced similar losses like to have a record of their loved one's life. One friend keeps a scrapbook of her deceased mother tucked away in a chest and pulls it out whenever she feels especially down or needs to feel connected to her mother.

Scrapbooks can also become a central place for family memorabilia. You can change junk and clutter into a family history. Instead of tucking certificates into boxes, I like to showcase them in my albums. That way I can look at them whenever I want (and my closets are a lot cleaner!).

It's also a good idea to work on scrapbooks with family members. Yvette's husband, Bob, ran his first marathon last year at the age of 65! To show support, Yvette not only went to the race, she took photos of him at several different points along the way. After she developed the film, she created a scrapbook for him that included his entry form and the number he wore during the race. This is a cherished gift that Bob loves to show off.

*I was working on some pictures from a tree decorating festival in our area and didn't have any accents that would go with the photos until I remembered the program on our fridge—it worked perfectly.*

Don't forget the kids! Although we like to make scrapbooks for them, it's even more fun to give them some materials and let them go to work. Though their creations might not be polished-looking, they are priceless. Kids enjoy making scrapbooks for grandparents and friends, and what schoolteacher wouldn't love a scrapbook page as a year-end gift?

Also, scrapbooks are a great way to stay connected to extended family. If your family is like mine, you've got aunts, uncles, and cousins you rarely see. They may send you Christmas cards every year. Instead of stacking them in the corner or throwing them in the recycling bin, organize them with photos in a separate album. This is the same album you'll use to put photos of the family reunion or other extended family events. This way, you can pull out the photo albums and teach your child who's who.

**Shortcuts**

If you are overwhelmed by the number of photos you have to work with, remember that you can simply use the extra-special ones. Be selective—you don't have to include every picture from the three rolls of film you took at Niagara Falls.

*My oldest son enjoys using the scrapbook supplies—the only rule is he uses them to create pages for his own album. This is one he made when he was five, and my favorite part is his writing.*

**Shortcuts**

Does the idea of compiling a family history seem overwhelming? Try this: Whenever your kids say something memorable, jot it down on your calendar. Now you've got some quotes to go on your scrapbook pages. This won't take much time, and you won't forget all the cute things your kids said.

Of course, if you're lucky enough to have family nearby, you probably have many photos of them intermingled with your immediate family photos. This is great! If you ever move away from each other, you'll have lots of memories. Even if there is a family member you don't particularly like, be sure to include a photo or two of them in your book.

# Letting Your Creative Juices Flow

One reason people don't scrapbook is that they think they are not "artistic." Well, in my three years of teaching scrapbooking, I have not had one artist walk into my class, yet each participant has taken home art. That's because scrapbooking is a skill that is easily learned. There are so many products available today. All you have to do is learn to put them together!

My favorite subject in school was art. I remember the funny smell of the paste and the frustration of those blunt safety scissors. I also remember the joy of creating something beautiful (at least to my young eyes) from nothing more than paper, crayons, glue, and scissors. I enjoyed the process as much as the end result.

Scrapbooking re-creates that feeling. The components are the same, just a little more sophisticated. Now I use acid-free paper, pigment pens, special glue, and decorative scissors, but I am still creating a thing of beauty.

### Anecdotes from the Archives

People like scrapbooking so much that some hotels and spas are offering scrapbooking retreats as a vacation package. One company offers traveling classes and a traveling store. There are even weekend retreats planned for scrapbooking. Check these Web sites for more information about scrapbooking trips: http://members.aol.com/DreamEvnt/index.html, http://www.scrapandspa.com, and http://www.getawaygals.com.

For most of us, creativity is a way to get away from it all. I know that when my twins were six months old and my older boys were three and four, creativity became a priority. I made it a point to get away and scrapbook once a week. It gave me great satisfaction. Not only was I able to take a break from my hectic family, I was creating something for that family. It isn't a matter of having enough time; it's a matter of making time for the things you like to do.

### Sticky Points

Many people give up on scrapbooking before they start because they think it is too complicated; continue through this book, and you will find the information you need to start and feel competent.

Being creative brings self-confidence and satisfaction. Many people do it as a retreat from the hustle and bustle of everyday life. My friend Debbie is going through a rough patch right now, but she always makes time for scrapbooking. "Scrapbooking is my sanity," she declares. "With all the problems I'm having, it's the one thing I do that makes me feel productive." I know many people with similar feelings; no matter what's going on in their life, they find time to scrapbook because they need to.

## The Least You Need to Know

➤ Modern scrapbooks are much more than photos and clippings. A scrapbook is an artfully arranged collection of photographs, memorabilia, and journaling that's fun to look at.

➤ Anyone can create a beautiful scrapbook; make one that reflects who you are.

➤ Scrapbooking is a terrific creative outlet that helps preserve your family history.

➤ The world is moving faster all the time. Scrapbooking is a craft that can help you slow down, reflect, and spend time with family.

# Chapter 2

# Scrapbooking Pioneers and Modern Methods

## In This Chapter

➤ The beginnings of the scrapbooking industry

➤ Why we don't use those magnetic albums anymore

➤ Adapting museum storage techniques for your photos

When was the last time you took a look at your old photo albums? I pulled out my magnetic photo albums 10 years ago, and the pictures were yellowing and faded. I tried to rip them out, but they were stuck! I swore I would never use that kind of album again, but, unsure of my options, I didn't know what to do. I knew that museums preserved artifacts in their storage vaults, but, unfortunately, I didn't have an entire museum at my disposal, and I'm laying odds you don't either.

People have been compiling family histories for years in Bibles and other ways, but these original scrapbooks often fell apart, creating a need for archival products. If you are like most people, you have treasures to preserve, and while they might not be considered valuable to an outsider, they are irreplaceable to you. Luckily, a scrapbooking supply industry has sprung up over the last decade that allows the layperson to take advantage of museum storage and presentation techniques. After all, as scrapbookers, you are just as interested in displaying your photographs as in preserving them.

So before you give up (or build onto your house!), read this chapter. Without turning your house into a museum, you can preserve your pictures and memorabilia while making them easy to view. This chapter gives some background on scrapbooking companies, the tremendous growth of the scrapbooking industry, and archival-quality products that you can find and use easily.

# Scrapbooking Origins

Scrapbooks were probably first made during the Victorian era. Scrapbooks got their names because they were often made from scraps of cloth and printed paper that were collected and pasted into blank books. These books were looked over as we would admire a stamp or coin collection today.

### Anecdotes from the Archives

Many scrapbooking designs now reflect an enduring fascination with the Victorian era. Decoupage, the art of decorating surfaces by applying cutouts and then covering them with varnish, was created during that time and is still done today.

When photography was invented over 150 years ago, people began to compile photo albums, typically using photo corners to adhere them to pages of blank books. In the early years of photography, photographs were most often taken by professionals in a painstaking process. Because film speeds were very slow, people had to pose perfectly still as the camera made its exposure. As film technology progressed, film and cameras became more affordable, and it became common for people to own their own cameras and to collect pictures in albums.

People have also commonly kept journals, diaries, and personal notebooks. Through journals that my own pioneer ancestors kept, I have learned about their struggles and triumphs. Modern scrapbooks are a melding of personal journals, old scrapbooks, and photo albums into one. What is unfortunate about many of the first-person accounts our ancestors kept that have told us so much about life hundreds of years ago is that many of them are faded and crumbling. Many documents that have been invaluable in piecing together information about various historical eras have been lost, even books that were only put together a few decades ago. This is largely because the materials that people used deteriorated and did not stand the test of time.

# First (Preservation) Steps

For a long time, it seemed that you could choose either to display your photographs by placing them in albums or to preserve them by packing them away in various storage containers. Now, because of some innovative companies, we have the techniques to do both.

Modern scrapbooking may have started with a Utah woman named Marielen W. Christensen, who put pictures, mementos, and journals together, though it is likely that others came up with the same idea around the same time. In 1987, two women, Cheryl Lightle and Rhonda Anderson, collaborated to begin a company called Creative Memories. This was the first company to offer photo-storage information and products directly to the consumer.

# "Is Your Paper Lignin-Free?"

After a few scrapbook supply companies raised consumer awareness, other companies became inundated with calls regarding their products. Questions such as, "Is your paper lignin-free?" became commonplace. The craft industry responded tentatively at first with a few products and then made many more as the demand increased. People wanted products that were not only safe for scrapbooking, but attractive too!

Many of the companies that responded were already established in the crafting industry. They made products for rubber stamping and paper crafting. They improved their products to make them appropriate for scrapbookers.

You know a crafting trend has reached major proportions when it has its own magazine, and there are currently several devoted to scrapbooking. Lisa Bearnson started *Creating Keepsakes* with Don Lambson in 1996, and it played a big part in connecting manufacturers with retailers and consumers with products. Another magazine, *Memory Makers*, was created around the same time by Michelle Gerbrandt. These magazines provide you with some great ideas for your scrapbooks, and really keep you up to date with the industry. You might want to pick one up at your local newsstand or even become a subscriber.

**Words for Posterity**

**Lignin** is a substance in paper that breaks down to become acidic over time. Paper with lignin is not suitable for archival projects.

On the heels of the big corporations were many cottage industries. Unlike the big companies that had all sorts of resources, these were companies that were created by people who saw a need and filled it. Most of these self-starters became successful by specializing in one aspect of scrapbooking. One small company was started by two women working on their scrapbooks who thought an oval shape cutter would make their work easier. They teamed up to develop a special tool called the Oval Cropper.

**Words for Posterity**

**Oval croppers** cut paper and photographs into oval shapes. After you determine the size of the oval by moving the blade, you position the cropper on the item to be cut and trim all the way around.

Scrapbooking has come a long way from gluing bits of photographs to paper, and one of the unique things about this craft is how it has been driven by the interests and needs of the people who enjoy it.

### Words for Posterity

**Archival** is a term describing an item that is considered safe for photos and long lasting.

### Words for Posterity

A **conservationist** is someone who makes a career preserving artifacts, artworks, or precious documents. Most museums employ conservationists to look after their works of art.

### Sticky Points

Remember those magnetic photo albums that have the sticky backs and the clear plastic sheet that covers the pictures? Do not use these books as photo or scrapbook albums—the adhesive used contains acid and emits chemicals that damage your photos.

# Keeping It All Safe and Sound

All the new scrapping supplies have one thing in common—they safely preserve photographs and other mementos. According to the American Institute of Conservation, preservation is defined as "the protection of cultural property through activities that minimize chemical and physical deterioration and damage and that prevent loss of informational content. The primary goal of preservation is to prolong the existence of cultural property."

Modern scrapbooking became archival scrapbooking when the pioneers in the industry adapted museum techniques to home preservation. Scrapbookers are indebted to this industry for all the guidelines we now have. Since technical books on archiving are a little complicated for the average person and museum storage spaces are a little big for the average apartment, it's fortunate that conservationists have done all the important research for us. More than the average scrapbooker, conservationists make a career of preserving memorabilia, spending years learning how to restore and care for precious treasures from the past; we have learned a great deal from them.

To protect priceless works of art from damage, museum conservators go to great lengths. Museums take strict measures against damage by light, pests, temperature, humidity, air pollution, and dust. Temperatures are controlled 24 hours a day with humidistatically controlled heating, ventilating, and air conditioning. Special light fixtures are installed to minimize damage by ultraviolet radiation, and because water damage is a major concern, museums are equipped with water alarms.

To keep photos and other paper items in good shape, museums store them in acid-free envelopes or sandwiched between acid-free paper in metal boxes, and most of the photos are matted with acid-free mats. Of course, photographs that are stored this way are rarely viewed, and when they are, it is mostly for research.

That's nice, you're thinking, but what does all this have to do with me? I'm not a professional, and I don't work in a museum. I just want to save a few photos. Obviously, family photos don't lend themselves to such rigorous methods because they are meant to be looked at and enjoyed—imagine your 12-year-old asking for a baby picture to take to school and you refusing to let him because your family photos are encapsulated in metal boxes! Thankfully, archival techniques have been adapted to suit everyday purposes.

As scrapbookers, we are concerned with three things: accessibility to our photographs, photo-safe quality products, and storage for supplies and completed books.

## Stamp of Approval

Initially, products available for archival scrapbooking were acid-free white or cream cardstock and black felt-tip pens. To satisfy the demand for more options—and more attractive options—companies introduced new products. Almost overnight there were so many new papers, stickers, and markers, it was hard to know which were truly safe. To simplify the process of looking for archival-quality materials without mastering museum-standard conservation requirements, the Creating Keepsakes company created a program called "CK OK," a stamp of approval that says the items are okay to be used in scrapbooks. Manufacturers of scrapbooking and craft supplies apply for the seal and submit their products for testing. If the product passes, the manufacturer can carry the CK OK seal of approval. This makes it a lot easier for scrapbookers to know what they are purchasing.

## Smart Storage

Even when you use good archival products, how you store your scrapbooks and photographs is important. These items are sensitive, but with a few simple precautions, they will be around for a long time. Here are few things to keep in mind when storing your scrapbooks.

➤ Moisture distorts and damages photos. If you have water-damaged photos, take them to a professional photo restorer.

➤ Acid causes paper to break down. Many kinds of paper (newspaper, for example) are highly acidic and need special treatment before being used in a scrapbook.

**Words for Posterity**

**Encapsulation** is the process by which a document or photo is surrounded by material to completely protect it from the elements.

**Shortcuts**

Look for the "CK OK" mark on products you buy for your scrapbook. These supplies have been tested and determined safe and long lasting.

**Sticky Points**

Try to wash your hands and have others wash theirs before handling photos; this saves a lot of dirt and oil from transferring from the hands to your pictures.

➤ The oils that are present in your skin are damaging to photos. Always handle photographs by their edges or copy the professionals and wear cotton gloves when handling your photos.

➤ Photographs can be damaged by temperature fluctuations, so keep your scrapbooks in a place where the temperature is fairly consistent, preferably around 75 degrees. Avoid storing scrapbooks in areas with high humidity, such as a basement or attic.

➤ Not only does sunlight fade photos, it discolors cardstock and stickers. Storing your scrapbooks in a dark place is a good idea, and remember to close your scrapbook when you are done looking at it.

## *Easy Access*

The second most important concern for scrappers is accessibility. My friend Susan told me that she had worked on a scrapbook for a year. It was a masterpiece, she said, but she was afraid to let her kids look at it. I had to convince her that scrapbooks are made to be looked at. The way to protect the photographs and other items in your book is to make sure that protective materials are used throughout. As safe as you want to keep the stuff in your book, there's no use going to all that work if you can't look at them when grandpa comes over.

Before they make it to a scrapbook, it's good to organize photos and store them in a photo-safe storage box. (These come in all sorts of cute decorator colors now.) It's also a terrific idea to duplicate photos and send them to faraway friends and relatives. With all of the new technology, photos can now be sent through electronic mail, as well as the good old-fashioned way. Nothing thrills grandparents like receiving pictures in the mail that they can start bragging about to their friends and neighbors.

**Shortcuts**

Kids can get a load of fingerprints on page protectors. To clean them, mist a paper towel with a little of your favorite window cleaner and wipe. The shine will return.

## Leaps and Bounds

Scrapbooking products are now available in most states, and a lot more people know about them. The professionals are taking notice of this hobby and recognize it as a trend, not just a fad. The question is where does it go from here? Hopefully, as many new products become available, prices will be driven downward a bit. This is great for consumers.

How far will this go in other countries? Creative Memories has consultants in Canada, England, and Australia, and with numerous online stores and hundreds of scrapbooking sites, I predict that scrapbooking will continue to grow internationally.

Modern scrapbookers are holding parties that people are calling modern quilting bees—people getting together for social interaction, while creating a lasting heirloom. Scrapbooking is definitely here to stay.

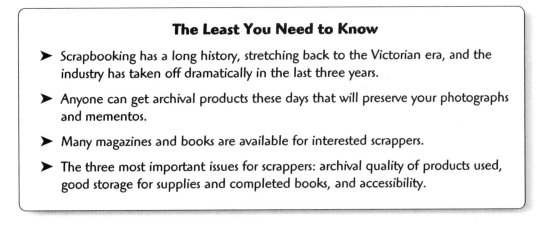

## The Least You Need to Know

➤ Scrapbooking has a long history, stretching back to the Victorian era, and the industry has taken off dramatically in the last three years.

➤ Anyone can get archival products these days that will preserve your photographs and mementos.

➤ Many magazines and books are available for interested scrappers.

➤ The three most important issues for scrappers: archival quality of products used, good storage for supplies and completed books, and accessibility.

# Chapter 3

# Absolute Scrapbooking Essentials

## In This Chapter

➤ Talking the talk—terms for the beginner

➤ How to begin organizing your scrapbooking essentials (without breaking your bank)

➤ Choosing adhesives, writing tools, and protectors

➤ Cardstock—the kind of paper you absolutely must have

Okay, you're convinced you want to scrapbook, and you've developed those dozen rolls of film that had been sitting in your kitchen drawer since last summer. You can't wait to put them into albums and show everyone your creative accomplishments. What now? Before you head out the door ready to buy, buy, buy, slow down and take stock of what you really need.

If you have an unlimited budget, you can go to the store and buy whatever you like without regard to cost. But if you're like me, you need to be careful with your money. This chapter shows what you absolutely must have to start a beautiful scrapbook and the scrapbooking terms with which you should be familiar.

## Scrapbookese: Terms Every Beginner Should Know

If you were to spend an afternoon with fly-fishing fanatics, you would most likely miss much of their conversation. Like many other hobbyists, scrapbookers have their own lingo. The first time I walked into a scrapbook store, I heard so many new terms that I was lost in five minutes. To help you seem like a pro before you have even mounted your first photo, here is a compilation of basic scrapbooking terms you will need to know before you go shopping.

➤ **acid**—A chemically reactive substance often found in paper that fades photographs. Products that are acid free help you preserve your photos and other paper mementos.

➤ **pH level**—This tells you how acidic or basic something is. For scrapbooking, you want to use products that are low in acid and have a pH level of seven or above.

➤ **PVC**—Polyvinyl Chlorides. All you need to know about this is that it is harmful to photographs. You should use products that are composed of polypropylene in your scrapbooks.

➤ **polypropylene**, **polyethylene**, and **polyester**—Stable plastics that are safe for photos. Look for these names on labels of products you purchase for scrapbooks.

➤ **lignin**—A naturally occurring substance in wood that can break down into acids over time. Lignin must be removed from the paper to make it last. An example of what lignin does is the yellowing of newsprint. Newsprint is low-quality paper that contains high levels of acid, as well as lignin. If you leave newsprint exposed to the sun for a few days, you can see how lignin is breaking down into acids because it discolors and becomes brittle.

➤ **acid-migration**—When an item that is acidic comes in contact with another item that is less acidic, the acid can transfer over. This happens when acid from paper, dirty skin, or any item comes in contact with other items, and the acid transfers over.

➤ **buffered**—A term used to describe products that are capable of maintaining the basicity of a solution; in other words, use buffered paper to neutralize acids that migrate from a photo to paper.

➤ **archival**—A designation for products and techniques that will prevent your photos and important documents from fading, deteriorating, and yellowing over time.

➤ **P.A.T. (Photo Activity Test)**—A test created by the American National Standards Institute that determines whether a product will damage photos. If a product passes the P.A.T., it is considered archival and safe to use with your photographs.

➤ **reversible adhesives**—These adhesives can be unstuck. Reversible adhesives are desirable if you think you might ever want to move an item in your scrapbook to some other place.

➤ **CK OK**—Designation given by a company called Creative Keepsakes; CK OK is the scrapbooking industry's equivalent to the Good Housekeeping Seal of Approval.

**Sticky Points**

You can't always tell *if* paper is acid-free by the label, so ask a store clerk for information. Many scrapbooking stores have policies regarding acid-free paper and will go so far as to guarantee that all their paper is acid-free, lignin-free, and buffered. So go ahead and ask!

**Shortcuts**

Why not start a scrapbooking club? If you don't have a store nearby where you can take classes, and you know some people who like to scrap, start meeting together at home or at your local library, or rent a place to meet. Some scrapbooking groups charge monthly dues that are used to buy new products that everyone can use.

### Anecdotes from the Archives

In order to clarify the scrapbooking industry's standard terminology, the CK OK team has written a book called *Saving Our Scrapbooks*, which has an industry-standard glossary.

If you need more details on these terms, check out the resources guide for a list of books. To make sure you feel completely confident in the company of hard-core scrapbookers, you're going to have to learn the following lingo. Do this and you'll really be able to "talk the talk."

➤ **crop**—1. To cut or trim a photo. 2. A gathering of scrapbookers working on album pages and sharing ideas with each other.

➤ **workshop**—A class in scrapbooking usually held at a store and taught by an expert. Participants bring photos and pages to work on and get advice from the instructor.

➤ **page exchanges**—These are fun activities in which participants are invited to create a page to share with up to 10 other scrapbookers. Sometimes, a theme is given, such as a holiday like Halloween. Each participant at a page exchange brings enough copies of an original page to trade with the others and goes home with as many different pages as there are members, as well as the inspiration of their fellow scrapbookers.

➤ **product swap**—If you've got duplicates of products, such as paper or stickers, or some tools that you don't use anymore, such as decorative scissors or paper edgers, gather them together and call some friends. Ask them to bring their unwanted scrapbooking items to trade. After it's done, you've got a clean closet and tons of new products—free!

➤ **scrapbooking club**—Any group of scrapbookers that meet together regularly to encourage each other and compare books. Their main goal is to scrapbook together and share products.

➤ **"pass the chocolate"**—A phrase commonly spoken by members of a scrapbooking club.

➤ **layout**—Grouping of pages in your scrapbook that go together. Most often this is two sides that lay side by side with the same theme, such as "Jacob's gymnastics program."

### Shortcuts

Use a pH testing pen to test the acidic level of paper products. The pen mark changes colors depending on the level of acid present.

Now that you know some of the technical terms and the jargon, you won't be confused when you go into a scrapbook store, open a scrapbooking magazine, or go to an online scrapbook chat room. Last of all is a list of scrapbooking terms that might mean different things to different people. Here is what they mean when I use them in this book:

**Words for Posterity**

An **adhesive** is any substance that is used to make items stick to each other—glue, paste, tape, reversible adhesives, and so on.

**Shortcuts**

Photo corners are a great way to get photos on a page without applying adhesive directly to the photos. See Chapter 9, "Extras: Goodies and Gadgets That Give Your Scrapbook Flair," for information.

**Shortcuts**

Several different weights of cardstock are available. Go ahead and experiment with them to find what you like, but keep in mind that different weights don't make a practical difference.

### Wendy's Lingo

➤ **mount**—Is what you do to your photo when you stick it on another piece of paper.

➤ **double mount**—To stick two pieces of paper together and adhere a photo to the top paper. This is similar to layered mattes in framing.

➤ **embellishment**—This catch-all phrase refers to stickers, die-cuts, and other extras that you add to your page.

➤ **heading**—The title on a page.

➤ **title page**—The page at the beginning of a scrapbook or section, such as Smedley Family Reunion, July 1999 or Kwaanza at Keisha's, December 1995.

➤ **theme**—The overall focus of the scrapbook, such as Family Vacations album.

➤ **Wendy's Wonder List**—Throughout this book, you will find lists of my original scrapbook ideas and favorite uses for products. Feel free to adapt them to your own scrapbooks.

➤ **page**—The bare paper that is the foundation of the scrapbook decorated with photographs, embellishments, and journaling.

➤ **memorabilia**—Items other than photographs that can be included in your scrapbook, such as documents, certificates, artwork, and souvenirs.

# Don't Get Stuck—Choosing an Adhesive

I'm going to confess something here that I don't even like to tell my scrapbooking students: I used rubber cement and scotch tape in the first scrapbook I made for my son! Of course, it was seven years ago, I was a first-time mother, and I had no clue about scrapbooking other than clip art and gluing pictures in. Years later and with much more scrapbook savvy, I know that rubber cement destroys photos, and I now use adhesives that are not only safe for photographs but also affordable and easy to use.

A variety of adhesives exists on the market, and as long as you use one designed for scrapbooking, your photos will be safe. Whether you choose to use glue, tape, or paste is a matter of preference, whatever you find easiest to use and easiest to find. Read on to find out what kinds of adhesives are available.

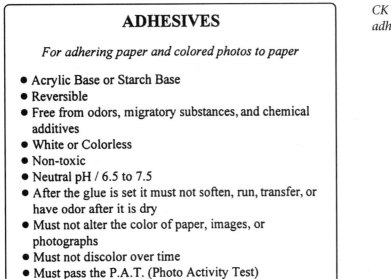

# ADHESIVES

*For adhering paper and colored photos to paper*

- Acrylic Base or Starch Base
- Reversible
- Free from odors, migratory substances, and chemical additives
- White or Colorless
- Non-toxic
- Neutral pH / 6.5 to 7.5
- After the glue is set it must not soften, run, transfer, or have odor after it is dry
- Must not alter the color of paper, images, or photographs
- Must not discolor over time
- Must pass the P.A.T. (Photo Activity Test)

*CK OK guidelines for adhesives.*

*A variety of adhesives is available for safe use in scrapbooks.*

## Singin' the Glues

Glue is available in different styles: There are traditional glue sticks, liquid glue pens, and bottled liquid glue. Some of these are stronger than others, so try out a few and see what works best for you.

**Sticky Points**

People sometimes ask why we don't use lightweight paper in scrapbooks. After all, it would seem to cost less. Of course you can use it, and there are some companies that sell light-weight paper, but heavy paper holds up better, and it doesn't always cost more.

➤ Glue sticks have glue in a stick form. They are a little messy but are reasonably priced and readily available.

➤ If you will be gluing many small objects, a liquid glue pen is a good bet. This type of glue comes in a pen form, and glue is distributed depending on the amount of pressure you apply to the tip.

➤ Bottled liquid glue distributes glue from a narrow tip that makes it easy to use with small items, such as tiny punches, die cuts, and scraps.

➤ Some glue pens come in a two-way adhesive. This type of glue has a very strong bond when it is wet. If you apply it and let it dry before adhering, the bond becomes temporary, meaning you can remove your photos and embellishments if necessary.

## More Sticky Stuff

Tape is my favorite adhesive to use in scrapbooks because it is neat and easy to use. A tape roller with its quick-dispensing capabilities and reversible adhesive is a great choice. You can buy refills for it, which also makes it cost-effective.

Double tape has adhesive on both sides. To use it, simply place the tape on your scrapbook page and stick the photo or embellishment to the other side. Double-stick tape is also available in rolls. Just peel it, tear it, and stick it! Nothing could be easier. Tape is great because it doesn't spill and won't dry out like glue. It is also reversible.

**Anecdotes from the Archives**

The Xyron machine is a popular, though relatively expensive, adhesive option. You run an item through two rollers in the machine, and the machine applies adhesive to one side. Without using heat or electricity, the Xyron can also laminate. You can even create your own stickers with a Xyron! If you plan to do a lot of scrapbooking, consider investing in one.

For precut adhesives, photo splits, sold by the box, are a good option. To use photo splits, simply pull out as many tabs as you need from the dispenser and apply them to your page. Peel off the top layer and apply your photo to the adhesive. That's it!

# The "Write" Tools

Be sure to purchase a few writing, or journaling, tools, because journaling is what makes a cute scrapbook into a storybook. At the very least, you need to record the names and dates of the photo subjects, so read on to discover the different options.

A simple, black felt-tip pen is definitely the best for journaling on your pages. The best tool for writing on the back of photos is a wax or grease pencil, which can be wiped off with a soft cloth, or a special pen called the Pilot Photographic Marker, which is a fine-tip, black permanent pen for use in writing on the backs of photos.

*CK OK pen guidelines.*

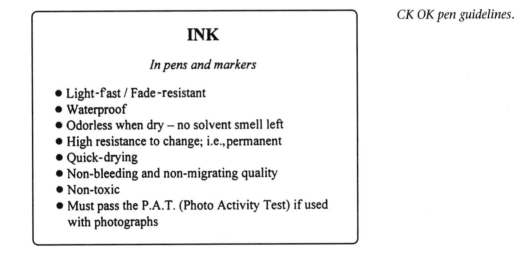

**INK**

*In pens and markers*

- Light-fast / Fade-resistant
- Waterproof
- Odorless when dry – no solvent smell left
- High resistance to change; i.e., permanent
- Quick-drying
- Non-bleeding and non-migrating quality
- Non-toxic
- Must pass the P.A.T. (Photo Activity Test) if used with photographs

# A Little Protection

Unless you consider fingerprints an embellishment, you'll want to keep your pages in protective sleeves. It is satisfying to finish an extra special page and place it in its protector, and page protectors are great because they're easy to move. You can purchase protectors in a couple of forms, from full-page to protectors with sections for photos. These make organizing your photos easy—just slip in the photo, add a note, and you're done. Try giving these protectors to grandparents so they have a place to put all those darling photos you send them.

**Shortcuts**

If you are unsure whether a protector is made with PVC, try the smell test—sniff the product. If it smells like a vinyl shower curtain, don't use it.

### Words for Posterity

**Page protectors**—these plastic sheets are a great way to display and protect your pages. They are available in top- or side-loading styles and come with holes that allow you to place them in a three-ring binder.

### Words for Posterity

**Economy, medium,** and **heavy weight**—these terms refer to the different weights of page protectors available. Economy is lightweight, medium is a bit thicker, and heavy is the thickest.

*CK OK plastic guidelines.*

Protectors are marketed in two different types: clear or nonglare. The nonglare type has an almost matte-like finish that reduces the glare from the page. I like the look of the clear page protectors, but they do tend to show little nicks and fingerprints more than the nonglare type does. This is, of course, a matter of preference, as both are safe for your books. See which you like best!

Page protectors come in three weights: economy, medium, and heavy. Although all are safe for your photos, there is a cost difference. Economy is the cheapest, and heavy costs the most. Again, this is purely a matter of preference and budget. While the heavy protectors look nice, they aren't essential to a good scrapbook. Buy what you can afford.

Do you have a special group of pictures that you don't want to split up? Then try the latest panoramic page protectors—they spread out to show four pages at one time. Try this for your vacation photos that include your oversized photos of the cruise ship you took along with your tickets and itinerary. These are also great to use with the before and after construction photos you took of your renovated house. Pick up a pack of these the next time you are shopping and create some great panoramic pages.

---

## PLASTICS

*For sheet protectors, enclosures, encapsulation*

- Made of plastic – Polypropylene, Polyethylene, Polyester (Mylar D® or Melinex® by Dupont)
- No Polyvinyl Chlorides (PVC) commonly known as "vinyl"
- Clear / Colorless
- Odorless
- Untreated – no coating on side next to photograph emulsion or negative
- Must not crack or break with age
- Must not contain any plasticizers, surface coatings, UV inhibitors, or absorbents and be guaranteed to be non-yellowing with natural aging
- Must pass the P.A.T. (Photo Activity Test)

# Cardstock: Backbone for Your Book

Now that you have the photos, some adhesives, and pens to write about your pictures, you need some paper to put everything on. Here is a rundown of basic mounting paper. For detailed information on decorative paper (you know, the cute stuff), see Chapter 5, "All Paper Is Not Created Equal."

The term "mounting paper" refers to cardstock—the usual choice for scrapbooking. Cardstock works well because it is thick and heavy—sturdy enough to mount all sorts of photos and textiles.

Cardstock is the backbone of scrapbooking. Because it is so sturdy, it holds everything together and is very affordable. Available from 8 to 25 cents a sheet, you can afford to use this paper for everything—from mounting paper to die cuts to borders.

Typically, cardstock is sold in solid colors, as well as marble and parchment styles. Hundreds of colors are available, so even if you can't find the perfect shade of red to match the photo of the brick on your new house, you'll be able to come pretty close!

**Words for Posterity**

**Cardstock** is thick, sturdy paper available in a variety of weights.

**Shortcuts**

When you use lightweight paper, such as a pattern paper, as a background, it is a good idea to slip a piece of cardstock into the protector so the page will be firmer.

*CK OK guidelines for paper.*

---

## PAPER

*For photograph albums, journals, photocopying*

**Papers that come in contact with color photographs:**
- pH 6.5 to 7.5 – not to exceed 8.0
- Alkaline buffered *(although unbuffered is recommended)*
- Lignin-free – 1% maximum
- Colorfast – No fugitive dye
- Must pass the P.A.T. (Photo Activity Test)

**Papers that are used with everything else:**
- pH 7.0 to 9.5
- Buffered with 2% minimum calcium carbonate, magnesium or zinc
- Lignin-free – 1% maximum
- Colorfast – No fugitive dye

# This Pen Has a "pH'D"!

I often find great paper at a craft store, but I'm not sure whether it is acid-free. That's when I use a pH testing pen. With a small stroke of the pen, I can tell if the paper is safe to use. It turns a certain color if the paper is acidic, depending on the brand of pen you have. Another use for it is to see if memorabilia, like certificates and cards, are acid-free and safe to put in your book.

---

### The Least You Need to Know

➤ Make sure to find out whether a specific paper is acid-free and safe to use in scrapbooks. Look on the package label, ask the staff, or contact the manufacturer.

➤ Choose adhesives that you find easiest to use and be mindful of reversibility, in case you ever want to unstick something.

➤ Black felt-tip pens are great for writing in your book, and there are special pens and wax pencils to write on the backs and fronts of photographs.

➤ Protect those pages you worked so hard on with page protectors. They'll keep fingerprints off and make sure that what is glued, pasted, or taped stays stuck.

➤ Cardstock is firm, sturdy paper that comes in a variety of colors and weights—use it for all your scrapbook pages.

---

# Chapter 4

# The Lay of the Land: Scrapbook Stores and Classes

> ## In This Chapter
>
> ➤ What you can expect to find inside one of those scrapbooking stores
>
> ➤ Advice on braving the checkout line
>
> ➤ What types of classes are available, what you should know before you take one, and what you should bring with you

I was overwhelmed the first time I walked into a scrapbook store. I couldn't figure out what all those people were doing buying stationery and fancy paper by the sheet. I thought I was in some sort of deluxe letter-writing place, and I couldn't figure out how to work the die cut machine. Ladies were lined up with paper in hand, holding these wooden things. I was too proud to ask questions, so I turned around and walked out. I finally got brave and recruited a few friends to take some scrapbooking classes with me.

I've come so far that now I teach scrapbooking classes and workshops. I've learned that many new scrapbookers feel the same sense of confusion I did, so before you run to the scrapbooking store (and run right back out), read this chapter to find out what products you can expect to find and how you can get into a scrapbooking class. After this tour of the scrapbooking store, you will be more confident than I was.

## Get to the Source

Where I live in Utah, there are 50 scrapbook specialty stores and over 100 stores that sell scrapbook supplies! For a state with a population of 2 million, that's a huge number (Utah and California are the states where scrapbooking is currently the most popular). Most communities don't have nearly as many of these shops, and it can be a challenge to find stores that sell materials for scrapbooking. Look for a limited but good selection at stores such as Wal-Mart, Target, Michael's, Hobby Lobby, and Fred Meyer. Following are some ways to find these scrapbook stores.

➤ Many of the major scrapbooking companies, such as Frances Meyer, have a locator on their Web site that tells you where their products are sold.

➤ Look in the backs of some scrapbook magazines for store listings.

➤ Word of mouth—do you have a friend who loves to scrapbook? He or she probably has a favorite place to shop.

➤ Internet message boards—post a query.

➤ You often can contact the manufacturers to find out where to find their products.

➤ Visit http://www.creatingkeepsakes.com for a store locator.

## You Better Shop Around

Once you get into a store, you may find that the owners have packed tons of stuff into a very small space. Don't be deceived by a small space; there are still plenty of items for you to look at—and buy.

➤ **Pens**—Most stores carry a huge variety of pens, all set up in different display racks. Pens are most often organized by brand, not type, so if one company doesn't carry a particular type of pen, check a different one. Be sure to test any pens you like on some scratch paper.

➤ **Die Cuts**—Head over to the die cut section. Make sure to look around for a pricing guide. If you can't see one, ask the clerk for help. Die cuts are sold in many different ways—singly, in packs, or mix and match. You can get more for your money if you buy the die cuts in sets, but there is no need to buy a pack of 10 teddy bears if you will use only one or two. Just be sure to avoid surprises by figuring out the pricing system before you head to the cash register.

➤ **Stickers**—Take a look at these. It's likely that there is a price guide nearby. Some of the stickers, like Mrs. Grossman's, have letters on the back that correspond with a pricing key. Some stickers are sold singly, others are sold by the sheet, but most stores insist that once you cut a sticker from the rack, you have to buy it.

➤ **Paper**—If you go to the scrapbook store to pick up a particular pattern or other kind of paper, only to find out that the store no longer carries it, let the clerk know. Often, staff can tell you if they have any more on order or if they've discontinued that pattern. A salesperson may even let you know of other stores in the area that carry that pattern.

➤ **Embellishments**—If you are looking for decorative embellishments, templates, or stickers that focus on a specific theme, such as bowling or hiking, the clerks in the shop can be very helpful. They know the store's inventory, often have a good idea whether they have anything that matches what you need, and can direct you to the product.

➤ **New items**—One of the most fun things to do when you walk into a scrapbook store is to go straight to the display of new items. This is where you can find the latest scrapbooking tools and products. Seeing these can give you motivation and inspiration to try something new.

## Divide and Conquer

If the store is divided into sections by items, you will probably find all of the cardstock together, which is helpful. Two choices are usually available for cardstock—by the sheet or in packs. I recommend buying cardstock by the sheet, except for the colors you know you are going to use often, such as white or black. It is commonly less expensive to purchase cardstock in a pack, but there is always a color in there that you won't use—guaranteed. I still have bright orange and hot pink from a pack I bought (I've used it up by letting my kids make paper airplanes out of it). Purchasing the paper by the sheet is my recommendation.

You will typically find pattern paper and stationery organized by the color or theme. If you need to purchase some pink pattern paper, for example, go right over to the pink section and find what you need. If you need birthday paper, then do the same. The price is often found on the back or on the wall above the paper.

**Shortcuts**

If possible, organize your purchases by product—stickers, die cuts, pens, and so on. This speeds up your check-out process because the cashier won't have to keep pulling out different price charts.

Now that you're loaded down with paper, pens, stickers, and more, it's time to head to the checkout. This can be scary, but remember, you are making an investment in your family.

Not only will the checkout be where you can buy all your supplies, it is often where you'll find information about upcoming events and places to sign up for scrapbooking workshops and classes. Most stores offer calendars with activities and workshops, so be sure to pick one up. If they have a mailing list, put your name on it; you'll be the first to know about any sales and specials.

**Shortcuts**

Some scrapbooking stores offer free basics classes to beginning scrapbookers—find out if your store does and take advantage of it!

# *The Internet Is Your Friend—Online Shopping*

Online shopping is great for those who don't live close to a scrapbooking store or don't have time to visit one in person. From the comfort of your own home, you can browse through all sorts of scrapbooking products. Some of these Web sites feature "shopping carts," which makes it easy to order directly from their sites with a credit card. Or, if you prefer, you can print up an order form, fill it out, and fax or mail it to them.

There are many different online stores. Some feature only one product, such as stickers or pens, while others sell one line of products. You'll discover many hard-to-find items online, so even if you do live close to a scrapbooking store, check out the virtual stores just to see what's out there.

While it is sometimes difficult to tell exactly what you are getting when you see it on your computer screen, most stores offer a product guarantee—if you aren't satisfied with what you purchase, they will give you a refund or exchange.

Here are some of my favorite online general scrapbooking shopping sites:

➤ http://home.earthlink.net/~heartstrings.

➤ www.memories.com—Has everything you need to scrapbook.

➤ www.creativexpress.com—Large selection of craft products.

➤ www.croppingcorner.com—A fun site with layouts, contests, and personal notes from the company updating you.

➤ www.scrapbooks.com—I like this one. They will send you a free catalog and let you order the old-fashioned way if you prefer.

➤ www.stampinscrappin.com—This is another fun site with stamps and other things.

➤ www.heartlandpaper.com—This site's retail store happens to be one of my favorites—especially since I teach classes there.

➤ www.remembermesb.com—This is a fun site to visit, with lots of exciting layouts and user-friendly ideas.

➤ www.thestickerzone.com—This site has loads of fun stickers.

➤ www.stickerplanet.com—Great friendly help.

These are just a few of the online store services. For more, see the resource guide at the back of the book. I suggest looking at some scrapbooking magazines for color photos of some of these products so you can check them out before you buy.

Online shopping tips:

➤ Order with a friend to save on shipping.

➤ Check the sites often for good deals.

➤ Utilize their message and chat boards to find some scrapbooking connections.

➤ If you are always looking for new products, most of these sites list their new items under a special heading.

➤ When you can, shop at non-peak hours to cut down on the waiting time.

➤ Search through the links to find helpful new sites.

➤ Empower yourself as a consumer and send comments and suggestions about what you want—this industry responds well to the consumer.

## Shopping at Your Local Hobby and Craft Store

Even if you are not close to a store that specializes in scrapbooking supplies, your local craft or sewing store will often have some products. Even Wal-Mart and Target carry some products in their craft section, so everyone should be able to find something. The great thing about these stores is their prices! Though they might have a limited inventory, they are reasonably priced.

When you are at a hobby or fabric store, head over to the craft section and see what products they carry. You can usually find lots of prepackaged kits. There might be a birthday kit, for example, that includes stickers, paper, and die cuts, as well as suggestions and instructions. Other popular kits include baby, wedding, vacation, and pet themes. These stores usually carry the basic scrapbooking accessories like scissors, adhesives, and trimmers. Sometimes, stores can special order things for you too—just ask. And many craft stores are beginning to offer scrapbooking classes.

## Shop Smart—Save Time

When shopping for a shirt to match your new blazer, you bring the blazer to the store with you, right? Of course! You can't tell what will match unless you have the item with you. The same holds true for scrapbooking. If you are shopping for a particular shade of orange or red to match the sunset in your photo, by all means, bring the photo with you.

**Sticky Points**

Unfortunately, people who go to the large stores to purchase scrapbook items sometimes find that stock is limited and the aisles are constantly a mess. Try talking with the store buyer to see when they get new shipments so you can get first choice.

**Shortcuts**

Make it a point to speak to the store manager about scrapbooking items and ask whether they are planning on carrying more. This input lets managers know there is a need and may convince them to increase their scrapbooking supplies inventory.

## Efficiency Counts

Many people waste time and money at the scrapbooking store when they shop without a purpose. They wander leisurely through the aisles looking for the perfect item to pop out at them. If you have time and money to spare, this is probably fine. But if you want to be a little more efficient, two methods work for me.

If you live near a scrapbook store and can make frequent trips for items as needed, bring the pictures you are working on to the store. That way, you can decide at the shop what items you want for a particular layout. I also make a list of basics that I need as I am scrapbooking. When I run out of photo splits, for example, I jot it down so that I know to pick it up on my next trip.

If you don't want to make frequent trips, buy in bulk. Make a list of what you need and want before you go to the store and stock up. There are a few items you'll always need—pens, page protectors, and adhesives—so go ahead and buy plenty of these. As for embellishments and other items, jot down what you need according to category. For example, for baby pages, you'll need stickers, die cuts, pastel paper; for pet pages: paw print stamps, bone die cuts, and sticker letters. Do this for as many pictures as you think you'll have time to complete before your next shopping trip. Bring a friend with you to make sure you don't go overboard and make sure you have fun!

*Make a list, check it twice.*

SCRAPBOOK SHOPPING LIST
1. *white cardstock*
2. *nautical sticker*
3. *die cuts for birthday/Christmas*
4. *glue stick*
5. *protectors*
6.
7.
8.
9.

## "Stick" to a Budget When Buying Stickers

Many people complain about how much money they spend on scrapbooking. When I ask them what it is they are purchasing, they usually give one of two answers.

Some people buy every tool available, including punches, puzzle mates, scissors, pens, and shape cutters, and then they purchase paper and other perishable items. When I ask them why they get all those tools, they say they just have to have everything. So I say, well, either budget yourself or don't complain. If you are someone who likes to have all of the latest tools, which can add up, give yourself a budget that you feel good about and stick to it. You will appreciate the tools you do buy even more.

Other people buy paper and stickers, take them home, and never use them, so of course it seems to them as if they are spending an outrageous amount when they aren't getting anything out of their purchases. If this is you, try to buy what you know you are going to use, even if this means going to the store once a week and spending only five dollars.

Remember not to overbuy, because you will get frustrated and laden down with too many products and choices. Purchase items you know you will use. Shopping sales, clipping coupons, and shopping around are some ways you are guaranteed to get more for your money. Good Luck!

# Workshops, Crops, Snips, and Snaps

I have taught scrapbook classes for the past three years in numerous stores, and I have also attended many classes. Scrapbook instructors typically are avid scrapbookers and enjoy the hobby so much they can easily inspire others. You can learn a lot from your instructor; so if you take a class, be sure to ask plenty of questions.

There are two types of scrapbook classes:

➤ **Specialty classes**—In these you work on a specific technique, such as making paper dolls. The instructor leads the class as she/he talks about a certain technique. Some of these classes include a project that participants complete that night with the help of the instructor, and, in some of them, the instructors teach something ongoing, such as photography or page design. You are sure to come out of these classes with great examples and idea pages.

### Anecdotes from the Archives

Scrapbooking classes are so much the rage at consumer trade shows that it is almost impossible to get a spot if you haven't signed up early. The instructors at these classes are the creators of scrapbook products, representatives for different scrapbook companies, and professional scrapbookers. You can expect all sorts of goodies at these classes and tips from the professionals.

➤ **Workshops, crops, snips, and scraps**—At these classes, a scrapbook store generally provides nonperishable supplies such as scissors, punches, and templates for you to use during the class. You'll also have an instructor who can help you with ideas for using the products you've bought and who can give suggestions to help finish those impossible pages.

**Shortcuts**

Ask friends who often attend classes who their favorite instructor is. You will be sure to have success if you go to a great instructor.

Don't have a store in your area that offers scrapbooking classes? If you already know a group of people who like to scrap, decide what you as a group are most interested in learning. Select group members to research and prepare a short instructional class for others in the group when you meet again. This can be a great way to learn in a less formal setting. You will definitely feel comfortable asking questions, and you will learn when it is your turn to present something to the group. If you get a large enough group together, you may be able to get experts to come to you. This is a great, inexpensive way to learn.

## Picking and Choosing—Deciding Which Class to Take

I enjoy learning new techniques but get bored easily, so the class I take had better be hopping or I won't recommend it. When deciding on a class, look for something that appeals to you. Don't waste your time taking a class on punch art if you don't own or like punches.

**Shortcuts**

Envious of your friend in a neighboring town who takes all sorts of fun classes at her local scrapbook store that yours doesn't offer? Go to the store manager or owner and tell them the classes you are interested in taking. Chances are they will even offer the class you are looking for.

I have often had people take my basics class who have already been scrapbooking for a year and are just looking for ideas. They are disappointed when I discuss the bare bones of scrapbooking—something they are already familiar with. When signing up for a class, ask the clerks what the class is about and what you will learn. Get the details before you sign up so you won't be wasting your time.

See what the store has to offer, and be selective. Don't be afraid to attend by yourself—you can often glean more from the class if you aren't chatting with your friends. If you are just beginning to scrap, start with a basics class and then attend a workshop. If you are looking for some inspiration, try a design class. If you find that you are suffering from scrapper's block, try attending a class where you make embellishments that you can use on your pages, such as die cut layering or a borders class. The idea is for you to leave inspired to try something new in your scrapbook and feeling as if you have completed something.

## Sharpen Your Pencils—Preparing for Class

1. So you don't attend the class unprepared and end up being frustrated, find out what you should bring with you when you sign up. Do you need to bring glue, scissors, pictures? Always bring your favorite pen and some paper to take notes on. You can accomplish so much more if you prepare your pictures before attending a workshop and select the photographs you are going to work on.

2. Categorize the pictures that you want to complete before the class so you can use class time more effectively. If you are working on your child's birthday pictures, divide the pictures into pages. For example, children playing party games, kids eating cake, party guests, opening presents, and so forth.

3. Get an idea of the embellishments you want to use—for a birthday page, do you want to use birthday embellishments, such as balloons, or do you want to stick with the dinosaur theme your child chose? Bring what you will be using to the class.

4. Bring only the necessary supplies to class. You don't need to bring your tackle box full of punches since you can usually use the store's punches. You will need your adhesives, both cardstock and decorative paper, and pens. The store does provide cutting tools, and, of course, you can purchase anything you need. (I like to bring my favorite cutters and straight-edge scissors with me so I don't have to share.)

5. When you are at the class, take advantage of having all of the materials on hand to select embellishments and colors that go well with your pictures. I like to gather all of the supplies needed to complete my page, such as paper, die cuts, and stickers, and put them in a protector to finish at home. That way I am taking advantage of being in the store. I can always glue and journal at home, but I don't have 500 pieces of paper to select from.

**Sticky Points**

Remember to be a little discreet at workshops, especially since the photographs and writing you are including tend to be very personal. (One participant in a class I heard about was having a good time looking at everyone's pictures and commenting on them until she looked at someone's album and saw her ex-husband with the album owner's friend! Oops!)

*With these supplies and a good class, you'll be ready to scrap the night away.*

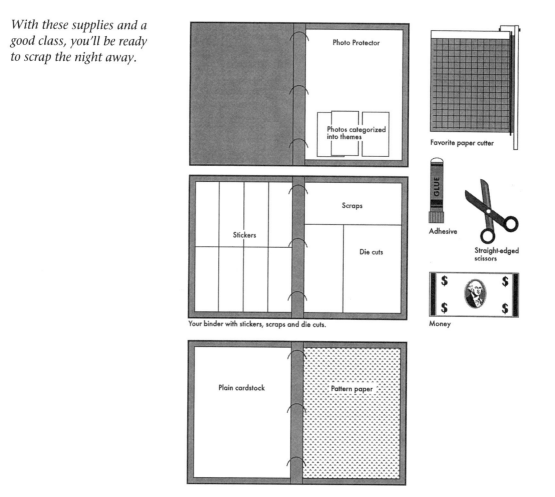

Photo Protector

Photos categorized into themes

Favorite paper cutter

Scraps

Stickers

Die cuts

Adhesive

Straight-edged scissors

Your binder with stickers, scraps and die cuts.

Money

Plain cardstock

Pattern paper

## The Least You Need to Know

➤ To find a store near you, go online to a store locator or post a message.

➤ Bring your photos along when you shop to avoid wasted purchases.

➤ Whatever stage of scrapbooking you are in, beginner or more advanced, try taking a class to learn new techniques and meet fellow scrappers.

➤ If there are no classes where you live, try starting one. Gather a group of scrappers together and find out what people would like to learn. Have everyone pitch in to create lessons for the others.

➤ Prepare for classes by finding out what you'll need and organizing photos and supplies beforehand.

# Part 2
# Setting Up Shop

*You'll be truly amazed when you discover all the products and services available to the scrapbooker. Every time my husband accompanies me to the scrapbook store he's utterly shocked to see the variety of paper, pens, and stickers available. In this part you'll read about the wide variety of products available to the scrapbooker and what you can do with them. Refer to this section often for ideas on using these products.*

# Chapter 5

# All Paper Is Not Created Equal

---

### In This Chapter

➤ Decorative papers and patterns—it's like having an artist draw in your book!

➤ Using patterned paper to tie together the theme of your scrapbook

➤ Pattern paper and stationery can be used for all sorts of craft projects

➤ Think texture—try using velvety, wavy, metallic, or handmade papers

---

My sister came with me on one of my visits to the scrapbook store. "Oh my gosh!" she said, "I love all this paper, but why do you need so many different kinds? I'm intimidated by all the choices!" I remember feeling the same way when I started scrapbooking. Not only are there different types of paper—cardstock, stationery, paper packs, and patterned paper—but each category has many variations. Between color choices, sizes, weights, and patterns, typical scrapbook stores stock anywhere from 500 to 2,000 different types of decorative paper! That's why an entire chapter is dedicated to this subject.

Scrapbooking paper can be used for more than scrapbooking. I've used it to make party invitations and greeting cards, and my friend Marcia sent me a lovely baby announcement made with scrapbooking materials. It's a good idea to be familiar with the different types of decorative paper, and after reading this chapter, you'll realize that quality paper is worth the few extra pennies.

When I was a cashier at a scrapbooking store, I loved seeing women come in with their boyfriends or spouses. I remember one particular incident, when a pregnant woman came in with her husband. He stood, bored, in the corner of the store as she oohed and aahed over the adorable baby-patterned paper. After half an hour, he cleared his throat, and his wife got the hint. She trundled up with a shopping basket overflowing with paper. He stayed motionless in his corner until I began ringing up her purchases. Suddenly he came to life, "Hey!" he said, "I think your machine is broken. There is no way that piece of paper costs fifty cents."

That's when I explained to him what I'm about to explain to you: All paper is not created equal.

# Are You Beginning to Notice a Pattern?

Though the rooms in my house are painted a neutral white, like many homes in the United States, I love patterns. My twins' bedroom sports nautical wallpaper, and my bedroom is decorated with a floral wallpaper border. Patterns are terrific because they give dimension and warmth to a room. From dots to checks to stripes, patterns are exciting. One of the best things about a scrapbook is that you can experiment with as many different patterns as you like without committing to painting a wall in your house with lime green and hot pink stripes. And since there are so many patterns to choose from, each page can be fresh and exciting.

## From the "Specific" ...

Pattern paper is by far the most popular scrapbooking paper. Everyone incorporates it into his or her books in some way or another. Pattern papers are described below in two sections, the first of which is called "specific pattern paper." This is paper designed to enhance pages that focus on a specific theme, such as weddings, graduations, or birthdays.

These types of pages can boost your scrapbooking power. For example, when my second son, Justin, was born, my husband was in school. Since money was tight, I didn't take many baby photos of him (something I still regret). To make up for it, when I did his baby book, I bought a lot of specific paper, like the baby's first step paper shown here. Although I didn't have an actual picture of his first steps, I managed to find a photo of him when he was about the right age and make a cute page out of it. This way I could still document his milestones and accomplishments. (Of course, now I take tons of photos, so many that my kids ask me to please put the camera away!)

### Words for Posterity

**Pattern** paper is paper with designs repeated on the entire page. Designs range from bold to conservative, funky to tasteful. Pattern paper is a fun addition for your scrapbook.

### Shortcuts

Specific pattern paper lets you use somebody else's artwork to enhance your pages. Many companies, such as Frances Meyer, offer coordinating stickers to match their pattern paper. With products like these, you can't go wrong! It's the next best thing to hiring a professional to draw in your scrapbook for you.

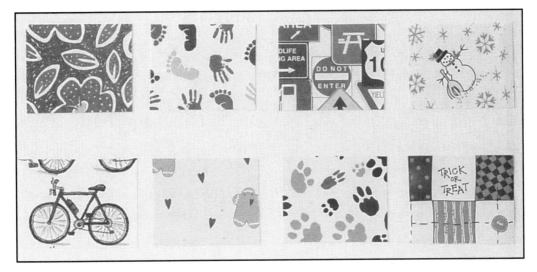

*This is just a small sampling of specific pattern paper that is available, from country gingerbread men to bicycles.*

One word of caution: Specific pattern paper is fabulous, but if a whole scrapbook is filled with it, your personality may be muffled a bit. To minimize this, some of the companies that offer specific pattern paper also offer coordinating general pattern paper. So, while your pages will match, they won't get the reaction, "Look at how cute these pages are, never mind the photos!" Another solution is to use some of the specific paper to mount your photos on and cut letters for your title out of the rest.

### Anecdotes from the Archives

It's best to buy this type of pattern paper only when you've got a definite use for it, although scrapbookers have been known to stage photos in order to use a paper they absolutely love.

## ... to the "General"

The other kind of paper is called "general pattern paper." This type of paper incorporates patterns, such as dots, florals, and stripes. This paper works great on any of your pages and can be used in all sorts of combinations. Try to echo the mood of the photo with the color and pattern of the paper you choose.

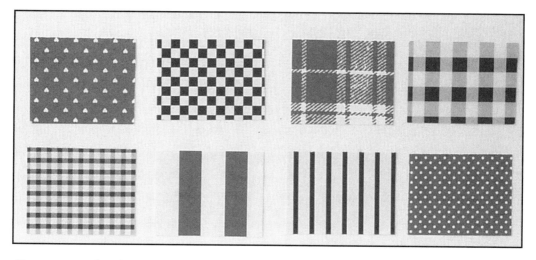

*Here are some favorite patterns—stripes, checks, dots, and more.*

General pattern paper is so versatile that one design can be used many different ways. Take the mini red dots for example: with this one kind of pattern, you can create pages for the Fourth of July, Valentine's Day, or Christmas. You can use it to record your college or high school days, make an "I Love You Because ..." page, or highlight an anniversary dinner. These are just a few ways to use one pattern. With all of the styles available, you can create an infinite amount of pages!

**Shortcuts**

General pattern paper is made to be used for any occasion. Go ahead and stock up on it—you can use it in hundreds of different combinations.

# Uses for Pattern Paper

The following are a few of my favorite uses for pattern paper.

➤ Individual photo mounts—Mounting a snapshot on pattern paper makes it pop out from the page. You can combine two coordinating papers for even more fun.

➤ Die cut layering—Die cuts are shapes made out of paper, and you don't have to stick to solid colors to make them. The key to using patterns for die cuts is to choose small-scale patterns; large-scale patterns won't show up well.

➤ If you're like me, you hate to throw out small scraps of pretty pattern paper but don't know what to do with it. Try using a punching tool to make little punches that will match your page. Punches are small tools used to punch out little shapes out of paper.

If you have more scraps left, place several colors randomly on a page to create a patchwork look.

➤ Paper piecing is a lot of fun. Paper piecing is the process of creating a layered look with templates by tracing and cutting different pieces of paper and combining all together for a layered look. While you need some solids for this technique, a few small areas with pattern paper will look great.

➤ Using pattern paper for your letters adds a special touch to your page.

➤ You can mount items other than photos on pattern paper—titles, captions, and journaling look great used this way.

For a simple layout, combine two different patterns (in this case, I've decided on thin red stripes and blue mini dots). Use one to mount the photos on and the other for background. With the addition of a couple of coordinating stickers you've got a great page!

**Words for Posterity**

**Punches** are small tools used to punch designs out of paper. The designs are also called punches. (See Chapter 9, for more on die cuts, punches, and other embellishments that make your pages look great.)

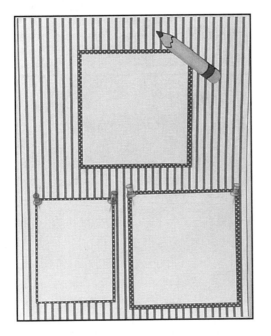

*This combination of patterns will make a no-fail page. Choose colors that match your pictures and you are done.*

Or you can use pattern paper to carry out the theme of your layout. Do this by selecting specific pattern paper for the background and a solid colored cardstock to mount your photos on. Add embellishments and some journaling for a beautiful page.

*You know right away that this page will be about soccer, and you don't have to draw anything.*

Many new scrapbookers are wary of using photographs they have had taken at professional studios in their albums. But properly preserved in a scrapbook, these pictures will last longer than if you put them in a frame or leave them in those cardboard mattes they give you. Besides, professional portraits look wonderful in albums. The trick is to choose a pattern paper that matches the theme of the portrait without overshadowing the photograph.

*This formal paper would flatter any professional portrait.*

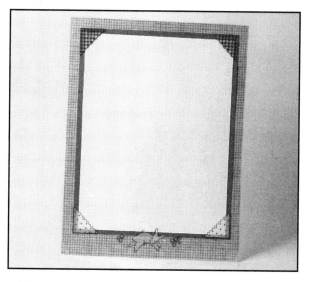

Pattern paper is just one type of decorative paper available. Read on to learn about other types.

# Stationery—Not Just for Writing Letters

The next most popular decorative scrapbooking paper is stationery. This paper is found in stationery and scrapbook stores and is a great way to create simple, fun pages in very little time. Stationery comes in all different sizes, from 8$\frac{1}{2}$-by-11, to 12-by-12, and cards of all sizes.

Stationery is marvelous for easy pages, especially when your pictures match the theme of the paper. Select your pictures and try to find stationery that coordinates with the theme and color of the pictures. Put pictures directly on the stationery or mount your photos on a coordinating cardstock color. What satisfaction!

A fun project you can do with stationery to jazz up your books is to create divider pages.

1. Decide how you want to divide your books. If you are doing a scrapbook about your trip to Europe, you can divide the book according to country. If you are doing a chronological year, you can divide according to season.

2. Choose stationery that goes with your theme. When I did dividers by the seasons in a year, I chose stationery with a border of snowmen for winter, gardening tools for spring, seashells for summer, and autumn leaves for fall.

3. Decide what you want to put on the stationery pages. I like to journal about what we do that time of year, important events, family outings—anything that gives a general idea about our history. A photograph depicting that season would work, too. Compile your pages and include them in your scrapbook. I think you will find this adds a great touch to your book.

### Words for Posterity

**Stationery** is paper with a decorative border that is blank on the inside. It makes great notepaper and wonderful scrapbook pages.

### Shortcuts

When mounting photos on decorative paper, cut out the inside of the paper that won't show to use in another project. This saves money!

Another favorite way to use these full sheets is to cut the designs out and use them as enhancements on your page. You don't need to include the entire design; instead, you can use elements from the stationery and adhere them to your page. Once, I was looking for frogs to put on a page I did of my little boys wading in water looking for frogs. Stickers weren't the right size and the die cuts I had were too large. I found some stationery with frogs on it and cut them out. Perfect!

*This is a classic example of stationery—great artwork, brilliant colors, and a definite theme.*

Stationery is fun to use for journaling, too. And remember, most stationery can be used in your computer printer, so you can type your text and print it directly onto the stationery.

*Here is a piece of stationery on which I've printed a poem to include in my scrapbook.*

When using smaller stationery, try pulling elements out of the stationery to embellish your page. For example, if you are using stationery with an illustration of the cow jumping over the moon with a photo of your baby sleeping, pull out the main elements of the card, such as the cow and the moon and stars. You can re-create those designs using punches, die cuts, or stickers. Make sure you stick with the same color scheme, though.

I like to look at stationery for ideas on how to lay out my own pages. The way they overlap the designs can be truly inspired. Use these as a guide to creating your own pages.

Stationery paper is for more than scrapbooking! Look at all the fun things you can do with it:

➤ Try this instead of sending a stuffy, formal thank-you card: Take a photo of the recipient using the gift. Adhere this to the middle of a piece of stationery that matches the gift. (If you received a book, for example, use stationery with a studious theme.) Write a message beneath the photo, sign, and send!

➤ Birth announcements take on a much more personal tone when you stamp the baby's feet on blue or pink stationery. Add baby's name and birthday.

➤ If you're tired of spending tons of money on holiday gift cards, take a different approach. Mount a photo in the middle of some cheery holiday paper and write a simple note. Add a sticker or two, and you've got a card that's sure to be appreciated!

➤ Children's party invitations look extra special on stationery. Use a computer to print out the information, but use stickers to spell out the guest's name.

➤ Stationery comes in a variety of animal themes—a perfect way to announce the addition of a new pet to your family!

**Shortcuts**

Stationery pages make great starting points for scrapbook pages about trips—write the dates of the trip and where you went inside the border ... and away you go.

**Shortcuts**

When making these cards, carry out the design of the card in your pages. For example, if the stationery border has a wavy edge, perhaps you could cut your photos with decorative scissors to mimic it.

# Take out the Guesswork—Specialty Paper Books

For those of you who have a hard time selecting pattern paper, several companies have a solution. They offer specialty paper books that come in specific and general pattern paper. There are layout examples with instructions that show the reader what to do. Some of them also have coordinating stickers and templates to use with these pages. I'll bet you don't leave these books sitting around—they are very user-friendly.

The best thing about these books is that they take the guesswork out of matching your pattern papers. Just choose a theme, and you'll find a book with all sorts of coordinating florals. If plaids are what you need, you'll be sure to find a book with plaids in it, too. Some of the books have matching punch-outs. Sold separately, the punch-outs are a more economical option than stickers, and they match the paper packs.

### Anecdotes from the Archives

This shows how scrapbooking has taken off—Hot Off the Press Paper Company introduced its first 15 Paper Pizzazz specialty paper books in 1997. They now sell 109 different books! According to them, their most popular theme books include Disney, wedding, and baby books.

*Specialty papers make for extra special pages.*

### Shortcuts

Velveteen paper looks and feels like velvet and adds elegance to any page. Try die cutting bows and flowers out if it for your baby pictures.

Don't forget to think of your kids' own scrapbooking projects when looking at these books. You can supply the scissors and glue; all the kids need is the paper in the books and the coordinating punch outs. Their books will look great because the paper and punch outs match.

# Shiny, Soft, Speckled, or Wavy— More Specialty Paper

Want to add a little elegance to your pages? Try vellum. This strong, translucent paper is currently available in a variety of solid colors and patterns, including speckled. I love to use it for journaling on a special page. Vellum can also be used as a unique embellishment. One of my students used it as steam rising off a bowl of soup. You can also use it as smoke from a chimney, clouds in the sky, or try some pink vellum as cotton candy! And vellum isn't just for scrapbooks—it also makes lovely baby announcements and wedding or bridal shower invitations.

Corrugated paper is heavy, wavy cardstock. It is a great way to add detail to your layouts. I like to use it in scenery layouts—as leaves or blades of grass, for example. Used sparingly, corrugated paper attracts the eye to a specific photo. Next time you go to make letter die cuts, think about using this paper instead of the flat stuff for words that pop out.

Another way to add texture to your scrapbook is using handmade paper. This paper often has flowers, grasses, or other natural-looking items pressed in it. It is a favorite choice for a unique and simple look.

Don't forget the bright, shiny, glossy, and metallic papers—a favorite of teenagers. These certainly attract attention. Take it from me, you won't be able to take your eye off some of these. It's great to use these papers, but remember, a little goes a long way. Use silver to make a mirror or use the glossy paper in your school colors for an original look.

There is also a growing selection of pre-embossed papers—cardstock with a raised design. You can color over the designs to add detail or leave them plain for a simple, elegant look.

One of the latest popular decorative papers is velveteen paper. Velveteen paper comes in about 10 colors and is simply gorgeous. Use it in your die cuts, for wedding pages, and to dress up that old prom photo. Vivelle paper is also interesting—it looks and feels like a terry cloth towel. Try using these on your beach photos as towels. These papers add great texture to your pages and will "wow" your scrapbook.

### Sticky Points

Since vellum is translucent, glue tends to show through, so you have to adhere the paper in a way that hides the glue. Try using a ribbon or other object to hide it. Just be sure to deacidify anything extra that goes on your pages.

### Shortcuts

If your wedding was a casual outdoor event, your photos will look beautiful set on handmade paper with flowers. Or why not use flowers from your garden to make some paper and then use it to mount your gardening photos. Talk about a do-it-yourself project!

### Words for Posterity

**Pre-embossed** paper, with raised designs, is an absolute must for an elegant, subtle look.

If none of the patterns suits your needs, you can always make paper, something the do-it-yourselfers love. Check the resource guide for paper-making directions.

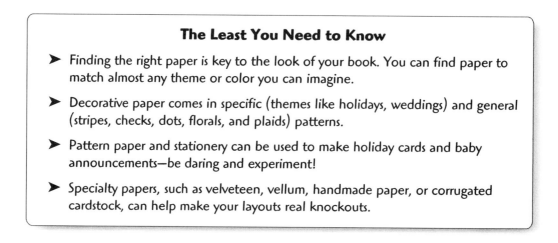

**The Least You Need to Know**

➤ Finding the right paper is key to the look of your book. You can find paper to match almost any theme or color you can imagine.

➤ Decorative paper comes in specific (themes like holidays, weddings) and general (stripes, checks, dots, florals, and plaids) patterns.

➤ Pattern paper and stationery can be used to make holiday cards and baby announcements—be daring and experiment!

➤ Specialty papers, such as velveteen, vellum, handmade paper, or corrugated cardstock, can help make your layouts real knockouts.

# Chapter 6

# Doodle On!

> ## In This Chapter
>
> ➤ Add life to your scrapbooks with writing
>
> ➤ What makes a pen safe (and durable) for a scrapbook
>
> ➤ Plain to fancy—pens, pencils, and other tools for drawing and enhancing scrapbook pages
>
> ➤ Lettering techniques for everyone

A scrapbook is more than pictures stuck on pages. It is a story, and although the photos are often the focus of the story, you need words to tell the reader who and what are in the pictures (see Chapter 12, "Tell Your Story: Journaling in Your Scrapbook," for more information on creating compelling text for your scrapbooks). When writing in a scrapbook, you must have the proper tools, tools that will let your ancestors read your writing in 100 years. Pens ought to have ink that is safe and lasting.

There are numerous types of archival quality pens in all sorts of colors, styles, and price ranges, so you'll find one to suit all your needs. The scrapbook store where I teach workshops has an entire aisle of pens!

If you've got neat, attractive handwriting, you're set. If you are like most people, you might be able to use a little help in the penmanship department so that your journaling will not only be legible, but charming, too.

This chapter describes the amazing range of pens available and what you can expect each type to do. I will also give you information on where to go for lettering techniques books, Web sites, and so on.

### Sticky Points

Make sure that the ink in the pens you use passes the P.A.T. (Photo Activity Test) if they will be used with photographs; P.A.T. determines whether a product will damage photos.

### Words for Posterity

**Fine-tip point pens** are pens with extremely small tips and are good for doodling and precise lettering.

### Sticky Points

Be gentle with your fine-tip pens— they're not designed to stay firm under pressure. When writing with them, press only as hard as you need to and use a thicker pen to color in broader areas.

# Permanently Safe

A pen is safe to use in your scrapbook if it is:

➤ Permanent

➤ Waterproof

➤ Fade-resistant

➤ Quick-drying

➤ Pigment ink

➤ Non-bleeding

➤ Non-toxic

Most of the pens found at a scrapbook store have all the above qualities, but look carefully at pen labels at your craft and other art supply stores because not all pens are suitable for scrapbooking. Many more options exist than just black, felt-tip pens, although it is the simplest and usually most legible option for recording history. Felt-tip pens come in a wide variety of tips, point sizes, and colors that can make a big difference in the look of the writing in your book.

Fine-tip point pens, for example, range in point size from .005mm–.08mm and are good for journaling and lettering. Fine-tip pens offers the widest range of small tip sizes and can be found at scrapbook stores, general craft stores, art supply stores, and stationery stores.

# Fancy It Up a Little

There are a number of elegant and interesting choices when it comes to pen tips that will give your pages loads of style.

## *Calligraphy Pens*

Calligraphy pens can create grand-looking titles and captions. The trick is in the tip of the pen, which is what is used to create formal lettering. They are available in different sizes and colors. The tips on these pens are flat and broad, so when they are held at a 45-degree angle, they produce letters that are beautiful and ribbon-like. Even if you've never taken a calligraphy class, you can still do some simple strokes with these pens that will add a lot of elegance to your page.

AT THE BEACH

*This was written with a calligraphy pen and has an elegant, traditional look.*

### Anecdotes from the Archives

Calligraphy comes from the Greek words meaning "beautiful writing." Before books were printed with movable type on printing presses, documents were painstakingly drawn by calligraphy artists. Beautifully leather-bound, illuminated calligraphic manuscripts can be found in fine art museums. Fine writing was so prized in the fifteenth century that a line of script by a Persian calligraphy artist named Mir Imad was sold for a gold piece!

## The Zig Writers

My favorite pen is the Zig writer, which has two tip sizes: 0.5mm for journaling and doodling and 1.2mm, which works wonderfully for borders, titles, and captions. You can't go wrong with this pen, which the company developed specifically for scrapbookers. The ink lasts so long, I often lose them before the ink runs out.

*Write it any way you like.*

### Anecdotes from the Archives

The most popular scrapbooking pen system is the Zig Memory System, made by EK Success. It has a comprehensive selection of markers: calligraphy, brush, fine, bullet, and scroll tips, each of which comes in 24 colors. They also have opaque markers, so pretty much anything you need, Zig sells.

## Fine and Chisel

The newest pen type is the fine and chisel, which can create all lettering sizes, is most versatile, and comes in a wide variety of colors. You can use this pen to create some unique lettering styles—my favorite is a rustic lettering for camping pages.

## Scroll and Brush

The scroll and brush pen is wonderful for the advanced letterer who wants to create more kinds of lettering. The tips enable you to create a unique look.

*Scroll and brush phrase.*

# Paint It on with Paint Pens

With many different tip sizes and over a dozen different colors, opaque paint pens boost your creativity. You can find them at scrapbook stores. Paint pens show up on dark cardstock where felt-tip pens can't. The gold and white paint pens are my favorites because they lend a royal look to my pages.

**Shortcuts**

Bring along some scratch paper to the store so you can "test drive" a pen before buying it. All the pens have different feels, and you'll want one that is comfortable to use and gives you the line you want. Buy extras of your favorite colors when they are on sale.

# Goof-Proof Gel-Based Rollers

If you like the look of paint pens, you'll want to try gel-based rollers. They come in a variety of tip sizes and colors, from basic black and green to outrageous fluorescent pink and purple. Be sure to try the milky colors on your dark pages. Don't overlook the lightning variety—colors mixed with silver—for a futuristic look. These pens are great for journaling and are goof-proof!

The one drawback with these pens is they get stopped up from time to time. If they do, keep scribbling on some scratch paper to get the ink started again. At around $1.49 each, they are affordable pens. Be on the lookout for sales on pen packs. You'll probably get a great deal!

# Coloring Inside (and Outside) the Lines

Aside from adding journaling, captions, and titles to your pages, you may want to draw and color something in them as well. Colored pens and pencils are the option for coloring in stamped images, clip art, or doing your own drawing.

## Coloring Pens

These pens are made just for coloring. Usually, they have two tips, including a brush tip. They come in a huge variety of colors, and you can also purchase blending pens to blend with these colors for an even larger range of color choices. It is sometimes impossible to get the perfect color, even with the selection you have; that is when the blending pens come in handy. You use them to blend two colors together to get that perfect color. Just color with the two colors and use the blending pen to mix them together.

Many coloring pens, such as my favorite Tombow, are acid-free but not permanent. They work beautifully for filling or coloring in, but be sure not to document with them because the ink will eventually fade. Use them for decorative purposes only.

**Words for Posterity**

**Fine and chisel pens** feature two ends—one small felt tip and one with a slanted tip. A must-have for the creative letterer, use it to create lettering in all sizes.

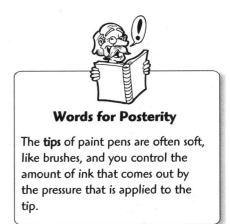

**Words for Posterity**

The **tips** of paint pens are often soft, like brushes, and you control the amount of ink that comes out by the pressure that is applied to the tip.

## Colored Pencils

Colored pencils are an exciting new addition to the repertoire of scrapbooking writing instruments. Zig and Berol Prisma make sets that are photo-safe and affordable. They come in kits of assorted colors. Many art-supply companies make colored pencils, too, but they are not guaranteed to be safe to use in scrapbooks, so be sure to check. Colored pencils can come in sets of 12, 24, 48, or 64 or more colors. Use them to doodle, write titles or captions, or color on your pages. Another great feature of using colored pencils is that you can use them to shade your pictures, something that is hard to do with pens.

*These come in some great colors.*

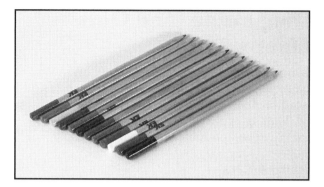

# It's Not All Black and White

If you ever sort through old pictures of your family, you'll notice that many black and white photographs from the twenties or thirties, especially those that look like they were taken at a professional studio, are colored—and this is long before color film was available. Those pictures were taken with black and white film and had color added after they were developed. This is sometimes done today with old black-and-white movies and is called "colorizing." Some people don't like the way colorized films look, figuring that black and white was the way they were meant to be viewed, but you can make some very neat effects by adding color to black-and-white pictures.

If you would like to add color to your black-and-white photos, tools are available that will let you to do it at home. Previously, only oils were available for this purpose, and they required a high degree of expertise—and a large investment (for more information on these, see the resource guide). But now you can get black-and-white, hand-coloring pens in a set that usually includes coloring pens in basic colors, pre-moistening solution, a dye-remover pen, a sponge, and some cotton pads. The dye remover pen makes the process fool-proof; if you mess up, all you need to do is correct your mistake with the dye-remover pen and try again.

**Shortcuts**

If the paint pens are too messy for you, try the milky gel roller pens on dark paper. You may find that when you are using these, you can concentrate on what you're writing instead of how you're writing it.

*It's easy as can be to "colorize" your black and white photos with these.*

# Lettering Techniques for the "Il'letter'ate"

When I am teaching workshops, this question inevitably comes up in the class, "Who has neat handwriting?" Most everyone answers, "Not me!" You may not feel confident now, but with some practice, you can create pretty, handwritten titles for your pages. By taking a class or practicing our alphabet below, you'll be able to whip up some great titles. Here are some basic steps to start yourself down the path to becoming a creative letterer.

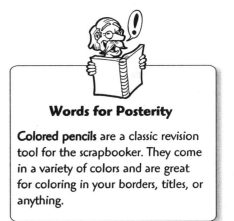

**Words for Posterity**

**Colored pencils** are a classic revision tool for the scrapbooker. They come in a variety of colors and are great for coloring in your borders, titles, or anything.

First, find some lettering styles that you like and want to duplicate. You may like the look of block lettering best, so focus on supplies and techniques that will help you draw block letters. If you like all types of lettering, pick a starting point. One lettering expert I talked to advises starting with a basic alphabet and practicing this alphabet to create a strong foundation for lettering that you can build on. Here are some of her suggestions:

1. Keep the spacing between the letters, words, and lines even; use a ruler to pencil in some lines if you need to.

2. Keep the size of the letters the same; pencil in lines at the top and bottom to give you an idea of your boundaries.

3. It is important to have an even slope throughout the letters. Keep your vertical lines parallel.

### Words for Posterity

A **basic alphabet** is the beginning point for other lettering creations.

### Words for Posterity

In lettering, a **serif** is the decorative line that extends from a letter, or its "foot." The typeface used in this sidebar is "sans serif," or without any decorative serifs.

*Here is a basic alphabet to create a strong foundation for your other projects.*

Keep these three basic suggestions in mind as you begin duplicating the alphabet. It is best to pencil in your letters first. This gives you a preview of how the lettering will turn out. Experiment with different pen tips to create different looks.

Keep on practicing the starter alphabet until you feel confident, then add to it. The ways are only limited by your imagination. Here are some sure-fire ways to get you going:

➤ Try different pen widths; the fat widths are bolder and attract more attention. The thinner tips are more delicate and soft. You can manipulate the lettering look simply with your choice of pen width.

➤ Add a simple serif style—such as dots, hearts, or squares—at the letters to the end point of each stroke.

➤ Layer the letters. You can do this by outlining in another color and then coloring it in, or you can outline part of the letters and leave spots to fill in with doodles or colors that match your page.

➤ Stretching your alphabet higher or lower will give you a different look.

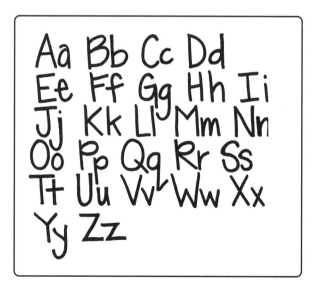

➤ Mix upper- and lower-case letters of the same alphabet to create a distinct look.

➤ You don't always have to keep your lettering in a straight line. Try curving it or tilting the letters for a playful look.

➤ Experiment with different pen tips—try chisel, calligraphy, or even an opaque marker to see what you can create.

Now that you have gotten the basic alphabet down, you are ready to move on. Throughout Part 5, "Theme Books and Great Pages," there are original alphabets for you to use in your scrapbooks. If you get frustrated, try purchasing some lettering books. Scrapbook stores carry a good selection. Look for books by Sandy Tyson, Lindsey Ostrom, Becky Higgins, Melody Ross, and Carol Snyder. Each of the scrapbook magazines also has a creative lettering section. Typically included in that section is an original alphabet, creative techniques, and page ideas.

Also, you can try taking a creative lettering class at your scrapbook store. If you don't have one nearby, many community education centers offer calligraphy courses.

**Shortcuts**

If you can't get the lettering down, you can always trace it onto your pages with a tracing table or tracing paper.

When incorporating creative lettering into your pages, remember that you don't want to use too many different styles of lettering on the same page. Pick a style that will support the theme of your pages. For example, don't use a formal script style for camping photos; save that for more formal events, such as weddings or graduations.

# Get the Red Out

Okay, imagine this: You take a great group photo where, miraculously, everyone is smiling and has their eyes open. It would be a perfect picture except for all those red eyes. We have all had this happen from the flash! A red-eye pen is the solution for this problem. Dab a bit of this ink on the red spots and, although it doesn't restore the true eye color, it does take the red away. If this is a frequent problem for you, it's definitely worth the investment. These pens are available in scrapbook stores and in camera equipment and supply stores. There are also ones available for pets.

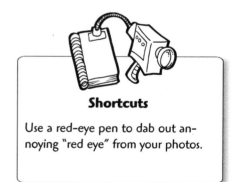

**Shortcuts**

Use a red-eye pen to dab out annoying "red eye" from your photos.

## The Least You Need to Know

➤ Writing and drawing tools should be permanent, fade-proof, water-resistant, and quick-drying.

➤ The right pen makes all the difference in the look of your writing, so be sure to try several different kinds first.

➤ Pens are available in different colors and types for different effects, including calligraphy pens, paint pens, gel-based pens, and more.

➤ Use colored pencils and pens for drawing and decorating.

➤ Anyone can learn to become a better letterer. First, try mastering a basic alphabet, and then experiment with pens and different techniques. You can also take a lettering class.

# Chapter 7

# Snip, Snip! Multi-Use Cutting Tools and Templates

## In This Chapter

➤ Not just scissors—different tools for cutting a straight edge

➤ How to get the most out of decorative scissors

➤ Cutting perfect shapes with a special tool

➤ Why templates can be a scrapper's best friend

Around the world, people are clicking their cameras an average of 46 million times a day. That's a lot of photos! Although many of these photos go straight into an album as is, many others are trimmed, cropped, or cut. And while some people grab the kitchen shears to do the cutting, dozens of tools can be found that are better-suited for the job.

This chapter updates you on the different straight-edge cutting tools and gives you the scoop on those funky decorative scissors. I will tell you all about templates, what they are, how they are useful to scrapbookers, and all the different kinds available, from letter to puzzle types. If you are a big fan of cutting your pictures into shapes, you are going to love tools called shape cutters, which effortlessly cut photos into all kinds of interesting and perfect shapes.

## Hey, Cut It Out!

I have been involved in many spirited debates with my students and friends regarding the merits of straight edges versus decorative edges on photographs. Straight edge proponents claim that the decorative edges look too fussy and clutter up layouts, while decorative edge fans declare that straight edges are boring and don't add anything to a page. As one student said, "Decorative edges draw attention to the photos, while the straight edges make them blend into the background." After hearing many such conversations, I maintain that it is strictly a matter of taste. Though I often use straight edges because it is quicker to make them, there are times when decorative edges add an extra something. I do recommend using decorative scissors on the mattes, though, and not the actual photo. Whichever you like, don't be afraid to combine the two looks.

## Straight-Edge Scissors

I like to have a large range of cutting tools at my fingertips when I work on my scrapbooks. Scissors are the most basic cutting tools for trimming and cutting everything from photographs to textiles to other documents you might incorporate into a scrapbook. You must have a pair of large scissors to scrapbook. While many people use their sewing scissors for this, I suggest purchasing paper scissors because they are designed for the job. Large scissors (with eight-inch blades) work well and are needed for cutting big shapes and templates. You'll also need some small, sharp scissors to cut detailed shapes from stationery and trim around tight corners. I also recommend a paper trimmer or paper cutter for absolutely straight edges.

If you don't like scissors, you can try a rotary paper edger. While it was originally designed for quilters, scrapbookers have fallen in love with this tool. The paper edger has ten interchangeable blades and is easier on your hands than scissors. It'll take a little practice to become proficient, so try it out on some scratch paper first.

A rotary cutting tool is easy to control when you are using the right tools. Use a hard plastic ruler with a metal edge to line up your paper and use a cutting mat under your paper. Cutting mats are mainly sold at fabric stores for cutting fabric on, but they are great to use for cutting paper. They are made of a hard plastic and come in a variety of sizes; I suggest a medium-sized one. You won't need the extra-large one, but the small one is too small. The ruler and mat each have lines and measurements to make straight cutting simple.

If you are a fan of decorative edges, you'll like the rotary paper edger because you can use it to get the lines perfectly even. See if you can try one of these out before purchasing to make sure you like the way it feels and cuts.

**Words for Posterity**

**Paper trimmers** are terrific tools that are easy to use. Simply place your paper in the trimmer, line it up on the grid where you want to make a cut, and move the blade down.

## Trimmers and Cutters

For straight-edge cutting, you can use anything from a lightweight small cutter to a large office-type cutter. There are two basic types of cutters: the type with an arm handle that you pull down to cut the paper and the kind that has a sliding blade. I suggest that when considering the purchase of a large paper cutter, you shop around and try some out. The difference between the two is minimal, and choosing one is a matter of preference. Trimmers with sliding blades seem to give more control over the cutting than arm handle trimmers.

Paper trimmers come in small and large sizes for small and large jobs and can be quite heavyweight, like the ones used in copy or photograph shops, or lightweight and more suitable for home use. These tools have precise grids and sometimes have rulers on their sides so you can determine the exact size of the paper you need—this is especially useful if you have an 8$\frac{1}{2}$-by-11-inch album, for example, and need to cut down larger cardstock or other paper to fit precisely. My favorite is the mini paper trimmer, like this one from Fiskars. Since it is portable and lightweight, it's easy to take with you when you travel or meet at someone's house for a scrapbook club.

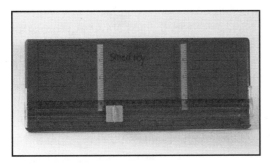

*This is my favorite travel cutter.*

# Scallops and Ripples— Using Decorative Scissors

"What are these for?" is a familiar refrain I hear from people who see decorative scissors for the first time. Decorative scissors were introduced by a company called Fiskars in 1994 with just six patterns. They were so well received that Fiskars has since created an additional 31 patterns. And with other companies creating variations and introducing new designs all the time, there is always something new to add to your supplies. Decorative scissors are a fun way to add a touch of whimsy to your pages. Since the scissors come in so many patterns, you can find one to match any mood and theme!

**Words for Posterity**

**Decorative scissors** are scissors with a fancy pattern on the blade. Use them on your photos or your paper for a fun look.

*Decorative scissors come in over 30 different designs. Here are some of the most popular: Victorian, Majestic, Scallop, Pinking, Ripple, corner-cut scissors, and wide-edge scissors.*

Here are the five most popular decorative scissors patterns and uses for each:

1. **Victorian**—These scissors have an elegant look with curves and waves that hearken back to the Victorian era. Use these scissors when doing wedding, heritage, or classic portraits.

2. **Majestic**—This is a bold pattern that can also be used to create an elegant page. I like to use these when I am doing pages that need attention drawn to the pictures. Try using these scissors with your favorite family portrait pages or to create stately borders for your heritage pages.

3. **Scallop**—You can use these playful scissors for just about anything. It can look like miniature bubbles for your tubby time photos, or you can use it with baby pictures to resemble the edge of a blanket. My favorite way to use it is to cut paper with it and then punch holes in the curve to look like lace.

4. **Pinking**—Try using it with your camping pages to reinforce majestic mountains in the background. I also like to use it when I am using a sun to highlight the sun's rays shining down.

5. **Ripple**—These are versatile scissors with a series of small curves in a variety of sizes. Use these to duplicate sand or water or to add depth to your pages.

*Here are patterns produced by Victorian, Majestic, Scallop, Pinking, and Ripple decorative scissors.*

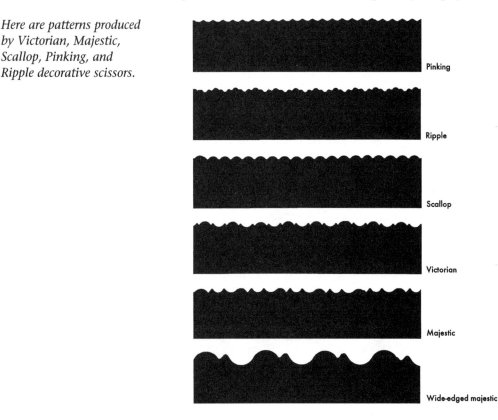

Pinking

Ripple

Scallop

Victorian

Majestic

Wide-edged majestic

Here are a few guidelines for working with decorative scissors:

➤ Choose a scissors edge pattern that enhances your page. For example, you could use pinking scissors to trim your photo mounts to coordinate with a die cut sun you are using on a page.

➤ It is difficult to keep decorative edges straight when cutting, so it's best to start with a straight edge or trace a straight line with pencil on the back of the paper you are cutting to give you a guideline to follow.

➤ Choose a design that's the right scale for the shapes you are cutting.

➤ Most decorative scissors allow you to make different designs by turning the scissors over. Try cutting strips of paper with the scissors to create borders for your pages.

➤ If you have the choice, purchase the scissors with the longer blades. They are easier to use and cut more paper with each stroke.

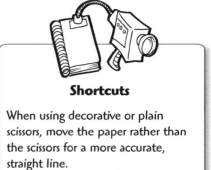

**Shortcuts**

When using decorative or plain scissors, move the paper rather than the scissors for a more accurate, straight line.

As fun as these scissors are to use, you need to make sure you try them before cutting something important so you can find out what the cut pattern looks like. Remember that some decorative scissors have a half inch or so straight edge at the tip—the decorative blade doesn't go all the way to the end. To avoid a break in the pattern, don't completely close the scissors. Rather, close them only three-fourths of the way or so and open them up again, making sure to line up the pattern before making the next cut.

Corner-edger scissors are designed to add flair to the corners of your pages, photos, or mounts. I like to cut the corner of the background paper with these scissors and cut out a photo mount with the same pattern. This gives my page consistency.

A fun new addition to decorative scissors is wide-edge scissors that make a cut up to five times as deep as regular decorative scissors. While you may not reach for this tool as often as your deckle-edged scissors, it is good to have a few of your favorite designs on hand. To create a stunning look, try cutting the sides of an entire scrapbook page with wide-edge scissors and placing a coordinating color of cardstock behind that to keep it flowing.

## Mix It Up with Shapes

Sometimes, seeing the same sized 4×6 photos lined up on a page gets a little boring, no matter how cleverly you angle the pictures. Cutting pictures into shapes can add

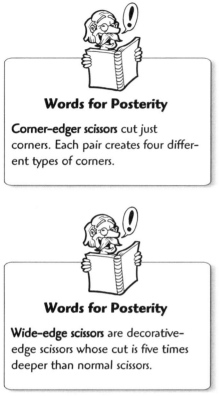

interest and flair to a scrapbook, but it can be frustrating to cut circles and ovals with scissors, even with a template to trace. Fortunately, shape cutters take care of this problem. Available in four shapes—square, rectangle, circle, and oval—shape cutters have a blade that cuts a perfect shape every time. My only suggestion is to try them before you buy. Different brands have different feels, and you want the one that works best for you.

One of the best times to cut your pictures into shapes is when you have gotten back a roll of film with parts that were overexposed or if the pictures turned out badly altogether but you still need to put them in. (Or try it if you want to cut out a relative or ex-significant others who are no longer "in the picture"!)

Recently, I got back some pictures of my two-year-old shiny clean from his bath, in his diaper, combing my sister's hair with an intense look of concentration on his face. To me, these pictures were irreplaceable. Unfortunately, they came back with the blurry edges. I definitely couldn't use them in the shape they were in, so I decided to cut them into shapes. I looked at the natural way the figures in the photos were displayed and decided to cut them into oval shapes. In order to preserve the majority of the figures, I had to leave in a little bit of blur around the edges, but it gave the photos an almost surreal look. The page turned out great, and you would never know that the pictures started out so awful.

## Tempting Templates

Templates have been on the scrapbooking scene from the beginning. Originally, templates were only available in a few basic shapes, but now you can find themed templates, too, such as medical, automotive, animal, and other unique choices, as well as letter templates and puzzle designs. While many scrapbookers use templates for their photographs, you don't have to stop there. Using templates on cardstock is a good alternative to die cuts.

If you don't have access to a shape cutter, use the basic templates to cut out squares, circles, ovals, and other shapes. To get the best results, trace over your photo with a grease pencil, cut, and wipe off the excess. If you get tired of seeing the same old rectangular photos on your pages, shape templates will quickly add interest to your pages.

## Letters to Trace

Letter templates are great! I love bright headings for my pages, so I use them frequently. I like to cut letters out of vibrant pattern paper. While this can be a little time-consuming, it produces a wonderful, crisp look. You can trace and color the letters, trace and cut the letters out, trace and decorate the letters using stamps or sponged ink, or trace and cut the letters out of more than one color of paper. The possibilities are endless.

**Words for Posterity**

**Basic templates** have shapes such as ovals and circles.

*Create page headings with letter templates.*

Letter templates come in a variety of sizes. The small ones are extremely time-consuming to cut out, so I like to use those when I trace and color. The medium and large ones are great to trace and cut or trace and color. Try overlapping the letters to create fun titles. When you have to do a poster for the PTA fundraiser, don't forget about your large letter templates. They definitely attract attention. Watch out, or you may be appointed the publicity chairperson!

Try using a variety of pens when tracing your letter templates. In the classes that I teach, I am

**Shortcuts**

Use a grease pencil when tracing your template onto your photos. After you cut out the shape, you can easily wipe off any marks.

73

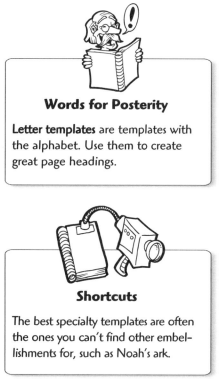

**Words for Posterity**

**Letter templates** are templates with the alphabet. Use them to create great page headings.

**Shortcuts**

The best specialty templates are often the ones you can't find other embellishments for, such as Noah's ark.

*Here's a fun layout made with a camping template.*

amazed to see what people come up with. Some of my favorite pens to trace and color the small letter templates are the milky gel-based rollers. It creates a great look and is fun to do. When your background paper is dark, imagine the paper in a Halloween layout, and do your letters with a white or yellow gel-based roller.

## Trace, Cut, Coordinate

If you don't have access to a die cut machine, specialty templates make a great substitute. You can purchase them in theme sets. They are available in diverse themes, such as Noah's ark, flowers, nautical themes, the great outdoors, Christmas, Halloween, gardening, stars and stripes, leaves, dress-up, baby, pool days, old-fashioned playthings, transportation, school days, and almost anything you can think of. The great thing about these templates is the coordinating borders that come with them. On the edge of many of these templates are border designs that you can use with your pages. For example, the pool days template comes with a border that resembles waves. You can trace this onto your page and color it or you can trace it onto some cardstock and then mount it directly on your page.

Remember, you don't have to use templates just to cut designs out. You can use them as stencils to trace a design directly on your paper and then fill it in with permanent pens or other writing utensils. Add some details for a personal touch. For example, if you have a template of animal designs and you are making a page about the birthday party your children threw for their pets or a trip to the zoo, you could trace the outline of a cat, dog, or elephant and add whiskers, eyes, ears, details of fur, and even a tusk with a colored pencil or pen.

If you'd like a more artistic look, place the template on the page, and, using a rubber stamp pad, sponge some ink in the design; you don't have to trace an outline because the sponged ink will be in the shape of the design.

## Picking Up the Pieces

For a playful look, try using a puzzle template. There are currently two designs available. The first is called a Coluzzle Collage Template System. Use it to arrange your pictures in different fun shapes, such as a teddy bear, Easter egg, or wreath, with each photo cut into pieces of a puzzle. I like to use this system when I've got a lot of different photos of the same pose that I just can't bear to part with. While this template is a little time-consuming, it can add a refreshing change to your scrapbook, and it is a great way to use up all of those extra baby photos.

Another kind of puzzle template is similar, except the photos aren't cut into interlocking puzzle pieces. Rather, you cut them into separate parts of a picture, with space between the photos for journaling.

**Words for Posterity**

**Specialty templates** have designs cut out that match a theme. A medical template might have items such as a stethoscope, bandages, crutches, and a doctor bag. Take the stethoscope and use it for a layout on your baby's first trip to the doctor. (And be sure to in-clude the growth charts you receive.)

## A Place to Write

Journaling templates are a must-have for all of you who like to write on your pages but can't keep your lines straight. My favorite is one called Journaling Genie, made by Chatterbox Publications. These templates provide you with writing guides for small, medium, and large lettering. You can even find lettering guides in different shapes. To use, simply trace the lines on your pages with a light pencil, write your captions, and erase the pencil.

**Words for Posterity**

**Puzzle templates** are simple tools that allow you to create puzzles out of your pictures—a fun look that can jazz up a layout.

*Star puzzlemate layout with template layout done by Julie Rasmussen.*

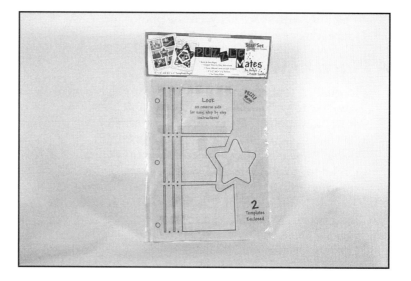

As a fun project, buy a small spiral-bound scrapbook and let your children trace in their favorite journaling genie shapes. Then they can write memories about their trips, stories, or whatever else they want. Placing pictures that go with the described events would be great fun. Use this scrapbook to emphasize the journaling. This helps encourage your child to have fun while writing and recording memories.

Those of you who love to create beautiful borders on your pages will love the decorative ruler templates. I have loved using the border buddies by EK Success. These rulers have a variety of edges on them to enable you to choose which one you want and then place and trace. You can use different sizes of the same design; simply overlap them and use a different tip size or color to trace the designs, and you have created something beautiful. Some of the rulers come with only two different edges to make, while others enable you to do numerous amounts with places cut out on the inside to trace and add doodles to your borders. When using the ruler templates, embellish them with your favorite stickers or punches to carry out the theme of your page.

### Sticky Points

Puzzle templates are a great way to use up all those extra birthday pictures to create a great page, but don't use pictures that are one of a kind because they all get blended in with these layouts.

### Words for Posterity

**Journaling templates** are templates made to create unique lettering. You can letter in different shapes or lines.

---

## The Least You Need to Know

➤ You can use decorative-edge scissors to create jazzy edges on your photos and paper. Try a Victorian edge or a Majestic look.

➤ Trimmers cut your photos into great shapes, such as ovals, circles, or squares.

➤ Templates come in a huge variety of shapes and designs, from letters of the alphabet, to fun shapes like animals and boats you can trace, to journaling templates with space for writing.

➤ For a unique page, try a puzzle template and have your child put the pieces back together.

# Chapter 8

# Cover the Basics: Choosing the Right Scrapbook Album

---

### In This Chapter

➤ Choosing an album size that is practical for you

➤ Matching the look of an album to the theme of your scrapbook

➤ Options to personalize your album cover

➤ Easy project—covering an album with a fun fabric

---

Choosing an album to house your scrapbook pages is important. You want the album to look good, of course, and you might also want it to match the theme of a particular scrapbook. A friend recently showed me a photo album of a trip to Greece—since the book focused on travel, she had decorated the cover with a map of the world, and it looked great. You also want an album to suit your needs for size and storage capabilities, and to be very easy to flip through (which, hopefully, you'll be doing a lot).

Scrapbookers can be a passionate bunch, and you'll find that album size ($8^1/_2$-by-11 or 12-by-12?) is a hotly debated topic within the scrapbooking world. The first thing some scrapbookers ask when they meet each other for the first time at scrapbooking clubs, stores, or conventions often is, "What size album do you use?" just as you might ask a new acquaintance where they live or what they do.

As for which album sizes and features are best, this chapter contains information on available sizes and features and the best ways to make your album look special on the outside, as well as the inside.

# The Ties That Bind

A primary difference among albums is the way the pages are bound into place. Some albums use a simple and effective three-ring binder, while others hold their pages with attractive and interesting posts or straps. The other major difference among albums is the paper size used.

**Words for Posterity**

An **album** is a blank book or binder used to store photographs and scrapbook pages.

When trying to decide which type of album to use, consider the following:

1. What kind of album is most accessible to you?
2. Do you foresee the need to move your pages around?
3. Where will you store your albums?
4. How many pictures do you want to use in each album?
5. Do you plan on using computer clip art directly on your pages?
6. Do you foresee color copying your pages for use in future books?
7. What is your budget?
8. Do you live close to a scrapbooking store?

**Shortcuts**

If you use a three-ring binder, try to find one that is a little longer than your pages. That way, the pages won't stick out when the binder is closed.

Once you make your choice and start, you may find that it is challenging to switch over to another type. I decided once that since I had always used the 8$\frac{1}{2}$-by-11 album size, I would use a 12-by-12 album for my children's baby books. I love the look of the large pages, and I just wanted to try it out. I went out and bought everything to make three baby books—even all the extra inserts and page protectors. The problem was that whenever I sat down to put a page down, I found that I couldn't create pleasing layouts. I was so used to using the other size that I found it frustrating to do larger pages. Eventually, I sold my blank 12-by-12 albums to a friend. I have talked with scrapbookers that successfully go back and forth between the two sizes. Mainly, they use the 8$\frac{1}{2}$-by-11-inch binders, and they use the larger-sized albums for theme books such as Christmas and vacation.

**Words for Posterity**

**Three-ring binders** look like loose-leaf notebooks and have three metal rings of varying sizes to attach the album covers and hold pages. They are affordable and allow you to rearrange pages easily.

Aside from size, when looking for an album you should think about what elements are important to you. Some people like large pages but want them to be easier to move around. A solution for this is to get three-ring binders and protectors that hold big pages.

## Three-Ring Binders

Three-ring binders are easy to use and very versatile. They come in a variety of premade covers, from padded vinyl to tapestry, are inexpensive, and the pages can be moved around without a hassle. The downside is that when you open the binder, the pages are not flush, but separated by the rings.

## Plastic Strap Bindings

Albums that have a plastic strap binding can be expanded. One of the nicest things about these albums is that, unlike three-ring binders which have gaps in between the pages, these pages lie flat, with no gap, so your layout is continuous. The only drawback with these albums is that it can be challenging to move pages around since you put pictures on both the front and back of pages. If you ever need to take the pages out for a school poster or something it is more complicated because you have to take all of the pages out to get to the one that you need.

**Shortcuts**

When you are looking at three-ring binders, be sure to get a kind of binder ring called a "D ring"—this type of metal ring has a flat side that allows pictures to lay flat when the binder is closed.

**Words for Posterity**

Books with **strap bindings** have plastic straps that run through a holder directly on the pages and keep the book in place.

*Plastic strap binding.*

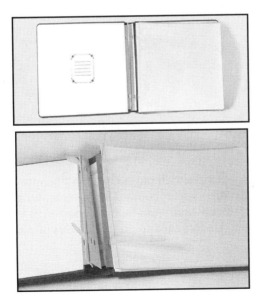

**Words for Posterity**

A **post-bound** album is held together with metal posts that run through the pages.

*Post-bound album.*

# Post-Bound Albums

Another choice is post-bound albums, which have a metal post that holds pages tightly bound together like a book. Many post-bound albums have printed designs on the album covers and are expandable by moving the pages. To fasten pages into these kinds of albums, you have to punch holes directly into scrapbook pages. This album is probably not the best choice if you are going to have little children flipping through it because the pages can easily tear.

# Spiral Binding

Spiral-bound books come in a variety of sizes with pages that can't be moved around. These books are a great choice for children's scrapbooks. The pages won't get lost, and for kids, the smaller sizes are perfect. These books can be purchased with writing and embellishments already on the pages. All you need to do is add your pictures, and you are done.

*A spiral-bound album.*

# Why Size Matters

Albums for scrapbooks come in two main sizes: 8$\frac{1}{2}$-by-11 and 12-by-12. Not sure which size album to use? Circle the answer that is closest to your style:

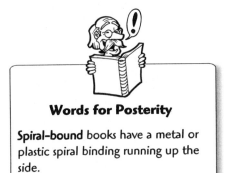

**Words for Posterity**

**Spiral-bound** books have a metal or plastic spiral binding running up the side.

1. My goal in scrapbooking is
    a. to get as many pictures on a page as possible.
    b. to make cute pages.

2. When it comes to scrapbooking, I am more concerned about
    a. keeping down the cost of supplies and equipment.
    b. the way my pages look.

3. An ideal scrapbook page is
    a. lots of pictures and lots of journaling.
    b. pictures and some scrapbooking.

4. When shopping for scrapbooking supplies
    a. I will look high and low for desired products.
    b. I want to be able to find everything I need without a lot of searching.

5. I want my scrapbook to
    a. look different from the rest.
    b. be the same as everyone else's.

See which letter you choose more of. More "a" choices, and you might want the 12-by-12 album. More "b" choices, and you may prefer the 8$\frac{1}{2}$-by-11 album.

Each has its own advantages and disadvantages. Advantages to using the 8¹/₂-by-11 books:

➤ There is a much larger selection of decorative paper.

➤ Paper for these books is usually less expensive.

➤ Books are readily available.

➤ Books are smaller and so are easier to transport.

➤ Smaller pages may be easier for some people to work on.

➤ It's easy to switch pages around.

Disadvantages of using 8¹/₂-by-11 albums:

➤ They don't hold as many pictures on a page.

➤ Pages don't lie flush so layouts aren't continuous.

➤ It's easy to spend a lot of money on paper because there is a larger selection.

➤ There is less room for large portraits such as 8-by-10 portraits.

**Sticky Points**

Still can't decide which scrapbook to choose? Talk to your friends and neighbors and see what they suggest. If you don't know anyone who scrapbooks, try going online and posting questions. You will be sure to hear opinions from many scrap-bookers on what album sizes they use and why.

Following are the advantages of using a 12-by-12 sized album:

➤ This size allows you to fit more pictures on each page.

➤ Layouts lie flush so the look is more continuous.

➤ Albums encourage you to be organized because you use the front and back of each page.

➤ Albums have a classic look because of their size.

Following are disadvantages of using the larger books:

➤ The albums and pages are typically more expensive.

➤ Pages aren't simple to move around.

➤ There is a smaller selection of decorative paper.

One of the most practical issues when choosing an album size, of course, is the number of pictures that you want to put inside. When using the 12-by-12, if you average 6 pictures on a page, you can get about 45 pages front and back in an album. Therefore, you can put as many as 540 pictures in that album! If you have that many photographs to put into a book, the bigger size is your best bet.

Using an 8¹/₂-by-11 three-ring binder, you'll average 4 pictures on a page. With 40 pages front and back in a binder, you can put approximately 320 pictures in an album. Either way, you can fit a large number of pictures into albums of these sizes.

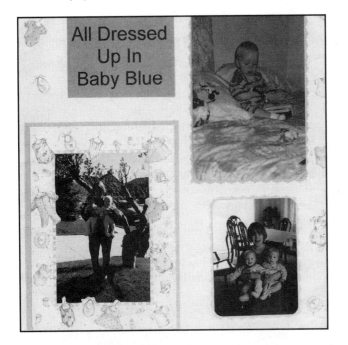

*Each of these 12-by-12 sheets can fit 12 pictures, six on the front, six on the back.*

*Each of these 8¹/₂-by-11 sheets can fit 8 pictures, 4 on each side.*

There are multiple small album choices out there with different types of bindings. These smaller albums are great for all sorts of projects, like making simple albums for your children, Grandma's brag book, any gift album, and for times when you just want to do something simple and fast.

# You *Can* Judge an Album by Its Cover

The cover of your album is the first thing people will see when they look through it. Like the cover of a book, an album cover can convey the mood and theme of the scrapbook inside. A cover can be a simple, classy leather with gold lettering—this says serious elegance. Or it can be a personalized cover with all kinds of artistic and decorative embellishments. Either kind functions to heighten a viewer's anticipation of what will be inside.

Of course, you can purchase your albums with already-made, nice-looking covers, or you can try to dress your covers up a bit. Here are some suggestions on how to decorate and personalize album covers.

## *Decorating Album Covers*

Some albums come with blank canvas covers that are great to personalize. There are many wonderful decorative options. For example, you can use stamps or templates on the cover—stamp or trace on designs and leave them outlined or color them in. If you are an artist, you can draw on covers to your heart's content. Since covers will be most exposed to the elements, don't forget that you always want to use permanent waterproof markers for cover art.

My son loves to use spiral-bound albums and decorates the covers using stickers. I have seen some albums made with wood covers—think of all the possibilities you have with a cover like this: tole painting, rub-ons, iron-on fabric, and wood stains. This is another great thing to use to decorate your covers.

**Words for Posterity**

A **brag book** is an album made especially for parents, grandparents, and other proud relatives. Anyone who will whip out pictures of their kids and grandkids at the drop of a hat will appreciate one of these. Use a small album they can carry around with them and fill it with pictures of the little ones. Leave some blank pages in the back and, every so often, send them updated photos.

**Shortcuts**

There are companies that make templates specifically for decorating album covers, so check your local craft store to see what is available.

## *Fabulous Fabrics*

Another nice decorative idea is to use fabric to cover an album; most stores carry already-made versions in tapestry, denim, and other types. Or try to make your own fabric-covered album. This is a great way to tie your cover together with the theme of the album.

If you want to do this, look at your photos to decide what you want to use to cover the album. For general scrapbooks, pick a favorite fabric that suits all needs, such as plaids or stripes. For books that have more specific pages or themes, get a suitable fabric. A travel book, for example, could be covered with a stamp tapestry, showing stamps from all over the world.

Here are some interesting possible covering fabrics:

➤ Plaid dish towels—I have heard of people using nice-quality plaid oversized dishtowels to cover their albums.

➤ Animal print fabric/fake fur—If you are an animal lover or just a member of the wild kingdom, try this one.

➤ Formal fabric—Try satin for a wedding, velvet for formals, taffeta for proms.

➤ Denim—You could use fabric or old jeans for a great cover.

➤ Flannel—Soft, cuddly, and rustic.

➤ Holiday fabric—for those pictures of your favorite holidays.

➤ Sports prints—For that album full of sports pictures, newspaper clippings, and ribbons.

*Fabric can make a beautiful cover for your scrapbook album.*

## Fabric Cover Project

After you have chosen a fabric you like, here are directions on how you can use it to cover an album front and back. These easy steps will work on a three-ring binder or with a post- or strap-bound album that will allow you to disassemble the album while you cover it.

Supplies you'll need:

➤ Depending on the size of your book, enough fabric to cut out fabric two inches wider than the album

➤ The album you intend to cover

➤ Tape

➤ Glue

➤ Scissors

➤ Decorative paper or cardstock for inside front and back covers.

Follow these steps:

1. Lay fabric out on a flat surface, printed side down, so that the pattern goes on the outside of the book. Open album and lay it out flat in the middle of the fabric. Cut fabric all the way around the album about two inches wider than the album.

2. When fabric is cut, begin folding fabric on the inside front cover. Snip the corners of the material and fold the fabric over each inside front corner. Tape the corner fabric down. Then fold down the fabric along the top and bottom sides. If you have to, make a small cut in the fabric so that it will fold down near the spine. Just tuck the fabric in under the metal that holds the ring binder. Tape down the fabric along all the sides.

3. When the inside front cover is done, fold the fabric along the back inside cover the same way, starting with cutting the corners, covering the book corners with fabric, and then folding the material over the inside back cover.

4. When both front and back covers are taped, try opening and closing the album. If it feels like the fabric is pulling too tightly when you try to close the album, loosen the fabric along the back inside cover and retape.

5. When there is enough slack in the fabric, permanently glue the folded fabric around both inside and back covers. After you have glued the fabric down, trim your two pieces of decorative paper or cardstock to a size about a half-inch smaller than your covers and glue them into the inside back and front covers. (This covers up the ends of the fabric and gives your book a finished look.)

Cover tips:

1. Try finding a material that conveys your album's theme. Fabric and notion stores usually have a great selection from kid's patterns to fancy satin and lace. And because you are buying a small amount, you don't have to worry too much about the cost.

2. Once you've covered the book, if it seems like there is too much extra fabric folded inside the covers, trim it down.

3. Use some of your fabric scraps inside your album for continuity.

# Creative Collages

Or try this cover idea: Assemble a collage of items that correspond with the theme of your book or that you just think look interesting together, make a color copy of it, and use it on the cover. Here are some ideas:

**Words for Posterity**

A **collage** is an artistic composition made of various materials (such as paper, cloth, or wood) and glued onto a surface.

➤ If your book is about your daughter's graduation from high school, put together a collage of photos of her from grade school to graduation, make a color copy of the collage, and make that part of the cover.

➤ For a book about a particular year in your family's life or in your life, gather newspaper and magazine clippings, pictures, and headlines of noteworthy news items from that year, make a collage out of them, make copies of the collage, and make this the cover.

**Sticky Points**

The adhesive on contact paper isn't safe, so try to avoid using it for album covers. Instead, use the Xyron machine to laminate and apply safe adhesive at the same time.

➤ Use postcards from your Alaskan cruise to make a cover for your travel album.

➤ Try using a map charting your route on the cover so you can look at where you traveled in comparison to where you live.

➤ For performers and musicians, paste your favorite piece of music or your playbills on the cover.

# Store Your Albums, but Not Too Well

The whole idea of having your photos displayed in an album is to contain the pages and protect them so you can view and enjoy your pictures any time you want. The best type of storage for your albums is a high-quality, acid-free album with a slipcase to keep dust, dirt, fingerprints, and light away from your photos. Store albums upright on a bookshelf where dust and dirt are unlikely to settle onto the pages.

Remember to store albums where temperatures don't fluctuate dramatically and they aren't exposed to bright light. Of course, you always want them easily accessible so you can look at them, but the kinder you treat them, the longer they will last.

*Make a collage that coordinates with your book's theme.*

---

### The Least You Need to Know

➤ Three-ring binders are convenient—you can rearrange your pages anytime you like.

➤ How many pictures do you have to present? Pick an album size that all your pictures fit into.

➤ Try personalizing album covers with fabric, stickers, painting, drawings. Tie a cover to the theme of your book and make it fun!

➤ Store your albums to keep pictures safe but make sure you can get to them easily. You want to enjoy looking at the albums you work so hard to make.

# Chapter 9

# Extras: Goodies and Gadgets That Give Your Scrapbook Flair

## In This Chapter

➤ Adding pizzazz to any page with stickers

➤ Die cuts are easy and inexpensive

➤ Using photo corners to make a photo pop out from a page

➤ Making your pages look professional with page toppers, handmade scraps, and frame-ups

Here is where the fun begins! Now that you know the basics of scrapbooking, from the essential tools to scrapbookese to making sure that the products you use are safe for photographs, it's time to learn about items that make your scrapbook fun to look at. Be warned that this is also the part that can add a lot of cost to scrapbooks. When you go into a scrapbook store, you will see so many stickers, die cuts, punches, and other embellishments that you won't know where to start. But don't worry—you don't have to spend a fortune to make delightful, personalized scrapbooks.

In this chapter, I talk about different scrapbook embellishments (that's the fancy word we use for things that make a scrapbook look pretty), where to find them, and how to use them to give your books personality, *your* personality. Although embellishments are not necessary for archival scrapbooking, they are what make scrapbooking fun. So read on to find what kind of embellishments are available.

## Stuck on Stickers

I have a friend who can draw any object or scene freehand. With a few strokes of her pen, she adds all sorts of details to her letters, scrapbooks, and cards. I don't have that talent. Besides a happy face and the occasional flower, my ability to draw is minimal. Luckily, I can use stickers to make up for my lack of artistic ability. Stickers are available in so many colors, patterns, shapes, and scenes that you are bound to find one to match any layout. Use a sticker not only to liven up your page, but to tell a better story, which, after all, is the purpose of your scrapbook.

*Check out the huge variety of stickers.*

If you use stickers created specifically for scrapbooks, you can rest assured that the adhesive is safe. But if you purchase stickers designed for other purposes, you need to check them out. Be careful with the stickers that you buy from mass-merchant stores. Some of them may have acidic adhesive that is harmful to your pages. You can always contact the manufacturer or use a pH testing pen to determine if the sticker is safe. In any case, try not to apply the sticker directly to any photo.

Right now, over a dozen companies specialize in stickers, and many other companies offer stickers along with other products. Each line has its own distinct style; for example, some companies, such as Suzie's Zoo, use only one artist's work, while others use the work of multiple artists. With all the new styles, you will probably find a favorite line.

To give you an idea of the variety of stickers out there, here are some popular themes and a few of the stickers to go with them:

➤ Christmas: Holly leaves and berries, ornaments, Santa Claus, gifts, poinsettias

➤ Halloween: Pumpkins, bats, ghosts, skeletons, candy corn, haunted houses, trick or treaters

➤ Easter: Dyed eggs, chicks, baskets, jelly beans

➤ Patriotic: Flags, firecrackers, stars and stripes, picnics

➤ Harvest/Thanksgiving: Turkeys, autumn leaves, acorns, pumpkins, cornucopias, Pilgrims

➤ St. Patrick's Day: Shamrocks, pot o' gold, leprechauns, gold coins

➤ Summer: Wading pool, swimsuit, sunglasses, chaise lounge, beach towel, seashell, sea animals

➤ Winter: Snowflakes, snowman, mittens, hot cocoa mug

➤ Kids: Crayons, tricycles, dolls, school bus

➤ Teens: Make-up, boom box, banners, cheerleader

➤ Baby: Footprints, bottle, diaper, teddy bear, baby booties

➤ Travel: Map, globe, airplane, ship, passport, city skyline

➤ Western: Cowboy hat, bandana, cactus, holster, lasso, steer, horseshoe

➤ Sports: Baseball mitt, bat, basketball, hockey stick, uniform, soccer, gymnastics, karate

➤ Characters: Disney, *101 Dalmatians*, *A Bug's Life*

**Words for Posterity**

An **embellishment** is a decorative item that is not essential to your scrapbook. Stickers, die cuts, and punches are a few examples of embellishments.

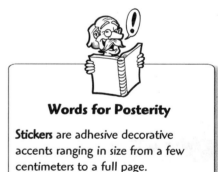

**Words for Posterity**

**Stickers** are adhesive decorative accents ranging in size from a few centimeters to a full page.

This is by no means a comprehensive list as there are too many stickers to name, but now you have an idea of the vast amount of stickers and themes out there.

**Shortcuts**

To title your page, try using some of the sticker letters that are available. They come in a large variety of colors as well as designs—match the style of lettering to the theme of your page.

You can also buy sticker letters, which are perfect for captions, headings, or titles and are great if you have poor penmanship or just want to brighten up your page. Use these to add a heading, write a caption, and to draw attention to your page. Multiple styles are available, extending from simple letters to funky letters to regal-looking letters, all of which come in many different colors. I like to match the theme of my pages with the sticker style. For example, I use puffy cloud-like letters for the title of a spring day layout or those rustic stick letters to go on a camping page. These stickers are mistake-proof since most of them can be repositioned—if you don't like the position of your stickers, you can move them around.

*Letters come in a huge variety of styles. Use them for titles, headlines, and to label your photos.*

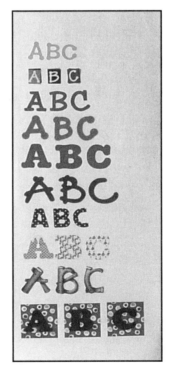

Wondering where to find all these stickers? Scrapbook stores sell a big variety, and new stickers come out all the time. One secret is to make friends with the store staff so they can alert you when they get a new shipment. Don't forget to check out sticker catalogs and Web sites, many of which feature ideas of how to use them—a great way to get those creative juices flowing. One of my favorite sticker on-line sites is Sticker Planet at http://www.stickerplanet.com. They have a wide selection of stickers and a brilliant Web site with lots of shopping options and ideas. You can order their sticker catalog by calling 800-555-8678. Check it out. (See the Resource Guide for more on-line sites that sell stickers and other embellishments.)

Stickers are a great way to restate the theme of your page. If the page looks a little blah, try using a festive sticker to perk it up. You can use anything from simple primary-colored balloons for a birthday page to an Eiffel Tower sticker to go with your honeymoon in Paris photos. The only thing to worry about with stickers is going overboard. I know those stickers are cute, but remember, you are trying to highlight your photos. I see many of my students try to use every single sticker that comes with the sheet in their layouts. My advice to them? Stickers randomly placed on a page are not nearly as appealing as stickers placed with purpose.

If you are a big sticker fan, make sure you keep your purchases organized to avoid overpurchasing one particular sticker. Just last week, I bought a sheet of stickers that I loved. When I brought it home, I found I already had three identical sheets!

### Shortcuts

Before making a sticker purchase, check to see if instructions accompany the stickers. Many stickers are sold with ideas for using them right on the back. Look for coordinating stationery and pattern paper as well.

### Sticky Points

Experience has taught me that it's important to buy spare stickers. If you buy too few, it's easy to run out of stickers before you finish a layout. Don't let this happen to you!

### Anecdotes from the Archives

Mrs. Grossman's Paper Company started in a 50-square-foot playhouse. Mrs. Grossman had only two employees (her 12-year-old son and his friend). In a little over twenty years, it grew to become one of the most popular sticker companies and now employs over 150 people!

# Any Way You Cut It, Die Cuts Are Great!

I love die cuts! You can customize them to your page or layer them to give your page some dimension. They come in thousands of designs, intricate to simple, and the sizes vary from 1 inch to an entire 8½-by-11 sheet.

*Here's a sample of the variety of die cuts you can use.*

Many scrapbook stores give their customers access to their die cut machines, often free of charge if you use paper purchased at the store. If you don't have access to a die cut machine, don't despair! You can buy the designs precut for a small price. And while precut designs don't have as large a range of color options, you can still purchase some great die cuts. Remember, if you want to layer these, buy more than one color.

Tips for doing your own die cutting:

➤ If you have a chance to cut your own dies, get to the store early so you can choose your paper.

➤ Die cutting goes more quickly and takes less effort if you use more than one piece of paper at a time in the machine.

➤ Go to the store with a list of colors and patterns in mind (or better yet, written down) so you won't waste time during your appointment.

➤ Place the paper in the die with the pattern side down to ensure a clean edge on the finished product.

**Words for Posterity**

**Die cut designs** are cut from paper. The process begins when a die is inserted into a die cut machine and pressed onto paper, cutting and perforating it into a design or shape. Die cuts can be used to embellish your page.

### Anecdotes from the Archives

Die cut machines and dies were originally made for use in schools. Teachers used the fun shapes for decorating their classroom boards, art projects, and classroom borders. Now there are two large die cut companies that sell the machines and the dies. Many designs are now created just for the scrapbooker.

Now that you know about die cuts, let me give you some of my favorite ways to use them:

➤ Embellishments on your layout.

➤ Use die cuts as a journaling block.

➤ Title for your page.

➤ Cut the dies into a wreath or make one by layering the dies.

➤ Use the jumbo dies to create great title pages for your books.

➤ Use one design and turn it into something else. For example, if you have a pumpkin die cut, cut it in red, add some small vines and leaves, and presto—you have a garden-ripe tomato that would be perfect for your harvest pages.

➤ Use small die cuts for great borders.

➤ Combine them with other accents. For example, place sticker apples in a die cut bushel.

## Guide to Die Cut Layering

One of my favorite uses of die cuts is die cut layering. This technique combines patterns and colors to make a more exciting die cut. I took a die cut layering class from an expert named Kim McCrary three years ago. The basic idea is to create a more realistic-looking die cut. Using patterned and textured papers is one sure way to get the look. Also, using stickers and other tools adds to the look.

Follow these steps to die cut layering success.

1. Decide what layers you want to add. If your layout includes photographs of kids in a wading pool and you are using a wading pool die cut, look at the photo for layering ideas.

2. Choose paper colors, patterns, and textures.

3. Choose your base die cut. This is the one that will be the foundation—everything else will be glued on to it.

4. Cut the layers from the different papers.

5. After the paper is all layered, you can add finishing touches.

*You can layer your die cuts for a really nice textured look.*

### Anecdotes from the Archives

Some scrapbook stores create their own custom die cuts, based on what customers say they want. The stores send the designs to die cut companies and have them prepare special dies. This way, shapes that are interesting to scrapbookers are available.

# Punches: For a Knockout Scrapbook

Punches are great, like having your own portable die cut machine. They are similar to a basic hole punch, except you press down on a button rather than squeezing the handles together. They make all sorts of different fun shapes, from small simple hearts to large frogs.

To use a punch, simply punch out the design and adhere it to your page or, for a different look, punch out the design directly into your scrapbook page and glue a coordinating colored or textured paper underneath. This technique is especially breathtaking with the corner lace punches, which are punches that you use on the corners of your pages.

I like to use punches to round the corners of my scrapbook pages. Some of the corner rounders punch out little designs in the corner as well. It's little touches like these that give your scrapbook flair.

**Words for Posterity**

**Punches** refer to the tools used to create small shapes as well as the shapes created by the punches.

*Here are some of the designs that can be created with punches.*

These punches come in several different types, and each type of punch has many different patterns:

➤ **Basic shapes**—circles, hearts, and trees

➤ **Silhouettes**—this punch cuts out the surrounding space so its shape is outlined

➤ **Corner**—these are designed to cut the corners of your pages

➤ **Border punches**—thinner punches used to create borders along the bottom of your page

Punches range in price from $2.99 to $13.99 each, depending on the size. A more economical option is the punch wheel. With six punch patterns on one instrument, this product is easy to store and fun to use. Be sure to buy some of the basic punches for your supplies before adding some of the specialty

**Sticky Points**

If your punch jams up, punch through a couple layers of waxed paper to lubricate it. To sharpen it, do the same thing with some fine grade sandpaper. Some of the intricate punches get paper stuck in them from time to time; you can use a small crochet hook to get it out.

ones. You'll always find a use for hearts, circles, and stars, but how many times will you need a car punch?

Here are some great uses for punches:

➤ As accents on page.

➤ As a border on page.

➤ As a frame around pictures.

➤ To create a different design. You can make different ent punches by layering just as you would a die cut. A great punch idea I saw in a punch art book had a house punch cut in half and placed in half of a circle—it looked like Noah's ark!

➤ Use in your title to add spark; for example, add some star punches to your Fourth of July title page.

*The punch wheel is a valuable tool.*

*Punches can add fun to any page in your scrapbook.*

100

# Just for Scrappers

While many of the scrapbooking supplies we use are borrowed from other crafting arenas—rubber stamps and stickers, for example, are stationery items—there are a few items that were created strictly for scrapbooking.

## *Top It All Off*

If you want to add a fun title to your page but don't have great lettering skills, there are a few options. One of my favorite product lines are Page Toppers. These have themed titles drawn in all sorts of innovative and creative ways that draw attention to your page. For example, "Father's Day" is spelled out with letters made of neckties, and "Snow Fun" features a snowman for the letter O. Available for around 40 cents each, these add a lot of character to your page for a small price.

**Words for Posterity**

**Title sheets** are pages with a variety of premade seasonal titles on them.

**Shortcuts**

Handmade Scraps makes embellishments that have color added to them so they have a layered die cut look without all of the work.

*Top off your pages with flair.*

# You're En"titled" to Use Title Sheets

If you need several titles with the same theme, look for title sheets. These have anywhere from 5 to 10 titles on one page that you can cut out and use on your page for captions, as well as titles. If you are creating a theme book, it's a good idea to buy one of these title sheets to give your book a little professional continuity. Available in seasonal themes such as Christmas, Halloween, and Spring, you can find one for any book.

# Punch 'Em Out

Perforated punches are fun accents that you punch out and adhere to your page. These make darling embellishments, are sold in books, and are included in some specialty paper packs. Hot Off the Press sells these punches in many different theme books. These are great and so easy to use—all you do is punch them out and adhere them to your page. If you need help deciding where to put them, check out the included idea page.

# Cut 'Em Out

A variation on the perforated punches is cutouts, which are sold in books (many from Provo Craft and Keeping Memories Alive). They are made to be cut out and are sold in a huge variety. They make fun frames for your snapshots, and many include a space to journal in. Since you can often find coordinating paper (like the bear paper shown here), you can mix and match the cutouts until you find the look you like.

Because cutouts are available in many of the popular Disney characters, like Mickey Mouse, Winnie the Pooh, and Simba, from the *Lion King*, these are a favorite for kids' scrapbooks. My son Nathan is a big fan of Winnie the Pooh and loves to look at his pictures on the Pooh paper.

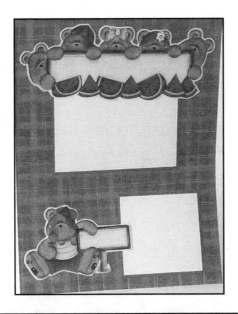

*Cutouts are great for kids' scrapbooks.*

*Handmade scraps and punchouts.*

## *Don't Sweat It! Specialty Die Cuts*

Handmade Scraps is a company that creates specialty die cuts. You can purchase these exclusive designs already layered and ready to go. Think of them as die cuts with detail—the boy doll they make has hair and a face, and the penguin is in three colors. Use these to get the layered die cut look without the time and work you would use making them yourself.

**Words for Posterity**

**Photo corners** are used to adhere photos in scrapbooks and photo albums without applying adhesive directly to the photo. Many scrapbookers like photo corners because photos can be removed from them without any damage.

## You've Been Framed

The latest on the scene of great products just for scrapbooking are Frame-Ups. These are hand-illustrated precut frames that fit pictures sized 3-by-5 and 4-by-6. The colors coordinate with all of the scrapbooking products already available and add instant flair to your page.

*Frame-Ups.*

## Colored and Clear Photo Corners for a Modern Look

If you are fortunate to have an old family photo album, you've probably realized that photo corners were a popular way to adhere photos to a page. For that reason, photo corners are the quickest way to add an heirloom quality to your scrapbooks.

Even if you aren't fond of the old-fashioned look that photo corners give, you'll still want to check these out because scrapbooking companies have given this product a facelift. While they are still available in traditional black, you can find them in four other colors and many designs! If you are really hooked on this look, try using one of the matching borders to make an ordinary photo look extraordinary.

**Shortcuts**

If you like the idea of photo corners but not the look, try clear photo mounting corners. Available in many different sizes, they are an invisible way to mount a photo to a page.

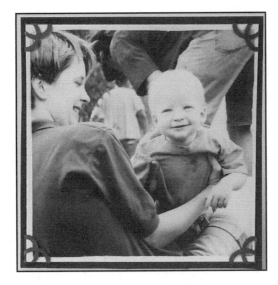

*Photo corners are easy and convenient to use. You can always take a picture out without any damage.*

## The Least You Need to Know

➤ Embellishments give your pages a polished (and fun!) touch.

➤ Be on the lookout for new stickers, punchouts, and cutouts to coordinate with the theme of your pages. Remember to highlight your photographs; and be careful not to overwhelm them.

➤ You may be able to use a store's die cut machine to customize these embellishments.

➤ Seasonal pages look great with coordinating page toppers or title sheets.

➤ Photo corners aren't just for old-fashioned books—they come in colors and clear.

## Part 3
# Getting Started

*When I began this project, the acquisitions editor informed me that writing the outline would be the most challenging part. She was right! For the scrapbooker, sorting and organizing their photos and collecting their stories—sort of like writing the outline for your scrapbook—is the biggest challenge. For some it can take a weekend, for others it can take months. But take heart—once you've done this you've taken a big step toward creating the scrapbook only you can create. To keep you inspired I've included some basic photography tips you'll want to refer to often. Good luck!*

# Chapter 10

# Photography 101: Taking and Organizing Terrific Pictures

Photographs are the heart of most scrapbooks. Even without embellishments of any kind, photos tell a story. In this chapter, you'll learn tips on how to take terrific pictures. The process isn't mysterious, and it is amazing to me the difference well-taken photos make in a scrapbook. We'll cover things like camera, film choice, and composing photographs to get the best possible pictures.

This chapter also covers important information on storing, filing, and sorting your pictures in ways that make the most sense. I know many people who want to scrapbook but don't know where to start. My mom told me, "I have too many pictures and documents and souvenirs to organize them. I'm just going to leave them all in boxes, and when I'm gone, you can take care of them." (Thanks, Mom!) Whether you have one hundred photos to work with or one thousand, follow these steps for gathering and sorting your photos, negatives, and other memorabilia. And for those of you who have very old photos to work with, I have included special instructions because these photos are easily damaged and need special care.

# Choose Your Weapon

The two most popular types of cameras are "point-and-shoot" and "single lens reflex" (SLR) cameras, which both use 35mm film. Digital cameras are also becoming increasingly popular. The one you choose depends basically on how much control you would like to have over your images versus how easy it is to take pictures.

### Words for Posterity

The **aperture** is the opening in a camera that lets in light. The aperture opens and closes when you snap a picture. When light hits the film, an image is made. Setting the aperture wider allows more light into the camera, while setting it smaller allows less light in.

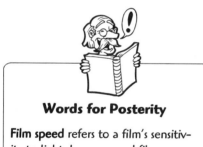

### Words for Posterity

**Film speed** refers to a film's sensitivity to light. Lower-speed films are less sensitive—use these on a bright, sunny day. Higher-speed films are more sensitive—use these in low-light situations.

➤ Point-and-shoot cameras are extremely easy to use. Point the camera at whatever you are taking a picture of, make sure the flash is on if you need it, and push the button. These cameras usually come with a built-in flash, focus automatically, and advance film automatically. These cameras are light and relatively inexpensive.

➤ Single lens reflex (SLR) cameras are somewhat more complicated to use but allow you to control your images in a way that is impossible with point-and-shoot cameras. Although you can buy SLRs that are fully automatic and as easy to use as a point-and-shoot, you can also set most SLRs to manual. Manual controls allow you to focus the camera yourself, control the exposure duration, and set the camera's aperture wider or smaller. You can also change lenses on an SLR camera, something you cannot do with a point-and-shoot.

➤ Digital cameras allow you to snap images that are stored directly onto computer disks. There is no film to develop, and the pictures can be viewed on a computer and then printed. Digital camera controls are similar to SLR cameras and produce high-quality images. If you have a computer and a high-quality color printer and money is no object, this may be an option for you.

➤ Polaroids are *not* a good choice for preservation because the processing chemicals are retained in the finished prints. Use this for a fun second camera, but not to record your family's history.

# Capture the Moment—Choosing the Right Film Speed

A film's speed tells you how sensitive the film is to light and is indicated by an ASA (or sometimes an ISO) number on the film's container. The higher the ASA number, the more sensitive the film is to light. What that means practically is that slower film speeds (ASA 64–125) are good to use outdoors in bright light and higher speeds (ASA 400–800) can be used in lower-light situations.

### Anecdotes from the Archives

Before the invention of 35mm film, photographs were made one at a time on large, heavy glass plates. Each plate was coated with light-sensitive chemicals just before the photograph was taken and then developed right away. Today's film, though much smaller and lighter, works on the same principle—it is covered with emulsion that is light-sensitive. When light hits the film through the camera's lens, it creates an image. The film must be processed to see the image (that makes a negative) and then printed onto photographic paper.

In addition, faster film speeds can capture movement without blurring (good to know when you are taking pictures of your child's softball game), but may lose detail and produce a grainy print. Slower-speed film will let you capture fine details in portraits but is not good for action shots. Below are recommendations for using different film speeds. Very slow film (ASA 25–32) can be purchased but may be hard to find and is not generally useful to the average picture taker.

➤ Medium speed (ASA 64–125). Recommended uses: Great for taking pictures of a newborn where there is plenty of light (if the baby moves around there will be some blurring on the photos—this isn't all bad because it conveys a sense of movement). Prop the baby on a blanket on the lawn, hold the camera steady, and snap away.

➤ Faster speed (ASA 200–400). Recommended uses: Good for situations where there isn't a lot of available light, such as early evening, or using indoors in a bright room without a flash. Fast-speed film can also capture movement without blurring.

➤ ASA 200 is an all-purpose film speed. Take it along to the beach, to the park, to any outdoor, medium- to bright-sun activity. It's medium-fast speed will allow you to capture detail without much blurring.

### Shortcuts

Consider asking employees of photo labs to recommend brands of film—a lab in a mall might develop on average 30–80 rolls each day. Without even knowing it, those employees become experts in the types of film. So ask lots of questions. What they like to develop should be the film in your camera.

### Sticky Points

Always remember to check the expiration date on your film—after that date, film likely will not perform well.

➤ Use ASA 400 in low light or situations where there's a lot of movement (good for sports events or snapping the kids running around under the sprinkler). Keep in mind that some of these pictures may have a grainy quality, especially if you make enlargements.

➤ Very fast speed (ASA 800–1600). Recommended uses: Good for extreme low-light conditions, such as a wedding indoors when you don't have a flash. Film this fast can let you take pictures that would otherwise be impossible, but pictures may be grainy even if they are not enlarged. You can try using ASA 1600 in near total darkness as long as there is some available light source, such as a candle, a lamp, fireworks, or even moonlight (on an SLR, set your camera to a long exposure).

It's a good idea to carry a few different kinds of film with you—weather conditions and light can change, and it would be a shame to miss a great shot because your film can't handle the existing light conditions.

It's also a good idea to consider getting your pictures developed at a photo lab—the difference in the quality of pictures that you'll get back versus pictures developed at the corner drug store can be tremendous. Photo labs are more expensive, but they are the best choice for developing important pictures. You'll be pleased by the results.

## Taking Great Portraits

Creating wonderful portraits is a challenge for any photographer. Great portrait photographers speak of a "moment of truth" that reveals a person's character. Sometimes, all you need is a quick snap that captures a spontaneous moment; other times, you'll want to be more careful and try to capture a person's mood and character.

➤ **Lighting**—The most important element in a picture. The most flattering light for portraits comes from a bit above and off to the side. Other lighting can be used for interesting effects, such as creating silhouettes.

➤ **Posing**—Make sure the people or person is relaxed. If your subject is nervous, chat with him or her to put them at ease. If you are shooting a group, don't make them stand rigidly; let them relax into their poses.

➤ **Props/background**—You can use these to interesting effect. Sometimes, you'll have to make due with what is around; other times, you'll be able to pick these to create a theme.

➤ **Direction**—Head-on shots can appear stiff and unnatural, while placing a subject off to the side might be more relaxed. Profile shots can be interesting and dramatic.

➤ **Position**—When taking pictures of kids, keep in mind that they are small and short—so don't be afraid to move in!

*These shots make creative use of props.*

# Top Ten Tips for Taking Terrific Pictures

Eliott Erwitt, world-renowned photographer, once said, "All the technique in the world doesn't compensate for the inability to notice." The best way to improve your photographs is to work on becoming a world-class noticer—watch out for interesting images, and your photography will improve. A photographer friend of mine suggested these 10 ways for anybody to take better pictures.

1. Change your point of view. Don't always plop down right in front of your subject. Try changing your angle, tilting your camera, getting on one knee, or standing on a ladder.

**Shortcuts**

Try using props to accentuate the character of the person whose portrait you are taking. For instance, if you are taking shots of a good friend who plays the violin, consider posing her with the instrument or against a background of musical notes—not anything too distracting, but something that shows who the subject is.

If your camera has autofocus, don't even look through the view finder. Guesstimate and be surprised at what turns out.

2. Get closer. Get in close to your subjects. People are sometimes afraid to get up close, resulting in a subject being a mere dot in the photo.

*Make sure your subjects aren't dots in your pictures—get in close.*

3. But not too close. On the other hand, there's such a thing as too close—hey, it's a camera, not a medical probe. This happens most often with newborn babies—remember that most autofocus cameras require you to be about three or four feet away. Any closer, and your baby is one very cute blur.

4. Follow the law of thirds. Here's an old photographer's trick—put your subject in the left or right third of the frame instead of dead center. These compositions are more pleasing to the eye.

5. Compose as you snap. You can easily crop photographs after they are developed, but try to frame the image in your mind's eye as you are taking it. Make sure all the elements are within the lines of the camera's viewfinder, and take a picture that already contains the balance, subjects, and shapes you want.

6. Get a 35mm camera. If you own a disk or 110 camera, it's time to toss it out. The negatives from disk and 110 cameras are so small they can't help but take poor pictures. A cheap 35mm can be purchased for less than $40—they're not the best cameras, but if you're on a budget, they're great. First learn to take good pictures, then graduate to a better camera.

7. Use your flash outdoors. Ever take a photo of your family underneath a tree and notice that half of the faces are covered in shadow? A flash used outdoors is called "fill flash" and can reduce this problem. If you are taking pictures of people outside, try using your flash on every picture (usually your subject needs to be less than 15 feet away).

8. Take some candid shots. It's so intrusive to constantly ask people to stop what they're doing to "say cheese." Candid pictures capture people's expressions and activities wonderfully. And if you do take posed photos, take them quickly—get the flash ready, make sure the film is advanced, and the lens cap is off.

9. Be mindful of your backgrounds. For instance, when taking photos of a newborn baby, try not to pose the baby on a solid-color blanket. Unless you are getting your film developed by a custom developer, the baby will take on the color of the blanket. In any shot, ask yourself if the background will flatter or detract from your subject.

10. Take lots of pictures. If a professional photographer gets one picture they are happy with on a roll of 36, they are ecstatic. Follow the photographer's rule and carry your camera around all the time. A picture may be worth a thousand words, but if you don't take the photo when the moment arrives, it's worth only one word—"Darn."

# Get It All Together—Establishing a Gathering Place

So you've taken a ton of pictures, and you have even more sitting around in boxes. Before you rush from room to room, unearthing all your family treasures, you need to establish a gathering place.

If you have an entire room for your scrapbook project, great. Stash everything in there. Or find a corner where you can leave your photos for a few days while you are organizing them. In my house, this is the floor on my side of the bed, but if you have a table or countertop that you can use, great. If you don't have small kids or pets running around, go ahead and leave them anywhere they won't be disturbed by drafts or wind. Just be sure that they aren't in the way of heating vents, as this is damaging to photos.

Now, go through your house looking for photos and souvenirs. If you are well organized, this shouldn't take long, but, if you're like my sister, you have five or six places where you stash important items. I still remember the thrill of discovering my long-lost program from my eighth grade viola recital. Looking at it brought back the excitement I felt at receiving a superior rating for a piece a group of us did in junior high. Suddenly, I am there playing the viola, and I am winning all over again. This is a great memory for me.

Call up your extended family to see if they have photos you'd be interested in. Look through your journals and diaries for documents, such as birth certificates, death certificates, school records, and other things you'll want copies of.

**Sticky Points**

Because photographs can be damaged by sunlight, keep the room dark if possible by closing the blinds or drawing the curtains.

**Sticky Points**

If you are working with very old albums that are tearing apart, handle pictures gently and try not to move them around or leave them exposed when you aren't examining them. It isn't a bad idea to wear photo gloves to handle these, and watch out for dust.

**Shortcuts**

Don't overlook the history that goes along with your old photos. As you are looking through these scrapbooks with your family, record their memories of the pictures and events either by taking notes or by recording the conversations.

**Shortcuts**

Use a soft, clean cloth to wipe off dirt and fingerprints. Do not use facial tissues or paper towels—these items have microscopic fibers that could scratch your photos.

Look to these sources for photos and other mementos that you, or people close to you, might have stashed away:

➤ Kitchen drawers

➤ Closets

➤ Mixed with school projects (this is often where I have found the class pictures that I forgot to take out and place with photos)

➤ From grandparents

➤ Hawaii pictures from the couple you went with

➤ Cedar chest

➤ Other relatives

➤ Your children's friends' parents

➤ Your favorite photo developing lab—maybe you forgot to pick up some film

➤ Old family friends

# Treat Old Photos and Mementos Gently

Most of us have photos that have been improperly stored. Photos of mine that were once stored in magnetic albums are yellowing and faded. And other old photos and mementos that have been stored in the bottom of closets or in drawers can show their age. What can you do about this? I've gathered advice and information for you.

## Old Photo Albums

If you're working with old photo albums where the pictures are fastened with photo corners, you're in luck. Usually all you have to do is remove the photo; the adhesive will often have already worn off some, if not all, of the corners. If the pictures are brittle, proceed carefully. Consider copying them so you won't damage the originals. Take them to a photo preservationist if you want an expert opinion. If you decide to copy your old photographs, beware that some copy machines are too hot for photos and can damage them and make sure that the one you use is safe.

## Magnetic Albums

So-called "magnetic" albums are destructive to your photos because the adhesives emit harmful chemicals. If you've got photos in these types of albums, get them out as soon as possible. Here are a few different ways to remove them. Some photos are really stubborn, so you might have to try several techniques.

➤ Pry up a corner of the photo with a table knife or other flat object. Aim a blow dryer set on low under the photo to loosen the glue until you can remove the photo.

➤ Slip some waxed dental floss under the photo. Use a sawing motion to loosen the glue.

➤ Try the adhesive remover Undu. This dissolves the glue used in magnetic photo albums.

➤ If all else fails, see a photo expert. Remember, you don't want to be rough with your photos—you can ruin them!

**Shortcuts**

It is a good idea to keep a wax pencil or photographic marker with you as you are removing photos to jot down notes on the back of the pictures. Any original captions should be recorded.

*This will become your new best friend if you are removing old photos.*

## Restoring Old Documents

If old documents are soiled, you can try cleaning them off using small bits of an eraser. If the documents have any rips, use a special document tape that is available through archival sources. Do your best to handle these items carefully. If all else fails, take the documents to a copy store.

Remember to store these precious documents flat with a piece of acid-free paper in between each document rather than standing them up in files; this prevents them from bending. If you are going to use these documents in your albums, make sure they are in sheet protectors to prevent further damage.

**117**

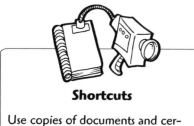

**Shortcuts**

Use copies of documents and certificates as background paper in your scrapbook.

# What "Sort" of Stuff Have You Found?

Now think about the type of scrapbook album you are working on. Are you doing a master one for yourself? Are you doing one for each of your children and grandchildren? Are you working on a family Christmas album? What if you just want to organize all your photos and use a select few in one special scrapbook? The important thing is to decide what your ultimate goal is before you begin sorting.

## Step 1—Make It Manageable

Divide the pictures into manageable increments. If you are working on a collection of 40 years' worth of photos, start by dividing them into decades, then work on each decade separately.

Pile the pictures into boxes that are labeled by decade and divide each of those boxes into years within that decade. If you only have three or four years' worth of photos, you can sort first by year, then by season, and so on.

## Step 2—Who ARE These People?

Step 1 works perfectly if every picture you have is nicely labeled with the year it was taken and a neat narrative about who is in the picture, where they are, and what they are doing. But this is unlikely—if we were all this organized, our photos would've been in albums long ago! Figuring out the year and what is going on in the photos is half the fun, especially if you haven't looked at the pictures in years. What can help you figure out when the pictures were taken?

➤ Check the background of the picture for clues—maybe you can just make out a banner in the background that says "Happy New Year 1977." (Perfect for the first picture in that album!)

➤ What type of clothes is everyone wearing? Coats for winter, swimsuits for summer, bell bottoms in the early seventies (fashions can often help determine what year it is, as well as the season).

➤ How old are the children in the pictures? If you can figure out even approximately how old the children in the picture are, you can probably figure out the year.

➤ Who is everyone hanging out with? If the photo is of you, say, with your friends Sharon and Marie from an old job, that'll help you guess when the picture was taken.

➤ Who are these people? If you're having trouble identifying some of the faces in a picture, enlist your family—maybe your brother can recall an old friend from your high school years.

# Step 3—Pictures and Keepsakes Go Together

Finally, all the photos are sorted according to the chronological order. The next step is to decide what type of memorabilia you want to include. I like to store my mementos in separate containers. One idea to help remember which memento goes with which pictures is to make a corresponding note or tag to place with the photos that correspond to the era or event the memento comes from (just don't use sticky back notes because the adhesive is damaging to your photo.)

Let's say you have pictures of your honeymoon trip to Spain, and you find ticket stubs for the romantic train ride you and your spouse took from Madrid to Barcelona. Note this on a piece of cardstock that you file with the photographs. Store the tickets in a separate container in the same chronological order as the photographs. When you are ready to make the album, you'll see the reminder among the pictures and find the old tickets in your file.

**Shortcuts**

There are many ways mementos can be sorted—chronologically, but also by topic (such as sports, awards, trips, pets), and by person (have a box labeled with someone's name and keep together all the mementos and souvenirs that have to do with him or her).

# Step 4—Focus On a Theme

The next step is to determine the type of album you are creating.

My next-door neighbor decided she wanted to do scrapbooks for each of her grown children. She took a couple of weeks gathering photos, another couple of weeks sorting the pictures, and then became frustrated. Because there were so many good pictures of the family and many of the photos were of all the kids together, she couldn't decide which child should get which photos.

If you come across this, you have a few options. You can divide the pictures up evenly and just give child A different ones from child B and C, and so forth. Another option is to copy the photos and create different layouts for all of the children. While this is time-consuming, it is nice to create a one-of-a-kind scrapbook for each child.

**Shortcuts**

When you are making multiple albums of the same time period, consider creating one master page and having it copied for all of the albums.

Another good idea is to create a master family album. This kind of book contains all the family pictures, including school photos, portraits, family vacations, and everything pertaining to your family. These are best organized in chronological order. The nice thing about these albums is everything is in one place. You are not creating duplicate pages, and none of the children feel left out.

### Words for Posterity

A **master family album** holds pictures of everyone in the family and family documents, typically in chronological order.

Theme albums are also popular. Just recently, in one of my classes, a mother and her two daughters were working on a theme album for their father. They combined their efforts in gathering the photos and put the album together in less than four weeks. He loves to fish with his grandchildren, and he loves to take pictures. So they surprised him for Father's Day with a 50-page album of him fishing through the years and ending up with the last 15 pages of him fishing with his grandkids. After they gathered as many pictures as they could, they went through them together and sorted the photos according to year and category: fishing as a child, fishing with friends, fishing trips to Montana, and so forth. Each family member then took a couple of sections and worked on them. Later, they got together to put on the finishing touches and compile all the sections. It was a wonderful gift and a fun project.

### Words for Posterity

A **theme album** is a scrapbook devoted to one idea. Some popular theme albums focus on birthdays, weddings, and school days.

Theme books are a great idea for anyone who wants to scrapbook but doesn't want to include 40 years of photos. There are many options. Consider doing a holiday album for Christmas or Hanukkah, or, if you have a special family reunion, creating a scrapbook with the photos from the event. Just be sure to include written memories and mementos, as well as pictures from everyone. These really help to personalize the event or celebration.

### Words for Posterity

A **photo display album** has a combination of special scrapbook pages along with photos displayed in regular sheet protectors.

A photo display is a kind of album that displays your photos on scrapbooking pages, as well as in page protectors with photo sleeves. This is a great option if you want to display your photos in a binder but you don't want to scrapbook every single picture. Do some of both. First you'll need to sort your photos chronologically, then estimate how many albums you will need. Go ahead and start by placing the pictures you want to scrapbook in plain sheet protectors and the other photos in the protectors with photo sleeves.

# They're Sorted—Now Where Can You Keep Them?

Two photo storage options exist: long-term and temporary.

Short-term or temporary storage usually is not safe for photographs to stay for too long, but pictures will usually do all right for a little while, say a month or so. For short-term storage, I like to use plastic shoeboxes for my photos because they are inexpensive, lightweight, and see-through. I use scraps of cardstock to divide my photos into categories. Since the plastic isn't acid-free, these containers will damage your photos in the long run, so use them only for current projects.

**Sticky Points**

As convenient as it might seem, refrain from using paper clips, rubber bands, or other office supplies to organize your pictures. These can leave damaging and unattractive imprints on your photographs.

Good long-term storage options:

➤ The cropper hopper photo storage case—this can hold up to 2,000 photos and is very compact and easy to store. Because it is made with archival ingredients, you can store your photos in here indefinitely.

➤ For projects such as theme albums or ongoing books or for any type of book, use your binders as your storage. Slip the categorized photos in your sheet protectors in the order you want them in.

➤ Be on the lookout for photo chests made from acid-free cardboard. These are available in decorator styles and keep your photographs organized and safe.

➤ Some scrapbook stores carry expensive storage items that are made for long-term photo storage. Try www.lastingimpressions.com for a good selection of long-term storage options.

# Store Negatives Safely

Negatives last longer than color photographs, so you want to make sure that you store all those slippery negatives in a safe place. You never know when you'll need reprints of lost or ruined pictures.

The easiest way to store negatives is in negative holders. These are similar to photo sleeves, but they have pockets sized to hold an individual strip of negatives. Many of them include space to label the negatives (a good idea) and have holes punched along their sides. Place these pocket pages in an album, and you're set.

**Sticky Points**

Though it's easier to store negatives in the house, it's not advisable. In the case of burglary, flood, or natural disaster, you'll want copies of your precious pictures. It's a good idea to store at least the most precious ones in a safe deposit box or in a fireproof safe at a family member's house.

Buying tabbed protectors to put in your negative albums will help keep them organized. Place the date of the negatives on the tabs, and you'll have an easier time finding negatives when you need them.

# Copy Precious Photos and Documents

If you decide that you'd like to present a valuable or one-of-a-kind document in your book but you are wary of using the original, take the document to be photocopied. Make sure the staff copies it on acid-free paper. Include the document in your scrapbook. If you want to use the original document, treat it with some of the deacidification sprays on the market. Then either store the document in your scrapbook safely or store it between layers of buffered cardstock.

Color copiers these days have an amazing variety of capabilities. Kodak has a color copying machine that copies photos and allows you to add color, delete red-eye, even add a decorative border. Many mass-merchant stores are carrying these, or you can go to your local copy shop for affordable color copies.

---

### The Least You Need to Know

➤ Photographs are the heart of a scrapbook. Anyone can take better pictures by following a few simple guidelines.

➤ Take your important film to be developed at a good photo lab—you'll be happy with the results.

➤ Enlist friends and relatives to help you gather pictures and mementos and identify people and eras in your pictures.

➤ Sort photographs and souvenirs according to the type of scrapbook you want to make. Possibilities include master family albums, celebrations of special events, like holidays, birthdays, trips, and family gatherings.

➤ Be gentle with old photographs and albums and figure out good storage for photographs, keepsakes, documents, and negatives until you are ready to use them.

# Chapter 11

---

# Saving Souvenirs

---

### In This Chapter

➤ Using souvenirs in your scrapbook

➤ Making souvenirs safe with deacidification products

➤ Neat projects for saving keepsakes

---

Souvenirs—we all have them. And we hate to part with them. After all, who wants to throw away your six year old's drawing of the family cat or the tickets from your junior prom? What about the program from your college graduation? Well, you don't have to throw them away nor do you have to shove them in that shoebox crammed under your bed because there is a better way.

Memorabilia adds a new dimension to scrapbooks. What better way to tell a story about a family trip to Disneyland than displaying a photo of your family at the entrance to the park, along with the actual passes you used to get in? Or how about the receipt from the bed and breakfast you stayed at in London? These mementos are fun for future generations to look at, and they add a three-dimensional element into your scrapbook.

But you may have some questions about saving keepsakes: What items are good to save? How do I save them? And, of course, where on earth can I keep them? You'll find the answers to these and more questions in this chapter.

## Holding On to Yesterday

Tickets, programs, maps and the like are often printed on low-grade, highly acidic papers. Despite all your efforts, souvenirs can threaten the archival environment you've worked so hard to create for your photographs. Because they are so important to the story that you are telling, you must include them, but how can you make them safe and lasting?

# Dropping the Acid

Thanks to some incredible products, this is now a fairly simple task. Sprays on the market, called deacidification sprays, actually neutralize the acid in your mementos, making them safe to use in your scrapbook. To use these sprays, flatten and spread out the items you want to spray. Keep items as close together as possible without overlapping to use the spray most effectively. Go ahead and spray on an even coat, covering items but not soaking them. Do not pick up the sprayed items until they are completely dry and then handle them with care so that you don't introduce any more acid to them.

While these sprays can be expensive, they are a good investment. After all, the items you are preserving are priceless.

### Shortcuts

Need an interesting background for your Halloween pages? Try color copying candy for the background. You can use a tray to place the items in and then copy away.

### Sticky Points

When scanning in items to use in your scrapbook, the color probably will not be as true as a color copy. For instance, white will tend to have a green tint. Experiment to see what you can get.

# Copy and Scan

The other thing you can do is to go to your local photocopy shop and make color copies of the items onto acid-free paper. This way you can place the copies in your scrapbook and safely store the originals. You can also reduce or enlarge these color copies to make whatever it is you're including just the right size for your page.

Color copying isn't just for souvenirs, photos, and documents—you can color copy almost anything. Don't just copy photos and documents. Try copying fabric, your wedding dress, or even flower petals. One of the sweetest baby pages I've seen was created by color copying a portion of a baby blanket and using that for the background to display a picture of baby wrapped in the blanket.

If you own a scanner that is attached to your computer, use it! Besides photos and certificates, you can also scan clothes and other items into your computer and then print them. Try doing this with blessing or christening gown. Making a scouting album? Scan those merit badge patches and print them out on paper to display alongside the photos.

# Encapsulation

The other choice for preservation of memorabilia is to encapsulate. This process involves enclosing the document between two sheets of stiff Mylar polyester plastic, then sealing the edges with a special double-sided tape. Next, finish up with a zigzag sewing of nylon thread on the sides of the plastic to protect and support the document. This way, you've preserved the document but left it accessible. If you ever need to get to the document, all you need to do is trim an edge. You can also purchase ready-made encapsulation pockets in a variety of sizes.

# Saving Your Budding Picasso's Works of Art

Anyone who has been the recipient of children's artwork knows how precious and heartwarming it is. When children express themselves through art, the results are touching. Here are a few different methods for saving artwork. See which works best for you:

➤ Create albums of your child's artwork. Spray each piece with deacidification spray and place them in a page protector. Put the protectors in an album.

➤ Choose the special pieces to display in a child's chronological scrapbook. Take a photo of him holding his artwork and put it in his scrapbook next to the original.

➤ For oversized art, go to the color copier and have the artwork reduced so that it can fit in your book.

➤ Arrange the artwork on the floor and take photos of your child with it.

➤ Try scanning the pieces into your computer and keep files of the scanned images to keep track on disc.

*Your refrigerator is too small—save your child's artwork in a special scrapbook.*

# Keeping Documementos

If there is a helpful copy shop near where you live, you can have a lot of fun with your certificates, or *documementos*. Try taking in card-sized stationery and having the shop print your daughter's birth certificate in the middle. That would make a great page, and you can reduce or enlarge the certificate to fit your needs. Some of the most creative uses of documents I have seen were pages copied from the phone book to show a fun ad or home number.

*You can use this certificate in your scrapbook.*

If you don't want to go to the expense or trouble of deacidifying some ticket stubs or greeting cards, at least make sure that you put them on their own page—not directly next to your pictures. You can also mount them onto buffered cardstock for added protection (and spraying them with deacidifying spray would also make them safe.)

This is a great time for pocket pages, too. Create a simple pocket out of two sheets of cardstock to hold items such as Valentine cards or ticket stubs.

*Make a little pocket on a page to store mementos.*

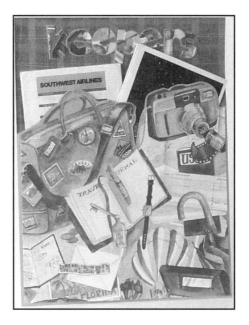

# Three-Dimensional Memories

Those baby booties your daughter wore when she was three weeks old are too cute to stash in a box somewhere. The same goes for the pet rock you had that your mom kept all these years. Believe it or not, these can be displayed in your scrapbook too!

There are special pages called 3D keepsake holders that are three-dimensional pages you can place objects into. Try saving items from your childhood or a favorite vacation. The 3D pages slip right into your scrapbook and are available for both 8¹/₂-by-11 and 12-by-12 albums.

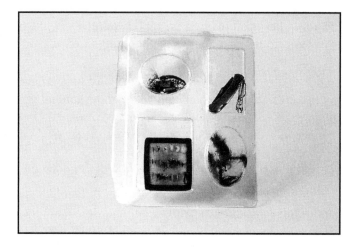

*Keep 3D objects in special pockets.*

Memorabilia pockets are another fun way to display souvenirs in your scrapbook. They come in a variety of sizes, from 2-by-2 inches to 8¹/₂-by-11 inches. People love to use these for locks of hair, but with a little creativity, you can put in anything: a rosebud from a special bouquet, the key from your first car, or a name tag from that silly summer high school job.

# Sowing Ideas—Make a Special Garden Scrapbook

Flowers are some of nature's most brilliant items and often hold special meaning to people. Here are some ways to preserve flowers in our scrapbooks:

➤ Insert dried and pressed flowers into memorabilia pockets and stick right on page.

➤ Color copy petals from a special bouquet or corsage.

➤ Adhere dried and pressed flowers directly to the page and gently place photos around it.

➤ Laminate dried and pressed flowers using an acid-free lamination, such as Xyron.

A lovely project would be to create a scrapbook that covers a year in the life of your garden and incorporates pressed flowers or color copies of flowers and plants. Here are some ideas of how you could go to town (or country!) with this book:

1. Start making your album during the fall clean-up and bulb-planting season:

   ➤ Title page: You might make a color copy of autumn leaves that you take from your backyard (keep them in a sealed bag on the way to the copy shop to preserve the color because these dry up and crack quickly).

   ➤ Include a diagram of the garden showing all the trees, shrubs, and perennials you've planted.

   ➤ Include journaling about how you planted spring flowering bulbs like tulips, daffodils, and crocuses—and include the pretty packaging of what you've planted.

   ➤ As the days get colder, take pictures of your garden in every stage: the stark beauty of the trees as they lose their leaves, and the way the garden looks in snow. In warmer climates, document what your garden looks like year round. If you live in a cold climate, use the winter to plan what you'd like your garden to include come the spring.

2. When spring comes, take note of the first flowers you see and take pictures and notes as everything comes into full bloom.

   ➤ You could turn your scrapbook into a gardener's almanac by including gardening tips along with the photographs. You can then refer back to the scrapbook when needed. Notes to include might be planting times, fertilization methods, growth success, where items were purchased, and watering methods.

   ➤ Include photos and colorful seed packets, clips from gardening catalogs, pictures of friends and family in the garden, your own drawings of flowers, pictures or color copies of prized flowers—and don't forget pictures of you in your gardening hat and gloves!

   ➤ Keep your book up through the summer, as perennials come into bloom and your garden starts to look lush.

3. When the fall comes, you, your garden, and your scrapbook will have come full circle. Imagine how nice it will be that winter to have a chronicle of your garden in full bloom. And in years to come, it will be wonderful to track the changes in your garden (when the tiny sapling you planted becomes a big apple tree) by looking back at your book.

# Treasure Boxes and Time Capsules

Scrapbooks are a great way to collect things to save for posterity, but they do have their limitations (it's kinda hard to slip the teddy bear you loved to bits or the guitar you first learned to play into a scrapbook). Below are two fun ideas for saving larger souvenirs, important sentimental items, and items for posterity.

## Yo Ho! Ho!—Making a Treasure Box

Creating a treasure box is a great way to compile an ongoing legacy for you and your family. You may not have a building named after you—or a flower, or a street—but everyone has things that tell about who they are. And your treasures don't have to be a pirate's ransom of gold bullion and jewel-encrusted daggers, just personal items that mean a lot to you and will mean a lot to your children.

A treasure box can also be a way of commemorating a loved one and telling their stories. Sadly, I have heard of parents who have buried small children and haven't been able to put any of their possessions away because of painful reminders.

Since we all have different lives and histories, we all want to include different things in our treasure boxes. I am going to share with you some of the items I have saved and what I want to add to my treasure box. My goal in doing this is mainly for posterity—I'd like my children to have tangible items from my life and an explanation for things I have saved. I want them to have a true sense of my life and what happened in it. As you see what is inside my treasure box, jot down what you want to include in yours in the space provided and set a goal to compile it.

**Sticky Points**

Although it is not easy to scrapbook difficult times, they are an important part of your history. Be respectful to others' needs, though, and carefully choose what is appropriate to share.

*Save whatever is most special to you in a treasure box.*

Following are the contents of my treasure box:

➤ Childhood journal—This has bits and pieces of my early teens, along with report cards and letters from friends.

➤ A toy I played with as a baby.

➤ High school yearbook—This is more for the interest of clothing styles and the era than for any sentimental meaning.

➤ College papers—Personal essays and papers written for college courses contain my thoughts at that time.

➤ Wedding dress—Since I have all sons, I'll have it forever.

➤ Matchbook from our honeymoon suite—The first time our names were together on a document.

➤ Maternity dress—Looking at it reminds me of being pregnant, the anticipation and excitement.

➤ Baby outfits from each of my children.

➤ Handmade presents—From love letters from my husband to my children's handprints.

➤ Books—I love reading, and I have saved a few books that have been very significant to me.

➤ Letters from my parents.

➤ Documents—Certificates, stories written about me by my family members, cards, and so on.

*Jot down items you'd like to save in your treasure box.*

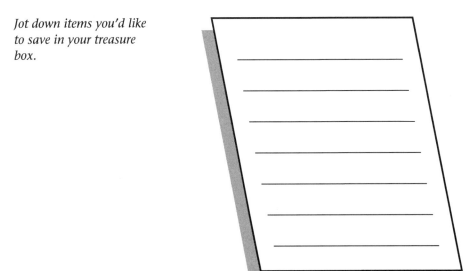

# Time in a Bottle—Making a Time Capsule

How about creating a time capsule? A time capsule contains objects that represent life in the year and era when it was created. It is intended to be sealed up and opened when at least a few decades have passed. Especially now that we are approaching the turn of the century, it'd be interesting to make a capsule with objects representing the 1990s. Image the fun you will have when you open it in ten or twenty years.

To make a time capsule, first find a container to seal it in. Make sure it is something that is going to be difficult to break into so you won't be tempted to open it up. Gather together everyone you want to participate, make a list of items you want to enclose, and decide how long you want to lock them up for.

Compile your items in the container, label the container with the date when you are to open it, and lock it away. Bury it in your back yard, put it on a high shelf in the garage, or some other place where it's out of the way. Make sure at least a few people know where it is so you'll be able to find it in the appointed year!

Items that would be fun to include in a time capsule are

➤ Current newspapers and magazines detailing current events

➤ For children, a recording of height and weight

➤ Tracing of children's hands and feet

➤ Listing of favorites, such as music, movies, food to eat, places to go, hobbies, books, and clothes

➤ Articles of clothing, CDs, something that captures that year

➤ Photographs of everyone involved

➤ Baby clothes

➤ List of goals for the next 20 years

➤ Family predictions for everyone

➤ Predictions

**Words for Posterity**

A **time capsule** is a container holding historical records or objects that represent the culture that deposited it for preservation. If you make a time capsule and intend to open it up sometime, make sure someone remembers where it is!

**Shortcuts**

You can purchase commercially prepared time capsules that come with the container and a list of everything to include.

Include anything that would be significant to you and your family. This is a fun undertaking and makes a great excuse to have a party in 20 years!

*Imagine how fun it would be to open up a time capsule in twenty years.*

- video tape
- audio tape
- family photos
- newspaper clippings
- predictions
- family member interviews
- favorite items
- etc.

### The Least You Need to Know

➤ There are deacidification products you can use to save many kinds of souvenirs.

➤ You can also keep mementos in 3D page protectors or sealed up packets.

➤ Try color copying documents so that you can include the items in your book without using fragile originals. You can copy anything—try color copying candies for a sweet Halloween page.

➤ Save your child's artwork by making a special scrapbook just for art.

➤ Use the ideas in this chapter to make a year-round garden scrapbook, a treasure box, or a time capsule.

# Chapter 12

# Tell Your Story: Journaling in Your Scrapbook

> ### In This Chapter
>
> ➤ Write for the kids, for the family, for the future, and most of all, for yourself
>
> ➤ Great suggestions on where to write stories
>
> ➤ Getting-started exercises for those who need help writing
>
> ➤ A guide to creating a one-of-a-kind scrapbook that focuses on your family's history

No scrapbook is complete without journaling. Future readers of the scrapbook won't recognize all the faces and will need names, dates, and details. You can write as much or as little as you like in your scrapbook, but you must write something! If you're wondering how to get started, read this chapter for guidelines, tips, and a few ideas to make journaling fun. You can include all kinds of writing in your book, like poetry, stories, jokes, cartoons—anything!

If you are looking for a fun and interesting scrapbooking project, this chapter includes a guide for creating a scrapbook that focuses on an oral history of your family or community. This kind of album could include photographs, souvenirs and documents, interviews written or recorded on audio cassette, writing, and art. While this project may sound overwhelming, it is extremely rewarding and can be completed in no time at all once you get started. Get the kids involved with interviewing grandparents, digging for photos, and compiling their favorite family stories in this album. So gather all the help you can and get started.

# The Who, What, When, Where, and Why

What you write in your scrapbook depends a lot on what type of book you are working on. If you are doing a baby book for your daughter, you will probably have all sorts of feelings and memories you want to record; the way you felt when you first laid eyes on her, who received her first smile, and the day she took her first step. But if you are working on an album with pictures of your grandparents, you might not have as many details to include.

For your everyday albums, remember to record the who, what, when, why, and where of your pictures.

➤ *Who* is in the pictures is an important place to start. Record both first and last names, especially of people who aren't in your family. In the years to come, you may not remember their last names.

➤ *What* is important because it explains what you are doing and helps the reader to understand the pictures.

➤ *When* is a must to record so you can look back and not drive yourself crazy because you can't remember when you went to Uncle Jack's cookout. This helps to establish your family history. Every summer, we go to Jackson Hole with my husband's family, and my kids love to look at pictures of us sitting in front of my favorite restaurant. Always include the date somewhere on your page.

➤ *Where* is a must to include because someday you will forget where you were that year. Give as much detail as possible, especially on trips. A great idea is to include restaurant and hotel locations. Make sure to write down the address. Another great addition is to take pictures of signs or landmarks that add to the story.

➤ *Why* are you wearing the same shirt in all your pregnant pictures? Why is your cat sitting on top of the refrigerator? Why is your mom wearing a hat made out of a paper plate on her head? The "whys" (and the "why on earths?") tell much of the story—don't leave them out.

**Shortcuts**

When traveling, take some time to jot down the events and fun times you want to remember. Have your notepad on hand when you are compiling those vacation pictures to help you remember the details.

## *Include the Sublime and the Ridiculous*

Make sure to include any interesting stories about the photos. I remember when my husband and I were in a group shot for a magazine article illustrating different types of jobs. I was the mom holding a small child. At the time, I was a few months pregnant, and by the time we were all settled and ready to take the picture, my son had had it. So in the picture, I have a very odd expression on my face because I had to go to the bathroom, my 18-month old was squirming, and I was very anxious to leave. My family finds this story about that picture very humorous.

## Jog Your Memories

When showing pictures of family treasures, such as your parent's first house, journal the stories of their first years together. Do the same for some of your children's treasures. I have a page of my twins' blessing outfits with a letter to them from me about that time in our life and how much I love them. Someday they will appreciate that.

What if you don't have pictures of important events in your life? This has happened to all of us, whether you forgot the camera, or you were so caught up in the event that taking pictures was not on your mind—until later when you regretted it. You can still record these events in your scrapbooking through journaling. You don't need to have a picture; just write the story down and place it on some fun paper, and you have a nice recollection of the event.

A scrapbook can give modest mothers a chance to brag about their children's accomplishments. You can include a picture of your toddler, his or her age, and current vocabulary. Show your child holding a favorite book and write down the words she recited from the story. When my son Justin was three, he began a love affair with dinosaurs. It would make a great page to show this three-year-old with his favorite dinosaurs and listing all the names of the ones he could say. Your child could also attempt a little journaling himself by writing right in the book.

### Anecdotes from the Archives

Do you want to record the voice of your children reading their favorite story? Get the Memory Button. It has a digital recording capability and fits right on your scrapbook page.

# So Maybe You're Not Hemingway ... You Still Have a Story to Tell

Some people like to make writing as much a focus of their books as the pictures. Want to tell a story but aren't sure where to start? Here are some exercises to loosen up the storyteller in you.

## The Setup, the Meat, and the Caboose

When recounting a story or event, use the three following parts as guidelines to get the information organized. Use humor when sharing stories if appropriate. Add more detail than you think is necessary—you won't believe what you will forget. Whether it is a paragraph or a page, this information is crucial to a scrapbook. This way, you will be the one to have the last word.

### Shortcuts

Try keeping a small notebook with you at all times so that when you are waiting in the doctor's office or watching soccer games, you can outline or jot down funny stories that you want to include in your scrapbook. When you start doing your pages, pull out the notebook to jog your memory.

➤ Part 1—The setup: This is the who, when, where of the photo or story.

➤ Part 2—The meat: The what, the details of the story.

➤ Part 3—The caboose, the why: The significance of the story or why this is funny to you or your family. If you want to make a point with this story, this is the place.

## Try Analysis

If you still have a difficult time remembering what is going on during that time, try photo memory therapy. To help you remember certain events, look through your photographs. These will help jog your memories and help you think of things to include in your writing. Try asking yourself a few questions about the photo to get you thinking.

➤ Why did I take a picture of this person, thing, or event?

➤ Who is in the photo and what is my relationship to them?

➤ Is there anything funny or interesting going on that the photo doesn't show?

➤ When was this photo taken?

➤ What were my relationships with these people like?

The only mistake you can make is to feel that you're incapable of writing down events and feelings—the more you write, the better. Keep on, and it will get easier. Use simple, everyday language when recounting an event. Write down what you remember from specific events.

If you are still having a difficult time, try these simple fill-in-the-blank questions to help you formulate your story:

The people in this picture are _____.

They are important to me because _____.

I was _____ years old at the time of this picture.

We are doing _____ in this picture.

I like this picture because it reminds me of _____.

You can also set the photo aside and show it to another family member to see what they can remember.

# A Clean, Well-Lined Space for Writing

Now that you know what to write, you may be wondering where to write it. The most popular way is to create a journaling block by using a blank section on your page and writing in that spot. Or cut out a piece of paper, write the story on it, and mount it in your book.

➤ If you don't have a ton to say about your photos, you can simply include captions around your pictures in blurbs. You can write under or next to your photo you are describing.

➤ For a different look, try writing on a die cut. Use a die cut that matches the theme of your page, such as journaling on a school page on an apple die cut. Or trace a shape from a template and write inside it.

➤ Incorporate journaling into your page decorations by journaling around the border. Add some stickers here and there, and you've got a cute page.

➤ Be creative and use journaling as an accent, as well. Make a journaling puzzle that leads the reader through the story in a unique way.

*A lengthy piece of writing in a layout.*

*Captions only.*

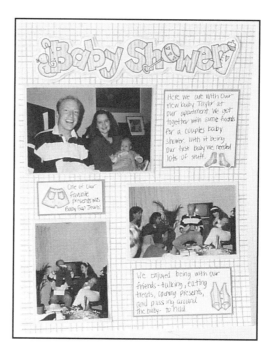

# A Heading Is Worth a Thousand Words

A heading is the title of your layout. It says a lot about your page and is a fun way to include journaling. I love to use fun headings on all of my pages. You can do so much with these!

Just as a headline is critical to a newspaper story, headings are a critical part of journaling because they can tie everything together and control the presentation and written aspect of the page. It's best to make headings short and sweet, easy to read, and eye-catching. For Justin's birthday pages, some of the headings I used were, "Presents, Presents, and More Presents," "Time to Celebrate," and "Digging Into My Cake."

### Anecdotes from the Archives

Melody Ross, the creator of many journaling tools, was called Chatterbox as a childhood nickname because she talked so much. That is now the name of her company. Look for Chatterbox books listing different heading suggestions and much more.

Coming up with cute phrases and headings used to be a hard part of scrapbooking. Fortunately, there are now reference books with great scrapbook titles included, listed by category, as well as many Web sites with topper ideas. Page toppers are also perfect for this. Some scrapbook magazines include titling ideas that you can copy into your scrapbook and color.

# Decorative Tools for Journaling

For journaling, don't just stick to black pens and blank paper. You can choose from numerous pens and colors to journal in. (See Chapter 5, "All Paper Is Not Created Equal," for more on the range of writing tools suitable for scrapbooking.)

Journaling templates are fun shapes with lines for journaling. You can also buy templates that have lines for straight, no-fail journaling.

*A journaling template can help create room for writing on your page.*

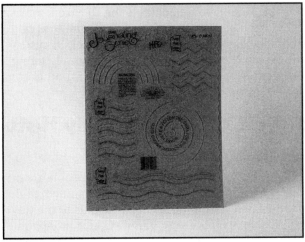

If you like rubber stamps, there are stamps available that have designs with lined places for journaling. Stamp on your page, and you have an instant place to add your story.

Some people ask if they should use their own handwriting for journaling or if they should use those cute computer fonts? This is a personal choice, and you can do some of both or go one way, but remember that your handwriting is precious to future generations.

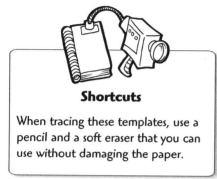

**Shortcuts**

When tracing these templates, use a pencil and a soft eraser that you can use without damaging the paper.

## The Handwriting on the Wall

My mother does not like her handwriting, but the rest of us like it because it reminds us of our mother's love. To me, her handwriting evokes memories of handwritten school notes excusing me for being absent, recipes I read of hers when I was learning to cook, opening Christmas presents that always said, "From mom and dad" (but we knew that mom picked them out), and the day's to-do list written by the phone, reminding her to wash laundry and drive us to the orthodontist's office.

Now my mother's handwriting means a carefully packed care package full of hand-sewn pajamas, discounted chocolates for me, crayons and markers for the kids, to-do lists detailing what tasks she wants to accomplish at my house, reminders for craft projects she wants to complete when she gets home, and a running grocery list for my house. I love my mother's handwriting because it reminds me of my mother's sacrifices and love for her children. So take this into consideration when trying to decide whether to include your own writing.

## Fiddlesticks and Scripts

If you want to have some other options for journaling, try buying some of the computer programs made for scrapbookers. They include fonts that are great accessories to your page. By far the most popular among scrapbookers is the DJ Inkers computer programs. These include clip art, as well as fonts that are perfect for the scrapbooker. My favorite fonts are Crayon (looks like little kids' writing), Fiddlesticks (a rustic-looking font), and Script (a more formal font). Creating Keepsakes has a lettering CD-ROM that includes 15 lettering fonts from their magazine. Look for other companies, such as Cock-a-Doodle Designs, to come out with lettering CDs.

# Putting It All Together—Creating a Family History Scrapbook

Genealogy, or the history of a family, has become something many people are interested in researching. Interest ranges from a desire to make a simple family tree that goes back three generations to a real interest in finding out the details of the way ancestors lived. (See Chapter 1, "What Is Scrapbooking, Anyway?" for more on researching the genealogy of your family, including resources.)

True/False quiz: Answer these questions to determine if you are a good candidate for writing a personal history:

I had a good childhood.

I had a bad childhood.

I am very young.

I am very old.

I received an extensive education.

I didn't go to school past the third grade.

I have several children.

I have no children.

I am close to my extended family.

I rarely speak to my relatives.

I am an excellent writer.

My writing is atrocious.

I had an eventful, colorful life.

My life was simple, filled with ordinary events.

If you answered true to any of these questions, you should write a personal history! Each person has a life worth recording, regardless of how ordinary it seems to you.

If you are interested in embarking on a project like this, why not make a scrapbook of your findings and make writing a focal point in the project. You will end up with a tangible and archival product that will be appreciated and enjoyed by generations of your family to come. There are many books solely devoted to the topic of researching family history, and after reading this, you should seek them out (see this book's resource guide), but here I have given a beginning guide to the process of gathering the information you'll need to create a memorable keepsake heritage scrapbook.

**Words for Posterity**

Someone's **heritage** is something that is passed down from generation to generation like a legacy or inheritance. It can also be thought of as the traditions that get passed down in a family or community.

**Shortcuts**

If you would rather, get a tape recorder and record your thoughts and memories on tape. Once you have recorded these things, you can save the cassette tape in your scrapbook in one of the 3D keepsake holders, or you can transcribe the words into text. If you are interested in creating a transcript of your interviews, you can do it yourself or pay a transcriber to do it for you.

# Step 1: Think! What Do You Already Know?

If you'd like to create a family history scrapbook, the first place to start is with you. Gather your childhood photos and write down what is happening in them. Don't worry about grammar or syntax, just write, write, write.

For example, let's say that the bare-bones facts you know about your family are as follows:

➤ Your father comes from a family that is of German and English Protestant background. Your paternal grandmother emigrated to the United States from Germany with her family in the 1920s. She came with her mother and great-aunt, and they settled in New York City.

➤ Your paternal grandfather's family had been in this country for a long time and were of English descent. He died when your father was 10, and you don't know much about him except that he was a commercial artist.

➤ Your mother comes from a Russian Jewish family. Your maternal grandmother's family emigrated to the United States from Russia at the turn of the century and also settled in New York. Her father (your great-grandfather) was a rabbi.

➤ You don't know anything about your maternal grandfather.

These explorations might leave you very curious. You might be interested in finding out what area of Germany your grandmother came from and exactly where they settled in New York. Both sides of this family likely came through Ellis Island in New York City—what was this like? Where in Russia did your mother's family come from? The religious background of this family might interest you—what was the rabbi grandfather's life like in the old country? You might want information on your maternal grandfather. And where did your paternal grandfather learn his trade as a commercial artist? What kinds of places did he work for?

Think about where you could go to fill in whatever information you are interested in finding out.

### Anecdotes from the Archives

From 1892–1954, Ellis Island in New York City was the entry point for 12 million immigrants to the United States. Today, over 40 percent of Americans, 100 million people, can trace their roots to an Ellis Island ancestor. At the Ellis Island Immigration Museum and Immigration History Center, people can find information about their families. You can even honor an immigrant relative by having his or her name put up on the Ellis Island Wall of Honor.

# Step 2: Focus Your Efforts

Once you have mined yourself as a resource for the project, the next important step is to decide on your parameters: What will your time frame be for the exploration of your family's history? How many generations do you want to include? Do you have access to oral or written history or photos? It's a good idea to create a time frame for your project according to what you are going to include.

Some of us come from families that have been in a certain community for many generations, others are from families whose ancestors came to this country during the great immigrant waves in the early 1900s, and others came from recently immigrated families that have been in the United States for only a generation or two. Your focus will depend on your access to resources, and your interests. If you don't have any historical information further back than two generations, then focus on two generations and include what you know of the previous ones. If you wish to go back further and have the resources, do it.

# Step 3: Gather Your Resources

Gather materials that will help you compile this history, such as journals, documents, photographs, old albums, old family bibles, favorite books and poems—anything that would give you an idea of your history. If anyone in your family has items they are not willing to part with, ask them to photograph or copy them to send to you for use in this project.

See if you can interview family members. This can be a great job for the kids. Sometimes older people are more willing to talk to children than to adults. If you'd like to make a history of your parents, sic one of your kids on them! Arm her with a few loaded questions, a tape recorder, and that irresistible grin, and you'll get all sorts of unexpected revelations.

Here is a list of questions your kids can ask to get the conversation rolling:

➤ What kind of pets did you have in your house?

➤ Did you get along with your siblings when you were growing up?

➤ What church (if any) did you belong to as a child?

➤ Tell me your favorite activity when you were growing up.

➤ Did you play with kids in the neighborhood? What were they like?

➤ Did you get in trouble when you were young? What for?

**Shortcuts**

When gathering family history, don't forget other family fixtures: your next-door neighbor, the lady who used to baby-sit you after school, or the man your family rented a cabin from every summer. They can give you a different perspective on events and people.

➤ What things did you do on your birthday?

➤ Tell me about the first time you met Grandpa/Grandma.

➤ What was it like when you drove a car for the first time?

➤ What were your favorite holiday traditions growing up?

### Anecdotes from the Archives

A book by Don Norton, *Composing Your Life Story*, includes 500 topics for taking a personal history. These topics include vocational choices, favorite family stories, favorite places, leisure activities, family shopping, naps, childhood friends, hairstyles, typical weekday routines, higher education, family recipes, and nicknames to cite a few. Choose a topic that is interesting to you and write what you can about it.

Don't forget to document these important family history items in your scrapbook:

➤ Family/community stories passed down

➤ Family/community legends

➤ Family tree chart

➤ History of who began the community

➤ Family traditions/holidays

➤ Family symbol

➤ Photographs of important family belongings along with written history about why it is important

It is inevitable when doing a thorough history of a family to come upon some difficult and sensitive subjects. My advice to you would be to document it in some way, but consider carefully who will be viewing this album. I suggest you be discreet; without entirely skipping over events and eras, be careful about including anything that might upset someone.

## *Step 4: Make a Timeline*

Once you see what kind of information you have to work with, you can decide what direction you want to go in. Make a timeline or outline for this scrapbook based on what you have gathered, which will give you a good base to start filling in the information you did not have about your family, and will give you a structure for how you want to present the information in your scrapbook. For instance, if you've gathered enough information about your great-grandparents emigrating to the United States at the turn of the century and what life was like for them when they arrived, your timeline might begin at 1905 and continue to the present. If you've decided to focus on a smaller time frame, begin your timeline at a later point.

As you are gathering this information, you need to have a place to store everything. I would suggest purchasing a good-sized plastic file box that would enable you to hang file folders and store documents and photographs. Organize the files to coordinate with your timeline and store documentation and photographs in separate folders in the same slot.

Now you have information, you're organized, and you know where you are going. What's next?

# Step 5: Start Scrapping!

The gathering process can take you anywhere from a few days to a few months, depending on how much you decide to do. Now you can actually put all this great material in a scrapbook.

You'll want to get your usual basic tools together:

➤ An album

➤ Paper—cardstock and decorative

➤ Tools for journaling

➤ Scissors

➤ Page protectors (recommended for use in this book, especially if some of the items included are fragile)

➤ Adhesives

➤ Embellishments you think you might want to use

➤ pH testing pen and deacidification spray

You'll want to choose an album and materials that complement your subject matter, and for this one, it is a good idea to keep the embellishments simple and tasteful. I would suggest using classic colors and classic embellishments, such as photo corners. Many embellishments have a selection of appropriate products for this. Take a look at some idea books to see how other people with the same type of project have designed their books. Remember, for this project, you want to focus on the history and writing, not the punch art.

Since this is a scrapbook meant to last, choosing archival-quality materials is of the utmost importance. You don't want to gather all these precious items, only to have them deteriorate. Be careful when handling them and be sure to deacidify any items, such as newspaper clippings, which might fall apart.

As you work on the book, make sure to include a lot of journaling that describes not only what is happening in the pictures you include, but also information about historical events during the time when the photo was taken, stories you heard about the people pictured, family legends, quotes and poems by writers of each era you cover, song lyrics that recall the times, and more.

When this book is completed, it will be a lasting, much-cherished tribute to your family—and will tell a story not only of the people in the family, but of the times they lived in. And for you, it will help you learn much more about people you know and the community you live in, and, by the way, it will help you hone your scrapbooking skills to a sharp edge.

## The Least You Need to Know

➤ Remember to include the who, what, where, when, and why when journaling the story.

➤ Include all the funny stories about pictures. These will have you holding your sides for years to come.

➤ There are some fun journaling tools to help you create great pages.

➤ Even if you don't like your handwriting, be sure to include some of it in your scrapbook.

➤ If you are interested in working on a scrapbook that documents your family's history, look in this chapter for ideas and a step-by-step guide.

# Chapter 13

# Create a Fun and Inviting Workspace

---

### In This Chapter

➤ Making the most of storage in your home and on the go

➤ Minimize frustration by organizing your supplies

➤ Making scrapbooking feasible so you aren't scrambling to find your supplies to sneak in some time

➤ Less is really more

---

Does this sound familiar? It's Saturday morning, and you have a few spare hours. Perfect time to scrapbook, right? So you drag your box of photos upstairs and place them on the kitchen table. You head back downstairs for your box of paper and notice the pile of dirty clothes outside the laundry room. After throwing the clothes in the washer, you head back upstairs, but halfway up, you remember your box and turn around to get it. After fifteen minutes of choosing photos for your layout, the phone rings. It's Aunt Ettie, reminding you to bring a potato salad to the church picnic. After disentangling yourself from her, you sit down again. You work for five solid minutes when you notice that your time is up, and you need to put everything away. Frustrated, you think, "Scrapbooking is so time-consuming!"

Some people prefer to do their scrapbooking at home and have plenty of space, others prefer to work on the go, and still others cram in their scrapping wherever they can. Whichever kind of scrapper you are, you'll need to organize your supplies, create a good and inviting workspace, store your materials, and, most of all, make the time for an activity you enjoy.

# Less Is More

Organizing your scrapbook supplies begins before you go to the scrapbook store. Remember, you don't want to buy things you don't need or duplicates of things you already have.

You know how they say you shouldn't go grocery shopping when you're hungry or without a list because you're likely to end up buying much more than you need? The same goes for buying scrapping supplies. A while ago, I went to my favorite scrapbook store to see what I could see. I found some great birthday stickers. "These will be perfect for Justin's birthday page," I told myself, "I'll buy two sets just to be sure I have enough." A few weeks later, as I was setting up my supplies, I found three more sets of those exact same stickers! That incident convinced me that I needed to keep better track of my supplies. Especially if you scrapbook often and have a lot of supplies, it's a good idea to keep an inventory of what you have and make careful lists of what you need before you step into the store.

After you have your supplies, the next step is to find good ways to organize them. To determine what your storage needs are, answer the following questions:

1. You do most of your scrapbooking:

    a. at home in a specially designated scrapbooking room.

    b. at workshops, crops, or with a scrapbooking group.

    c. anywhere from your next door neighbor's house to your kitchen table.

2. Which of the following describes your current storage situation?

    a. I live in a huge house and have unlimited space.

    b. I do all my scrapping outside my house so I need portable storage.

    c. All my supplies are crammed under my bed, on top of the fridge, and on the top shelf of my closet.

3. When selecting storage supplies:

    a. I want to use items I already have on hand.

    b. I use something that's easy to transport.

    c. I'm more concerned with being able to locate supplies than purchasing the latest gadgets.

4. What are your shopping habits?

    a. I'm a sucker for gadgets and tools that make scrapbooking easier.

    b. I don't purchase many tools because I use the ones at the store.

    c. I buy the products I like and know I'll use.

Add up your score using the following scorecard:

A = 3 points

B = 5 points

C = 7 points

What range do you fall into?

12–15 points = Home office scrapper

16–21 points = On-the-go scrapper

22–28 points = Kitchen-table scrapper

Using these categories as a guide, read the corresponding advice on setting up your own scrapbooking space. Each section includes advice for your particular needs, but remember to be flexible and creative. The last section contains tips on storing favorite products.

# The Home Office Scrapper— The Den at Your Disposal

Even if you have plenty of space for your scrapbook supplies, you may have a hard time keeping things organized. For example, do you wander into your scrapbook room and find it hard to remember where you put those back-to-school stickers or the embossed vellum paper for your wedding album? Well, read on for a description of an easy-to-use scrapbooking room for the home office scrapper.

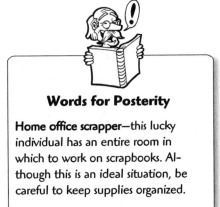

**Words for Posterity**

Home office scrapper—this lucky individual has an entire room in which to work on scrapbooks. Although this is an ideal situation, be careful to keep supplies organized.

## Workspace

The first item you'll need in the home office is a desk, preferably one with drawers of various sizes. If you don't have a desk, a table with a file cabinet and some storage containers would make a good substitute. Use the small drawers for things like pens and adhesives and place large supplies in the file drawers—templates, idea books, class handouts, and things like this work well here.

## Storage

I like to store my cardstock upright in a filing container so I can see the colors rather than storing it flat on shelves.

Another way to organize your paper is to purchase large accordion-style folders, which are sold at office supply stores. Use one to store paper sorted by color and the other to store paper sorted by theme. Following are suggestions for the color storage folder:

Red

Red combinations

Blue

Blue combinations

Yellow

Yellow combinations

Green

Green combinations

Violet

Violet combinations

Black

Neutrals

Metallics

Primary combos

Pastel combos

The theme file has folders labeled

Winter

Spring

Summer

Fall

Christmas

Halloween

Seasons (smaller holidays, all combined)

School

Kids stuff

Sports

Nature/camping

Animals/pets

Birthdays

Wedding/graduation

Baby

Miscellaneous

You'll want to put your templates in folders in the file drawers, arranged by category in alphabetical order. When placing several templates in one folder, place a sheet of paper between the individual templates to keep them from getting tangled up. If you've got a large number of templates, it's a good idea to keep a numbered list of them, with a corresponding list on each template. This helps you when you can't remember if you filed your soccer templates under *F* for fall or *S* for sports. For example, if the soccer puzzle mate is number 12 in your system, place that on your master list—having a master list makes things much easier to find.

The next necessary item is a bookcase or shelving system on which you can place binders filled with stickers, die cuts, and other small items, as well as your scrapbooks in progress. Boxes of sheet protectors can go on the shelves, too.

**Sticky Points**

Remember to look through your scraps before you cut up a new piece of paper. You can get a lot of mileage out of your scraps by using them for punches and other small embellishments.

Now for the scissors and punches. I have found that the best way to store them is a way that makes it easy to see them. Try mounting some inexpensive pegboard onto the wall and organizing your scissors in rows on the pegboard. You can mount tabs on the back of your punches (the kind retail stores use to display or hang small items on their walls) and hang the punches, as well. You will always be able to see what you have on the wall. One thing to keep in mind is that everything in your office should be within easy reach—if you have to get up on a step stool or crawl under the desk every time you want to reach your pattern paper, you won't want to use it. Make all of your supplies and equipment as easy to get at as possible, not too high up or too low.

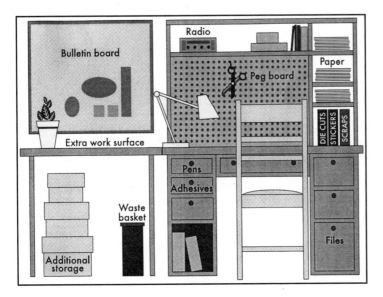

*Organization and good storage—a perfect workspace.*

## *Inspiration*

Keep in mind with the home office that you want to be inspired to create great pages. One idea is to hang a bulletin board where you can attach pictures of some of your favorite layouts, keep your running shopping list, and write down (and pin up) ideas as they come to you.

Create a nice ambiance in your office—it's as important as having the proper storage space and efficient files. Choose lighting in your space that provides both good overhead light for when you are looking through your supply bins and good bright spot lighting for when you are working up close with pictures and other items in your scrapbook. A good idea is to buy an inexpensive desk lamp to go over your work area—generally incandescent light is easier on the eyes than fluorescent light and provides bright, natural light. Try burning a scented candle to add to the atmosphere and help you relax. What a difference this makes. Also, why not bring a radio into your room so that you can enjoy listening to your favorite CDs or radio station if you are scrapbooking by yourself. This room is where your creativity comes alive, so make it as cozy and comfortable as you like.

**Shortcuts**

Do you have a friend who likes scrapbooking too? Try this: Each of you get subscriptions to different scrapbooking magazines and trade with each other. You'll be up to date on all the latest in scrapbooking without spending a ton of money.

The best way to stay organized when you have a home office is to take inventory frequently and put everything away when you are done. Good Luck!

# The On-the-Go Scrapper—Away You Go!

If you are an on-the-go scrapper, you first need to determine where you are going to store your scrapbook items in between crops and workshops. Even if you only have a small amount of space, you can store many things if you use the right products.

You basically have two options—purchase a storage item made just for scrapbooking products or use storage products that you can purchase at mass-merchant stores.

The following are some storage options made specifically for scrapbookers. My favorite is the "Crop in Style" bags. They come in three sizes and are like suitcases. You can fit an amazing amount of supplies inside and outside the binder. There are special pockets and slots on the outside for pens, scissors, cutters, and more. My favorite part is that these bags have wheels so you can pull it or use the shoulder straps to carry it.

There are also storage containers made out of hard plastic with compartments inside for adhesives, pens, scissors, and the like. These containers have handles to carry them and come in $8^1/_2$-by-11 and 12-by-12 sizes. You can use them for paper, as well.

Next is a rolling cart type of storage option that is made by Cropper Hopper. You can store all of your supplies in here, as well as your albums under construction. It has wheels so you can just roll it out, and you're on your way. I would suggest finding what is going to work best for you by determining how many products you are going to be purchasing. If you are going to go to classes where all of the nonperishable products are available, such as scissors and punches, you won't need to purchase them. If those items are not available, you are most likely going to purchase some tools. Some of my favorite storage options are not made just for scrapbooking.

**Words for Posterity**

On-the-go scrappers need supplies that can be stored in portable containers, making it easy to grab the stuff and go!

Plastic storage containers that I have used to tote around cleaning products at home work great for transporting pens and adhesives. Just place the items on either side—these are very transportable.

For paper and pages in progress, I use a plastic file bin. Place your paper in them, sorted by color, and put pages under construction in manila folders that expand and go up the sides—this is a great project idea. You have everything in one place, and you can also place binders in here to hold all of your die cuts and scraps, as well as stickers—they fit right in.

Some people have those oversized plastic bins with wheels attached to the bottom and carry all of their containers and products in those and just wheel away to class. If you decide to use this, don't forget to have someone help you lift it into your car.

# Kitchen-Table Scrapper—Wherever and Whenever

If you don't have much room to store your supplies, you need to be creative to think of new spaces. I had friends who lived in a two-bedroom apartment with three kids and used every available inch of space for storage, including raising their bed up with cinder blocks so they could use the space underneath. Look around your house: Is there room under your bed or in the linen closet? What about building some shelves in your bedroom to store your supplies? Just remember to keep in mind these storage rules: Avoid moisture, temperature fluctuation, and humidity. Try not to use the basement, attic, or garage for your supplies. Also, make sure you have put supplies where you can get to them easily.

**Words for Posterity**

The kitchen-table scrapper fits supplies wherever they can possibly go: in the closet, behind the sofa, or even in kitchen cabinets—wherever sup-plies are easy to grab and use. You'll find her scrapbooking at the kitchen table or on a card table in the family room.

Be creative when coming up with storage options. The most important thing is to keep things organized and readily available. I advise the kitchen-table scrapper to organize scrapping at home in a two-part process. First, spend some time grouping pictures together and deciding what you want to do with them, maybe sketching out layout ideas or creating a folder with your pictures and the supplies needed to create the page or pages. When you shop to get supplies, put them directly into the folder and store this in a file bin. Then, when you have your other supplies organized and stored on one shelf of a closet or bookcase, you will be ready to scrap at a moment's notice.

# Extra Storage Ideas for the Avid Scrapper

If you are an avid scrapbooker like myself and you have been collecting supplies for a while, you may find you have as much or more than a small store. You need extra storage savvy—here are some ideas.

## *Bind It Up*

Binders are so versatile, so easy to use, and so compact that you'll find they can fill many of your storage needs. For instance, you can buy binders especially designed to hold stickers, which have refillable pages that have different-sized pockets. The binder measures 12-by-12 and features a wrap-around zipper so your stickers cannot fall out. Or you can try the binders made to hold baseball cards. Use the different protectors with photo sleeve pockets for larger stickers. If you are ambitious, you can even make sticker storage sheets from page protectors. Simply sew some pockets of varying sizes onto the protector with your sewing machine, using a heavy-duty needle.

Templates are perfect to store in binders; just place a sheet of paper in between each one so they don't get tangled. Organize these by category, and you're set. If you have large templates, try punching a hole in a corner of each one and storing them on a metal ring. I also like to store a pencil, sharpener, and wax pencil with my templates so I don't have to look everywhere when it is time to trace.

**Shortcuts**

Make sure you label your binders on the spine so you can easily see what is in them.

Die cuts work well in binders, too. You probably went to a lot of trouble to make those die cuts, so make sure you store them in such a way that they won't rip or bend. You can use binders for storing your photo corners, punches, and scraps. I like to organize these by category, such as holidays, dances, or birthdays. This way, you can flip to find the supplies you need without any hassle.

## *Resealable Bags*

I have seen people organize their embellishments in resealable freezer bags. This is a smart, inexpensive way to store items like stickers, die cuts, punches, page toppers, and other small items that get lost in large boxes. Simply seal the items in a bag, punch a hole in the corner, and place them on a metal ring. Just be sure that you don't cram the bags full of stuff, or they won't lie flat. This can be adapted for use in binders, as well; punch three holes in the bags and place them in your binders. Remember, this method is only for short-term storage since it isn't acid-free.

## Storing Paper

You've got to have paper on hand when you want to scrapbook, but how do you store it without creasing it? Some of my students use expandable folders, but that doesn't work well for me because my paper always gets crumpled. I like to use a plastic file box because it is sturdy enough to protect my paper but lightweight enough for me to haul around with ease. I store it lengthwise, so I can see at a glance what colors and patterns I have to work with. If you must store your paper on a shelf, try not to stack it more than three inches high, or it will have a tendency to slip and fall.

If you don't have large amounts of paper to store, use an oversized sheet protector and organize your paper by color. Place the protectors in a binder, and you've got all your paper at your fingertips! This works well for paper packs, too.

Paper that is size 12 by 12 inches is difficult to store because there aren't many ready-made commercial products that come in that size. You either have to buy products made for 12-by-12 scrapbooking or improvise. Some of the best storage options I have seen are oversized storage containers with a lid—paper is placed on its side and other supplies are next to it. Also, for those who have lots of 12-by-12 paper, try using your cleaned-out pizza boxes to store your paper in for temporary purposes. This can be successful and is a good way to recycle those boxes.

## Storing Cutting Supplies

You can certainly toss your scissors in a box, but if you have a lot of scissors, you'll probably get frustrated when you have to fish through all your scissors to find the needed design at the bottom of the heap. I store my scissors on large metal rings, according to their use—one ring for corner-edgers, one ring for wide-edgers, and one for

**Shortcuts**

If you go to crops or scrapbooking parties and bring your supplies with you, mark your initials on them with a permanent pen to avoid losing them.

**Sticky Points**

Remember, you don't need to bring every pen you own to crops and workshops. When other participants see your collection, they'll want to borrow them. That's fine, but these pens can be misused—too much pressure will ruin many pen tips. Try bringing only the essential pens to class—remember that you can always journal at home.

regular so I can easily find what I need. There are bags and shelves specifically designed to store scissors, something that might be worthwhile if you use scissors frequently.

If you are a punch fan, you ought to buy a tackle box (or if someone you know goes fishing, "borrow" theirs). Clear plastic make-up storage boxes with lots of little drawers are good, too. Another favorite for punches are the boxes designed for storing embroidery floss. This is a great way to store your punches and be able to see what you've got. You don't want to buy a punch on sale, only to find that you've got one just like it at home.

## *Organizing Writing Tools*

There are a couple options here. If you have lots of pens, you can store them upright in mason jars. If you need to transport them, there are several kinds of storage boxes available. I like to store mine upright so I can see the colors I have to work with. Of course, the scrapbook bags mentioned earlier in this chapter have clear pockets in which to store your pens.

# Housing Ideas—Storing Books and Magazines

Idea books and magazines are wonderful ways to motivate you and get your ideas flowing. The problem with these is that they tend to get spread out all over the house, so try to keep them in a central location. Most stores sell magazine boxes that you can store these in, and if you are really frugal, you can cut up a cereal box and cover it with contact paper for an original look. Better yet, tear out the layouts and articles you like and organize them in a three-ring binder. This way, you'll be able to find what you're looking for without searching through every single magazine.

**Shortcuts**

Keep small Post-it notes on hand when you are looking through a magazine. Whenever you see a layout, idea, or new product that interests you, simply peel off a Post-it and place it on the page.

Wherever and whenever you do your scrapbooking, it is a time for you to get creative and enjoy doing your own thing. If you meet with people to work on your scrapbooks, remember that the point is not to compete with the others but to share ideas and get inspired by the creativity of your fellow scrappers. Relax and enjoy the camaraderie. If you work at home, in whatever space you use, organization can be the key to making scrapbooking possible and making a little space for yourself in the midst of your busy life. Do it before the children are awake or when they are out with friends. Turn on the phone answering machine, turn up the Mozart, and have fun!

## The Least You Need to Know

➤ It's best to take note of supplies you need before you go shopping.

➤ Organization of your supplies and space is key to enjoying scrapbooking.

➤ Where do you scrapbook? In a home office? On the go? Or anywhere you can find space? This can determine what sort of storage is best for you.

➤ Scrapbooking is a wonderful, creative outlet—make sure your space is comfortable, and your time is your own. Enjoy it!

# Part 4

# Scrap It, Stick It, Store It

*You own the supplies and you've attended the classes, yet you still struggle when it comes to creating satisfying scrapbook pages. You're not alone. Many scrapbookers, long confident in their knowledge and use of tools, still struggle with design. As you read these design guidelines, think of your own pages and you'll be surprised at how many rules come naturally to you. In this part you'll get advice on making the best color choices for your scrapbook, evaluating the pros and cons of different album sizes, and even getting the kids interested and involved in your new hobby!*

*You won't be able to wait to display your pictures in this beautiful album. Its pages are 12" by 12" and the front and back covers are made from a $^3/_8$-inch-thick foam core with original watercolor art.*

*This portrait has little added to it—the soft colors convey the mood.*

*The great colors in this layout are based on the bear stationery. Notice that the edges are cut out to overlap on the picture and give it a more interactive look.*

BEARY GOOD

ON JUSTIN'S FIRST BIRTHDAY HE GOT TO HAVE HIS OWN CAKE ALL TO HIMSELF AND HE THOUGHT IT WAS "BEARY" GOOD. HE WAS A MESS WHEN IT WAS ALL OVER, BUT HE THOUGHT IT WAS SO MUCH FUN. I CAN'T BELIEVE THAT YOU ARE A ONE-YEAR OLD!!

Try taking portraits of your children. When the pictures are developed, select a large-sized print for a great layout. This layout is simple to keep the focus on the picture.

This page uses velvet paper as the background and the rub-on rope as an embellishment. One of the photos is trimmed into an oval shape to add interest.

This delightful page was done very quickly with scrapbook products. Don't be afraid to mix and match—it turned out very successfully here.

This page was featured in Paper Kuts magazine. The journaling is what works here—it tells the story of the day's events in a fun way.

Recipe for all American boy:

Combine
1 cup dirt
2 dimples
3 bursts of energy

stir in a dash of mischief,
let simmer for 4-5 years
stand back and enjoy

*Include all sorts of memorabilia items on your page such as these hand-tied flies. Be creative when adding spice to your page.*

*This page illustrates how to combine pictures with a straight edge with angular objects such as the snowflakes. They really complement each other.*

The kids could not wait until it was hot enough to get out Justin's new pool. They had so much fun and the pool was great- people stopped by and asked where we got the pool May 99

The brightness of the puper and stickers just scream summertime fun! Let the products do the work for you in this easy-to-create summer page.

Remember to take at least one roll of black-and-white film a year of your family. They last longer and capture the era better than color photos. When creating pages with black-and-white photos, stick with dark, classic colors and simple enhancements.

*Paper dolls are great embellishments for kids' pages. You can customize them to match your page or use generic clothes—whatever works for you.*

*This is an example of a theme album. These layouts stick with one color scheme and one line of stickers to keep the look the same.*

*These fishing pictures work well displayed together. The people in the pictures have changed, but the tradition continues.*

*When creating a memorial book, include precious pictures. If you don't have many, then enlarge some of your favorites. Be sure to include journaling in these pages.*

# Chapter 14

# Define Your Style, Determine Your Needs

---

**In This Chapter**

➤ Learn how to define your scrapbooking style

➤ How to make your scrapbook showcase your style

➤ Making time for scrapbooking in your busy life

➤ Streamline shopping by defining your supply needs

---

If you are like most of the first-time students who take my basic scrapbooking classes, you are overwhelmed by all the different layouts and products you see. The most common question beginners ask is, "Can you give me some ideas on what to do with all these pictures?" My answer is absolutely, positively, YES.

All you need is some direction, and that's what this chapter will give you. First, I'll teach you how to compile a favorites file. Then you'll take a short style quiz and fill out a favorite product checklist. This will help you define your style. Once this is done, you'll determine your needs profile, and you're ready to go!

## Vive La Différence! There Is No "Right" Style

It's important to take a little time before you begin scrapbooking to discover your style. When I teach a scrapbook class, I invariably hear people say they are intimidated by the layouts they see in magazines. Those professional layouts can seem so difficult that people would rather give up than try to do something that elaborate. Participants sometimes come to a six-hour workshop, choose a store layout idea they like, and spend the entire time painstakingly replicating the layout with their own pictures.

The real secret is that there is no one correct way to scrapbook, no one perfect pen, no one must-have product. The only "right way" is the method that you prefer—the one that gets you to your goal. In this chapter, I will help you define your style and clarify your direction as a scrapper. Once you get that taken care of, the fun begins!

To illustrate this, let me share this story with you. My friend Julie moved into a new house a couple months ago, and I eagerly accepted her invitation to take a tour. When I walked into the living room, I thought, "This room says 'Julie.'" Although I might not have made the choices she made with colors and furnishings (a little bold for my tastes), she had followed some basic design principles that made the room comfortable and a guest feel at ease. However, if I had tried the same decor in my living room, the results would have been much different—it just wasn't my style.

You can apply this same principle to scrapbooking. Though you need to follow some basic design principles, there is no right style for a scrapbook because we all have different tastes.

## Consult the Experts

When Julie was planning her house and décor, she spent months looking at magazines, stores, and friends' houses, making note of what she liked. You can do the same thing, on a smaller scale, when you plan your scrapbooks. Take a little time to flip through this book and mark the layouts you like with a paper clip or Post-it note. Do the same with layouts you dislike. Next, look at some scrapbooking magazines and idea books and tear out the layouts you like and dislike.

The major scrapbooking magazines are *Creating Keepsakes*, *Memory Makers*, *Paper Kuts*, and *Remembering*. You can find most of them at your local craft stores, but some of the smaller ones are more difficult to locate. Many of them can be found in the major bookstore chains. Looking through magazines can really motivate you to work on your albums. Besides that, these magazines help keep track of all the newest scrapbooking products. Browse through several to see which ones you prefer and don't overlook the other craft magazines while you're there. Check out the stamping books for the latest techniques in that arena. You can look at tole painting magazines to see the most recent designs (such as sunflowers or frogs). Make sure you look at the interior design magazines for the latest color trends. You can even find inspiration in sewing magazines!

### Sticky Points

While it's fun to look at your friends' and neighbors' scrapbooks, try not to get caught up in comparing your skills. What matters most is that your personality comes through. Remember, you are creating a unique scrapbook; let yourself shine through.

### Words for Posterity

Don't know the difference between a scrapbooking magazine and an idea book? Although they look similar, there is a difference. Idea books are larger and often focus on specific events, such as weddings or vacations. They have fewer ads than magazines and fewer articles. Magazines, on the other hand, are published regularly and have regular articles. It's a good idea to subscribe to a magazine and purchase idea books that suit your needs.

Now that you're familiar with available resources, you can decide which ones you'd like to buy and create a favorites file you can refer to. Now you are ready for the next step.

# Find the Common Denominator

Study the layouts you've chosen. What is common among them? Are the designs simple or complex? What types of products are used? Is there a unique style of lettering? Take note of the amount of embellishments used, as well as the style. Are there die cuts or stickers? Is there a lot of journaling or are the photos left to tell their own story?

Make note of these items. If all your favorites include stickers, then spend some time at the sticker rack next time you go shopping. If it's the lettering that catches your eye, you might want to purchase a lettering book or take a class. Whatever it is, you'll want to repeat it in your own book.

Take the next step in defining your style by filling out the following checklist to choose your favorite products. Put a check by the items you like to get an idea of your favorites.

**Paper Colors**

\_\_\_\_    Primary

\_\_\_\_    Bright/Neon

\_\_\_\_    Classic

\_\_\_\_    Muted

\_\_\_\_    Pastel

**Paper Patterns**

\_\_\_\_    Specific

\_\_\_\_    General

**Pens**

\_\_\_\_    Black Felt-Tip

\_\_\_\_    Colorful Gel Rollers

\_\_\_\_    Paint Pens

\_\_\_\_    Coloring Pencils

\_\_\_\_    Colorful Felt-Tip

**Words for Posterity**

**Tole painting** is painting on wood using patterns that you can transfer onto the wood, typically done in a rustic style and depicting country scenes.

**Words for Posterity**

A **favorites file** is a personal book of ideas and layouts that you compile. Organize the files in a three-ring binder, file folder, manila envelope, or whatever is easiest (there's no need to buy archival materials for this).

**Shortcuts**

If you've ever gone overboard purchasing cute supplies, you probably have a closet full of leftovers. The solution? Hold a "product swap." Invite your scrapbooking friends over and ask them to bring their leftovers. Trade back and forth. You'll end up with free products while cleaning out your scrapbooking collection.

**Decorative Tools**

___ Scissors

___ Punches

___ Stamps

___ Shape Cutter

___ Crimper

**Stationery**

___ Full Sheet

___ Varying Card Size

___ Punch Outs

**Page Toppers**

___ Pre-cut Shapes

___ Die Cuts

___ Handmade Scraps

___ Stickers

___ Letter Shapes

___ Frames

**Decorative Paper**

___ Vellum

___ Corrugated

___ Metallic

___ Specialty Packs

___ Handmade

___ Embossed

___ Pressed Flower

**Templates**

___ Basic Shapes

___ Elaborate Shapes

___ Alphabet

___ Border Buddies

___ Journaling Genies

___ Puzzle Mates

**Miscellaneous** _____

Once you've gotten a feel for what you like, you are ready to move on to the next step.

# Name That Style!

To further determine your style, take this fun quiz. Choose the answer to each question that best matches your personality. Remember that no one is looking, so be honest.

1. Your wardrobe consists of

   a. classic items—you want to dress like Lauren Bacall.

   b. up-to-the-minute styles out of fashion magazines.

   c. Laura Ashley jumpers.

   d. functional, sturdy clothes.

   e. bright colors and lots of accessories.

   f. whatever is clean and comfortable.

2. Your favorite activity is

   a. dinner and a movie.

   b. a trip to New York for a Broadway musical.

   c. ordering pizza and watching the latest video release.

   d. hiking and camping outdoors.

   e. riding roller coasters, bungee jumping, anything adventurous.

   f. a writing workshop at the community college.

3. Your bedroom is decorated with

   a. muted natural colors and fabrics.

   b. coordinating comforter, pillows, and curtains.

   c. floral pillows, cute knick knacks, and hand-made crafts.

   d. an antique dresser and a quilt your grandparents passed down.

   e. brightly colored curtains, funky pillows, and patterned lampshades.

   f. framed prints and a nightstand covered with books and papers.

4. Your makeup bag is

   a. neat and contains the bare essentials: lipstick, foundation, mascara.

   b. replete with all the free samples you pick up from the cosmetics counter.

   c. filled with coordinating items from your favorite makeup line.

   d. What makeup bag?

   e. overflowing with all the different colored mascara, eye shadows, and eyeliners. You have a separate bag for lipsticks.

   f. very small because you only wear lipstick, on special occasions.

5. Your hairstyle is

    a. an easy-to-do version of the latest trend.

    b. a complicated version of the latest trend, with highlights.

    c. a shoulder-length bob.

    d. very short or very long.

    e. always changing; you like to try different colors and styles.

    f. a little scruffy; you never have time to get it cut.

6. Your choice of purses is

    a. just a wallet—who wants to lug all that stuff around?

    b. a large tote bag; you never know when you'll need an extra pair of pantyhose or a 12-ounce Diet Coke.

    c. a cute medium-sized zippered purse.

    d. a backpack because you need to have your hands free.

    e. a brightly colored leather handbag with an overflowing wallet.

    f. a dog-eared planner with extra pens.

Now tally up how many *A* answers you gave, how many *B* answers, and so on. Whichever letter you choose most often defines your style:

A—Classic and Simple

B—Elaborate

C—Down Home

D—Earthy

E—Wild Child

F—Documenter

Read below to find a description of your style and a sample layout. This is your starting point. Let's take a look into each scrapbooker's likes and dislikes:

## Classic and Simple

The simple scrapbooker likes clean, straight edges, owns few, if any, decorative scissors, and relies on a paper cutter and wide variety of colored cardstock to enhance her photos. She also uses stickers, die cuts, and page toppers, but only sparingly. "Less is more" is her motto.

*Classic, simple layout sticks to the basics.*

## Elaborate

The elaborate scrapbooker carries a cropper hopper full of her latest purchases so she can set up in an instant. She likes action on a page; plenty of stickers and fancy lettering. Decorative scissors, punches are favorites. Even if you aren't an elaborate scrapbooker, try to befriend one; she always has the latest clip art, computer programs, the newest pen styles, and up-to-the-minute magazines.

*Elaborate layout with plenty of action.*

## Down Home

The down-home person loves cute clip art, paper piecing, and decorative scissors. Things with a handmade touch fill her scrapbook. She loves coordinating stickers and paper and enjoys stamping. Her scrapbook is consistent and relaxing, like reading a bedtime story.

*A layout with loads of down-home charm.*

## Earthy

The earthy scrapbooker carries her supplies in a well-worn duffel bag and stays away from computer-generated scrapbooking, preferring to use more natural products. She likes muted colors and torn paper edges. She even goes so far as to make her own paper with interesting flowers and foliage garnered from her various outings. The earthy scrapper uses raffia to adorn her pages and uses her own handwriting to document the photos. This scrapbooker is creating an heirloom.

## The Wild Child

The wild scrapbooker is flashy and hates rules. She doesn't need anyone to tell her what her style is! She likes bold colors and stickers and chooses patterns that are brash and bright. Her personality is evident on every page.

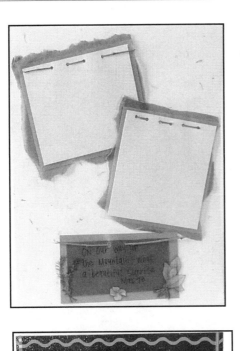

*This layout makes much of natural products.*

*WOW! Flashy and bright.*

## The Documenter

The documenter's goal is to get as many pictures as possible on a page, so she favors the 12-by-12 album that leaves plenty of room to journal on the layouts. Borders are popular, as are stickers. She is as concerned about preserving her family history as she is about creating artwork.

**169**

*Photos and journaling, that's what is important here.*

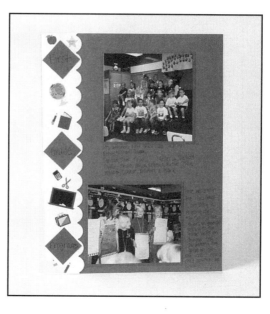

Once you've determined your primary style, you'll be able to streamline your shopping by focusing on the products you like. Of course you don't ever have to stick to one specific style. As a matter of fact, most people overlap into at least two categories, but by selecting what you generally like, you'll make your shopping expeditions easier and more purposeful. Why waste time looking at the newest stickers if you don't like them? You can head straight for the latest pen set if that's what you prefer.

## So, Whaddya Need?

After you've decided which type best describes your individual style, it's time to determine what kind of scrapbooker you are. Do you have lots of time and few photos? Do you have mounds of photos and little time? Is money a factor? Keep reading to find a profile that suits you.

➤ Hobbyist—The hobbyist is someone who dabbles in many crafts and enjoys using her talents to decorate her living space. She is a social scrapbooker and shares her enthusiasm by starting scrapbooking groups. Don't miss a chance to go to one of her scrapbooking parties because she will be able to help you learn the latest techniques since she loves to share her craft!

**Sticky Points**

If your handwriting is illegible, you might want to use a computer to type up some of your stories. But be careful because most inkjet printers don't use archival or permanent ink. Your best bet is to use a laser printer, but if you don't own one, you can save the material to a disk and take it to your local copy center to print on a laser copier on acid-free paper. Whenever you make copies, ask that carbon-based ink or toner be used.

➤ World Wide Traveler—This scrapbooker has been there, done that, and now wants to show it off! She needs methods to showcase her travel photos and brochures, as well as treasures she has gathered on her journeys. This scrapbooker's goal is to get the book done, as she enjoys the end product more than the process.

➤ Empty Nester—An empty nester has a house full of memories and a closet full of photos and partially completed albums. Overwhelmed by the huge task in front of her, she needs ideas for quick-and-easy pages and tips on preserving memorabilia, such as certificates and newspaper articles. This scrapbooker wants to finish her project so she can sit back and enjoy her efforts.

➤ Isn't He Adorable?—The proud parent. This mom or dad's kids are so cute that they take lots of photos to highlight all their kid's accomplishments. This parent enjoys scrapbooking as a way to relax with friends, and you'll often find her in an all-day workshop or even a 12-hour overnighter at her scrapbook store. Her scrapbooks are a work in progress.

➤ Me and My World—This teenager or child loves to record the fun events in his or her life: dances, birthday parties, field trips, school accomplishments, and best friends. With big dreams and a small budget, these scrapbooks have lots of personality.

➤ Career Track—This person is so successful in the workplace that she has little time for scrapbooking. For her, scrapbooking is a way to relax and get away from it all. Her albums document her accomplishments, friends, and pets. Seeing a new product in the store spurs her on.

**Sticky Points**

If you're a scrapbooker with a lot of other projects going on, you'll need to be extra careful to keep your scrapbook supplies separate from your other projects. For example, don't confuse your regular stamp pad with your archival stamp pad or your stationery stickers for scrapbooking stickers; these products are not interchangeable.

**Shortcuts**

Don't know how to preserve all those certificates and newspaper clippings? If they're not acid-free, take them to your local copy store and copy them onto acid-free paper with a laser copier.

Now you're ready to go! You know what you like and how you like to do it. Keep this in mind the next time you go shopping.

# But I'm Too Busy!

The key to having the time to scrapbook is knowing what you like and dislike, just as you have discovered in this chapter. Just imagine if there were only one clothing store that carried everything you ever needed—you wouldn't waste time shopping around in the mall because you'd go directly to that store, make your purchases, and be on your way. When you know your scrapbooking style, you can spend the time scrapbooking that you used to spend shopping. Try to set aside a chunk of time once a month or once a week for scrapbooking. Join a scrapbooking group, invite friends over, or go to a class. You will be surprised how much you can accomplish in this short amount of time.

## The Least You Need to Know

➤ Are you a Wild Child, a Documenter, or an Earthy scrapbooker? Everyone has a different style and different needs.

➤ Once your style and needs are determined, you can save time and money.

➤ Make a favorites file to store interesting layouts and page ideas.

# Chapter 15

# Color It Yours

---

### In This Chapter

➤ Learn about the color wheel and how to use it

➤ How color affects the look and mood of your scrapbooks

➤ Tints, shades, value, and intensity—why these matter

➤ Choosing colors that work with your photos and please the eye

---

Color is a large factor in our scrapbooks. Color creates the mood for a page, highlights or distracts from photos, and portrays who we are. Often, the difference between a great page and a mediocre page is color. Most people who work on scrapbooks don't refer to the color wheel; they choose by instinct. If that works for you, great. But some people (like my sister) don't have an eye for color. She gets frustrated shopping for her layouts because she has such a hard time choosing colors. And some of her color combinations are awful—even she admits it! So I taught her how to use a color wheel, and it has helped her create better pages.

Since you want to keep the focus on your pictures, it's great to learn how to manipulate color. Don't be afraid to look to the experts for examples and inspiration. My favorite color combination comes from my favorite part of nature—the skies and trees. I use blue and green over and over again in my albums because it portrays the feeling that I want portrayed, and I find it very pleasing. Look at the art around you in paintings, architecture, and, of course, nature to give you color clues.

## The ABCs of Color

Color is very important in setting a mood, both in the photographs you take and in the decorative elements of your scrapbook. Choices of color are everywhere, from the background paper you pick to the color of your embellishments. But what is color, exactly? If the last time you thought about this was in a physics class long ago, let's take a moment to go over a few color concepts.

# ROY G. BIV

Light is the source of color. Pure white light is composed of all the colors the eye can see. You have probably seen this demonstrated with a prism—if you pass white light through a prism, the light refracts, or breaks apart, to show the rainbow spectrum, or ROY G. BIV. You remember him, right? The letters stand for the major colors, each with a different wavelength, that can be seen when white light is sent through the prism: red, orange, yellow, green, blue, indigo, and violet. The same thing happens when light passes through a drop of water—the water acts like a prism, and we see a beautiful rainbow.

### Words for Posterity

When light is **refracted**, it is bent. Light refracted through a prism, a piece of glass or crystal with a triangular shape, shows the colors of the visible light spectrum: red, orange, yellow, green, blue, indigo, and violet.

## Refraction

When light hits any surface, some colors are absorbed, while others are reflected. The colors that we can see (and that the lens of a camera sees) are the colors that are reflected. Imagine a big bouquet of sunflowers. The bright yellow petals of the flowers reflect only yellow wavelengths and absorb all the other colors, while the green leaves and stem reflect only green wavelengths. The reflections of the yellow and green wavelengths hit our eyes, and we see the glorious colors. An object looks black to our eyes when its surface absorbs all color wavelengths and white when the surface reflects all colors.

### Anecdotes from the Archives

Even though colors can change depending on the kind of light we are seeing them in, your brain automatically makes adjustments so that we see the colors as they are in bright light. For example, if you know that a shirt you are wearing is red and your jeans are blue, even if you are in a dim movie theater where your clothes look like almost the same color of brown, your eye will tend to "see" the pants and shirt as blue and red.

# Colors in Nature

How can mood be affected by color? Researchers have shown that people react excitedly to "hot" colors, like red, orange, and bright yellow, and are soothed and calmed by what we think of as "cool" colors, like shades of blue and green.

Ever wonder why you are drawn to a certain item in your favorite department store? Wondering why you like to buy the expensive packaged food items instead of store brand? Color plays a role in everything we do, and those who are trying to sell us something have studied color and have it down to a science. They use color to get certain markets to purchase certain goods. You can find hundreds of books, online sites, and articles related just to the purchasing power of color. We can take their expertise and put it to work for us. Let's look at the basic colors in nature to see what mood they generate.

➤ **Blue**—When I was having my wisdom teeth out as a young adult, the oral surgeon's office was a blend of blues, from the furniture down to the fabric. He told me that blue is the most soothing and comforting color to humans—good to calm his anxious patients! Blues blend well with other colors, especially the bolder colors.

➤ **Green**—Green sends across feelings of growth. Everything around us in nature that is green is growing, and if it isn't growing, it changes color. The different hues of green work different ways. The softer colors are more mellow, and the darker colors are classic and go well with other classic colors.

➤ **Yellow**—Bright and sunny. Yellow, of course, generates energy and excitement, but use it in small doses because it can overwhelm and almost blind the eye. I love to use yellow when I am doing summer pages with my kids running around and playing—it captures the energy of their childhood.

➤ **Red**—Red in nature screams bold and brave. This is a color that dominates everything it is in. Many fruits and vegetables are this color, and they look great growing on the green trees or plants. Green and red is often a natural combination in nature. Use these colors to show power and control.

# Moods and Matching

People tend to associate certain colors with certain events and moods. For example, because people associate soft, calm, gentle colors with babies, baby clothes and other items are often made in pastels. By the same token, when people are making signs that they want others to see, they often choose bright, even electric colors, to get attention. People often match clothing to nature's seasonal colors—wearing fresh, light colors in the spring and summer, and richer, darker colors in fall and winter.

Unfortunately, though people often try to match with the seasons, they don't always match their socks to their pants. Certain colors don't seem to go together, but why don't those green, striped pants match those hot pink polka-dotted socks? It's a matter of color and pattern. If you know anyone over five years old who leaves the house sporting an outfit like that, you may want to make them a copy of the next section.

### Anecdotes from the Archives

Colors have tremendous cultural significance as well. In most Western cultures, black is the traditional color of mourning. In Eastern cultures, such as China, Japan, and Korea, however, it is white that is worn at funerals and times of mourning.

### Words for Posterity

The **color wheel** has the main colors laid out to show their relationship and placement to one another. You can use the color wheel to create successful color combinations.

### Words for Posterity

Red, yellow, and blue are called **primary colors**—they cannot be created; they just exist, which means that they are the base from which all other colors are created.

# No Need to Reinvent the (Color) Wheel

If you have ever taken a basic art class, chances are that you have heard the term "color wheel" and have even seen one. I first learned about the color wheel in a high school interior design class, and I thought the concept was boring. I rebelled against the idea of obeying all these "rules" about picking colors. Now that I understand the ideas of color better, I find the color wheel useful, although the concepts can be a little confusing at first. Here I've adapted the basic rules of picking colors to apply to scrapbooking.

## Decoding the Color Wheel

There are three basic color classes on the color wheel, which are referred to as follows:

➤ **Primary colors**—Names given in CAPITAL LETTERS.

➤ **Secondary colors**—Names given in lowercase letters.

➤ **Intermediate or tertiary colors**—These colors are numbered.

Primary colors are the three colors from which all other colors can be made:

A = red

B = yellow

C = blue

These colors are of vital importance to artists. With paint in the three primary colors, plus white and black, an artist can create virtually any hue.

Secondary colors are made up of blends of the primary colors. They are

Orange (a) = Red (A) + Yellow (B)

Green (b) = Yellow (B) + Blue (C)

Violet (c)  = Blue (C) + Red (A)

**Words for Posterity**

**Secondary colors** are created by blending primary colors. Orange, green, and violet are the secondary colors created by mixing combinations of red, yellow, and blue.

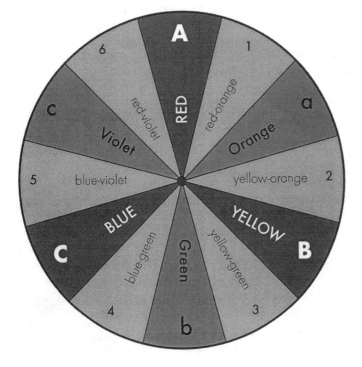

Tertiary, or intermediate, colors are made by mixing primary colors with secondary colors. Tertiary colors are indicated by numbers on the color wheel.

Red/Orange (1) = Red (A) + Orange (a)

Yellow/Orange (2) = Yellow (B) + Orange (a)

Yellow/Green (3) = Yellow (B) + Green (a)

Blue/Green (4) = Blue (C) + Green (a)

Blue/Violet (5) = Blue (C) + Violet (c)

Red/Violet (6) = Red (A) + Violet (c)

## Tints and Shades

The next important thing to understand about color is how colors are affected by adding white and black. The basics are this: If you add white to a color, you are tinting it. A tint looks like a lighter version of a color. If you add black to a color, you are shading it. A shade looks like a darker version of a color.

Color + black = shade

Color + white = tint

Pastel (or "pale") colors are color tints. Pastel yellow is yellow that has white added to it; pastel blue is blue with white added. Pink is the name for the tint of red—that is, red mixed with white.

## Color Intensity

Here are a few other terms related to color. You will sometimes hear the words *value* and *intensity* when people are describing a color. These terms are somewhat related. The value of a color is determined by the amount of light or dark in it. Intensity is how true the color is to the primary colors. So, the color red has more intensity than the color pink. Value is the component of color that describes its lightness or darkness.

Artists use intensity to evaluate the color of their paintings. Look at the works of two well-known artists, Picasso and Monet. Picasso used intense colors to create his bold paintings. Monet used a majority of less intense colors to create his soothing paintings. Picasso even had what is called his "Blue Period," where he almost

**Words for Posterity**

**Tertiary** (pronounced *TER-she-ary*), or intermediate, colors are blends of primary and secondary colors. Colors like red-orange and blue-green are tertiary colors.

**Words for Posterity**

A **shade** is a color with black added to it.

**Words for Posterity**

A **tint** is a color that has had white mixed in with it.

exclusively used that color in every shade, tint, and variation possible.

## Color Categories

The intensity of colors can be described either as bold or muted.

Bold colors are bright, high-intensity colors that demand attention. They reach out from the page and make you look at them. It is good to use these colors sparingly—when used as a background, they can dwarf your pictures.

On the other hand, muted colors are shades and tints of colors and are low-intensity, soothing colors. These colors are great as background colors, and using a lot of them is fine. The pictures will be emphasized when you use these colors.

You'll want to use combinations of bold and muted colors on your pages to create great effects.

# Color for Success

If you don't read any other part of this chapter, make sure to look this one over. Below are color combinations based on the color wheel that are balanced and pleasing to the eye. Hewing too strictly to certain traditional combinations (like using all primary colors) can make your layouts a little predictable, so try being experimental with the complementary, analogous, and triadic combinations described below.

Colors that are called "complementary" combinations are opposite each other on the wheel:

➤ Red (A) and Green (b)

➤ Yellow (B) and Violet (c)

➤ Blue (C) and Orange (a)

➤ Red/Orange (1) and Blue/Green (4)

➤ Yellow/Orange (2) and Blue/Violet (5)

➤ Yellow/Green (3) and Red/Violet (6)

Analogous combinations are those that are next to each other on the color wheel. I'm using just the six basic colors to illustrate, but there are other combinations.

**Words for Posterity**

**Intensity** is the strength of a color based on how true it is to the primary color.

**Shortcuts**

A painter might vary tints, shades, values, and intensities just by varying the amounts of colors that are blended together. Blending equal amounts of blue and yellow gives a true green color, which you can then shade or tint to your liking. Variations in amounts of color blended create variations in intensity.

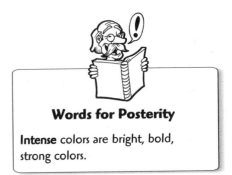

**Words for Posterity**

**Intense** colors are bright, bold, strong colors.

➤ Red (A) and Orange (a)

➤ Yellow (B) and Orange (a)

➤ Yellow (B) and Green (b)

➤ Blue (C) and Green (b)

➤ Blue (C) and Violet (c)

➤ Red (A) and Violet (c)

**Words for Posterity**

**Muted** colors are subdued tints or shades of colors and tend to be more suitable for backgrounds.

**Words for Posterity**

Colors that are opposite each other on the color wheel **complement** each other.

**Words for Posterity**

**Analogous** colors are next to each other on the color wheel.

Triadic color combinations form a triangle on the wheel. This combination of colors can lend a sense of balance to your pages, though it can be quite stark in the primary or secondary forms. I prefer using them as tints of shades; for example, the pastel versions of green, orange, and violet are mint, peach, and lavender, respectively.

➤ Red (A), Yellow (B), and Blue (C)

➤ Orange (a), Green (b), and Violet (c)

➤ Red/Orange (1), Yellow/Green (3), and Blue/Violet (5)

➤ Yellow/Orange (2), Blue/Green (4), and Red/Violet (6)

Different values of the same color are referred to as monochromatic. An example of this is blue, navy, and pale blue. Blue is the primary color, navy is a shade of blue (remember, blue with black added), and pale blue is a tint (blue with white added). Monochromes can be quite impressive when used together.

# Pleasing the Eye—Color Guidelines for Scrapbooking

The basic rules of color suggest that it is often pleasing to use colors together that are complementary, analogous, or triadic. Primary colors can also be used together in combinations and make a pleasing, if not sophisticated, statement. Approaching color in your layouts will be most successful if some basic color guidelines are followed:

➤ Use no more than three or four colors on a page, with one neutral color such as white, gray, or black.

➤ You don't need to limit your colors to traditional choices. One Easter, for example, I dressed my four sons in navy blue outfits. When I went to make a page for these photos, the typical Easter pastel colors just didn't work.

➤ Repeat your colors throughout the layout. Use it in lettering, enhancements, and captions.

➤ When choosing background paper, experiment with lots of the different colors available by holding your pictures against the choices to see what looks best.

➤ Use color to manipulate the story you are telling. Bold colors work well for a wild birthday party, while subdued colors might be better for an elegant anniversary party.

➤ Please, please, please shop with your photos! I cannot say this enough! Trust me, it will make the biggest difference in your pages.

Look around you when considering color combinations. Check out the packaging at the grocery store or department store. Look through retail catalogs to see what colors go together in those. Every season, I look to the Gap to see what colors they are putting together this time. Sometimes, I would never have put together the combinations they try, but I am always impressed with how they put combinations together successfully. Use the experience of the professionals to get good color combinations.

**Words for Posterity**

A **triad** is a group of three colors that form a triangle on the color wheel.

**Words for Posterity**

A **monochromatic** color scheme employs different values of the same color.

**Shortcuts**

Match colors to the mood of your pictures. While pale blue is soothing and relaxing for a beach layout, yellow is energetic and spunky for fun at the circus.

## Product Personality

This is an important part of color and basic design. When planning your layout and choosing colors, it's usually best to remember to stick within the same genre of products. For example, if you are working on a baby page, use colors that go with those pictures (stay away from metallics and wedding bells!). For a country page, stick with country products, such as a quilting pattern, sunflowers, and bumble bees.

Obviously, most of these "rules" are flexible—sometimes unexpected, unusual, or even outrageous combinations look great; sometimes, they are clashing disasters. And if children are working on scrapbooks, it's folly to expect them to pick colors that match—they won't, so let them color the way they want to. The great thing about anything in your scrapbook is that you don't have to glue anything down in a hurry. Play around with layouts and color combinations until you are satisfied.

---

### The Least You Need to Know

➤ If you don't have an "eye for color," a color wheel can be your Seeing Eye dog.

➤ Understanding a few properties of color can help you have the confidence to create very pleasing layouts.

➤ Shop with your photos to match paper and embellishments.

# Chapter 16

---

# Scrapbooking Isn't Just for Grown-Ups

---

**In This Chapter**

➤ Creative fun for kids using scrapbooking materials

➤ Projects that parents and kids can do together

➤ Tips for helping kids take great pictures

➤ Working safely with kids

---

Kids love to make scrapbooks. In fact, one of the greatest parts of my job is teaching kids' scrapbooking classes—partly because kids don't have the same inhibitions that adults do and get really creative with their books, and partly because I get to act silly, and the kids appreciate all the fun things we do in class. Kids like to scrapbook their vacation photos, photos of friends, and anything else they can think of.

Recently, we were doing baby pictures at a kids' class. I loved listening to the children describe what was going on in their baby pictures. I imagined their parents going through the pictures with them and telling their children what they remembered about them. One little girl described an incident where she got into her mother's lipstick and, even though her mother was frustrated, she took pictures of her. She did the cutest page with these pictures, and she thought it was great her mom captured her on film.

This chapter gives tips on scrapbooking with kids, as well as fun projects to do with them. If you are interested in teaching kids, there are some suggestions on how to make teaching scrapbooking fun with games and goodies.

# Kids Are Scrappers, Too

Sometimes, children see the whole picture of a project better than we do because they don't feel the same pressure to "get it done" that many of us do. Kids truly enjoy the process of making a scrapbook as much as the product. All children need is some encouragement and the freedom to use their own style. It's great when adults and children can work on scrapbooks together—either on the same book or each on an individual book.

If you are setting up supplies for some kids you know (or if you are a kid and you want to get yourself set up), here are some things you'll want to get prepared from a teaching curriculum I created for a kids' basic scrapbooking class:

➤ Be Prepared: Have supplies organized in some sort of container.

   1. To start with, you need scissors, paper, pens, embellishments, glue, and an album with sheet protectors.

   2. Have pictures sorted according to event, such as a birthday party, trip to the zoo, or best friends.

   3. Make sure you have a clean workspace.

➤ Get Started:

   1. Pick a theme for the pictures you are working on if possible (such as a camping trip, vacations, school, birthday, or friends).

   2. Help the child choose a color scheme, encouraging him or her to stick with three or four colors that match the photos.

➤ Shop 'Til You Drop:

   1. You need to have a plan when shopping with your child. Bring only a few photos to the store and don't stay too long; you want this to be fun, not stressful!

   2. Find embellishments that match the color scheme the child has picked.

➤ Cut and Color:

   1. If you want to trim your photos, encourage your child to match the pattern of the scissors to the theme of the page.

   2. Mount your photos on coordinating cardstock and trace and color borders.

   3. If desired, your child can draw some pictures to go along with the photos. This is especially good if the child is too young to write.

➤ Put It All Together: Teach the child a few designing guidelines to follow so they will be happy with their creative results and want to do more.

➤ Write It Down: I think this can be the most important part of the scrapbooking process. It is amazing what your child remembers about different events.

1. Ask questions and encourage your child to write responses in his or her own words.

2. Some children are self-conscious about their penmanship and are reluctant to use their own writing. A good compromise is to have a title and date for the page, and you write in the text. That way, you still get their cute lettering, but your child is happy, too.

3. If your child is too little to write, make sure you write down the things they tell you. Put the writing into a protector and keep on going.

# Color Control and Easy Extras—Kid's Guide to Layouts

I also teach a kids' design class. Here are some basic design rules for kids.

➤ **Eye catcher**—Every design needs a focal point and so do scrapbook pages. Carefully choose the picture that you want to be the focal point, usually the one that tells the story the best way possible.

**Sticky Points**

Children don't have the same concept of time as we do, so give them plenty of time to shop and see what all of their options are. You will be surprised at what they can come up with.

**Shortcuts**

Scrapbooking with kids is a two-step process: organizing and selecting items to use on a page and putting it all together. Depending on the age of the kids, it can be hard to do it all at once, so do it in parts. Place selected items with pictures in a protector, and you and the children will be ready to go.

**Anecdotes from the Archives**

Once, a mother of six attended one of my scrapbooking classes. At one point, she was so overwhelmed with compiling her family's pictures into a scrapbook that she taught her two oldest children how to do it. Now they do most of the scrapbooking, and even some of the younger kids are involved.

**Sticky Points**

When working with kids, give them the basic rules and let them go to work. They want to have fun, and if you are critical or push them too hard, they won't enjoy it. So if Susie wants to put a dozen Little Mermaid stickers on one page, let her!

➤ **Shapes**—Shapes are great for kids' pages, but encourage them to use shapes sparingly. Remember, if they don't want to cut their pictures into shapes, they can add interest to their pages with accents that are shapes.

➤ **Cool Colors**—Kids are often attracted to bright, bold colors. Help the kids to make their pages look cool—not too many and not too few. I think three or four colors is plenty. Teach kids to use colors to match the pictures and the mood of the pictures.

➤ **Theme**—Remember to use the book's theme as the finishing design so that everything works well together and tells a unified story.

➤ **Extras**—Help kids remember embellishments are extras. You don't have to use them on every page, and too many detract from your photos.

# Picking Pineapples and Making Friends—Fun Projects

While it's good to give your kids some tools and set them loose, sometimes it's a good idea to provide them with a little structure and a theme. Here are some kid-friendly projects:

➤ **My Best Friends**—Kids can use all of the pictures they take of their friends and class pictures that they get every year. Let them make a page with these photos, listing what they like about their friends and the fun things they do together.

➤ **Family Tree**—You can purchase some of the preprinted family tree paper or you can make your own. Let the children use pictures if possible to show as many generations as you have. This is a great project for any child.

➤ **100 Things I Want to Do When I Grow Up**—Did you ever make one of those lists where you wrote down that when you grew up, you'd like to go parachuting, pick pineapples, or be an astronaut? This is fun to put in a scrapbook. A variation of this is "100 Things I Want to Do Right Now." (Kids might include stay up all night, play Nintendo all day, and eat candy for dinner! Whatever they choose, this is a fun project for them and fun for you—maybe you can even make some of those things come true for them.)

➤ **Make simple gifts**—Kids love to give homemade gifts to grandparents and others. Try giving them some of your leftover supplies and letting them create a gift that could be preserved forever. My kids have made bookmarks, cards, pictures of themselves with the loved one on a cute scrapbook page, a set of thank-you cards, a recipe book, mini-scrapbooks, stories, gift bags, gift tags, and more.

➤ ABC book—Have kids use pictures and stickers to make their own ABC book, with a picture of something on each page that begins with one letter of the alphabet, and challenge them to pick unusual objects. For example, for the *A* page, there could be a photo of an accordion with *A*-shaped embellishments on the page; the *B* page could have a picture of a Band-Aid; and so on. This is a great summer project they can show the next year at school.

# Paper Dolls and Pocket Pages

Kids bored of just doing scrapbook pages? Send them off to do one of these easy projects. They will have fun and will utilize their creativity while completing these projects. Help them get the supplies set up and let them have at it.

## Kid's Project #1—Paper Dolls That Fish and Swim

You need the following supplies:

➤ Glue

➤ Straight-edge scissors

➤ Scraps of paper for clothes

➤ Paper dolls (if you don't want to create your own pattern, you can purchase these precut or die cut them yourself)

Paper dolls in a scrapbook can reinforce your photo story. If the pictures are of you at the beach, put your paper dolls in bathing suits and have them doing what you are doing. It's fun to duplicate your clothing onto the paper dolls.

1. Decide what pictures you are going to use with your paper dolls so you can decide how you want the dolls to look and what they should be wearing. Start simple; if you are fishing, have them wear fishing clothes and make a fishing pole.

2. Decorate the dolls. Make the clothes out of scraps of paper. Layer them for a realistic look. Add hair, eyes, and shoes. You can color these in or cut bits of paper to use. Glue the clothes onto your paper doll.

3. Time to accessorize. For a fishing doll, make a fishing pole and use a sticker for the fish. Look at what you have at home to add to the paper doll. Be creative and have fun.

*What I like about the paper doll on this page is that the child colored directly on the paper to create the desired effect.*

# Kid's Project #2—Put Dreams in Your Pocket Pages

This is a popular project, and you can find many inspiring ideas all around you. The concept is to create a paper pocket to go on your scrapbook page to hold items that you want to keep, such as report cards, letters, valentines, ticket stubs, and collector cards. You can keep all of these items in your scrapbook, and it is much easier to find the item when you need it.

You need the following supplies:

➤ Paper for pocket

➤ Paper for background page

➤ Stickers, die cuts, scraps of paper to decorate pocket

➤ Scissors

➤ Glue

➤ Pen

Here are the instructions:

1. Cut the paper for the pocket page in half the long way.
2. Put glue on three outside edges of the pocket and place on background paper.
3. Decorate your pocket any way you like.
4. Wait for glue to dry and gently place items inside pocket.

*Pocket pages are simple for kids to create and very useful.*

Following are some other ideas for pocket pages.

Put a pocket in the middle of the page. Just glue the sides and stick letters down the middle.

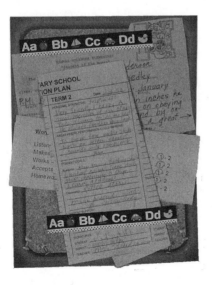

*This page is perfect for holding letters in place.*

Use large die cuts to make your pocket into a shape, such as a bus or school house.

**189**

*I love to put letters from teachers in this bus pocket page.*

*This is a great way to keep your items separate but all together on the same page.*

You can make small pockets throughout the page to hold special tickets.

## Kid's Project #3—Basketball, Bugs, or the Bassoon

My kids like to customize their books as much as possible. One fun project is to create dividers for your book ... whether it is a sports book or it is divided chronologically, the possibilities are endless. For one of the projects in the kids' scrapbook class we created seasonal dividers using stickers that depicted the four seasons.

*These dividers are perfect for a child to put their pages in.*

You need the following supplies:

➤ Glue

➤ Scissors

➤ Four plain protectors

➤ Four sheets of cardstock to go into protectors

➤ Scraps of paper to mount stickers on

➤ Sport stickers for dividers

➤ Clear contact paper/laminating paper

Here are the instructions:

1. Put stickers on scraps of paper and trim around them, leaving a small tab on the bottom to glue on the back of the protectors.

2. Decide how you will place the dividers. You want them to be seen, so lay out how you want them placed.

3. Glue on back of the protector on outside edge.

4. Decorate cardstock to go inside the protector.

5. Put paper in protectors and put it into the scrapbook.

## Parents and Kids Together

Children can be encouraged to join in the fun with mom and dad. Some innovative scrapbooking stores have realized that kids are interested in scrapbooking and are offering classes especially for them. Among the classes I have developed are a 12-week kids' summer camp, kids' basics, and kids' design. My latest is Baby-sitting Mania, which features projects and games to add to a baby-sitting kit.

Try holding a scrapbooking party for kids. If your local scrapbook store has space, use their classroom. If not, you can throw one at home. Here's how:

➤ Pick a theme (summer, picnics, poolside, beach, or anything the kids might like) and ask each guest to bring some related pictures. That way, you can have a packet of appropriate die cuts and stickers for them. Let the kids experiment with scissors and punches.

➤ Relate the party games to scrapbooking—Pin the die cut on the page, scraptionery, sticker match game, and so on. When I play scraptionery with the kids, I have a bunch of cards with scrapbook items written down on them, such as decorative scissors, stationery, memorabilia pockets, and so forth. While you may not be able to come up with hundreds of items to draw, the kids will have fun playing this game. Give them a set amount of time and let them draw.

➤ As part of the fun, make an oversized scrapbook page to give to the birthday girl or boy. Ask each guest to bring a picture of themselves and have them glue it on the page and write what they like most about the birthday child.

➤ Favor bags would be a breeze to come up with—they could include die cuts, stickers, pens, cardstock, and much more.

**Sticky Points**

Some of the smaller scrapbook stores are not yet kid-friendly. If that describes your local store, try to encourage them to start classes for kids or offer workshops.

Kids learn best from hands-on experience. In the tool section of my kids' camp curricula, I show them how to use different tools and different ways to use them. In addition to showing kids the right way to use the tools, you can also teach the kids to sharpen their observation skills and their eyes for color and pattern. For instance, give each child a pair of scissors and ask them to find some paper that would match the pattern or show them all of the different ways to use punches other than just punching the shape out and gluing it on.

# Photography Tips for Kids

As soon as kids start scrapbooking, they usually begin wanting to take their own photographs. I think you will be surprised at how much they love taking their own pictures. Here are some tips for getting children started taking their own pictures:

**Shortcuts**

If you aren't sure whether to buy a camera for your child, try purchasing a disposable camera to see how interested they really are.

➤ Make sure they know to hold the camera steady until they have clicked the button.

➤ Cameras with an automatic focus and an automatic flash are generally easier for children to use, but if the camera is manual, show them how to advance the film so they can take the next shot.

➤ Teach them to take the pictures at their level or to climb up (safely!) or crouch down if they are taking photos of objects higher or lower than they are.

➤ Instruct them on how to get everything in the picture by looking through the camera's viewfinder and making sure the things they want to take photos of are within the viewfinder's lines.

➤ Tell them to take their time and compose the shots—they don't need to rush.

Let them enjoy taking the pictures and putting them in their scrapbook. This would be a great summer project.

# Safety First

While having fun with the kids, don't forget to take precautions, especially since the children will be using scissors and other cutting tools. Show kids exactly how to use tools that they may not be familiar with and go over safety rules when you begin any project.

## Safe Cutting

Remind children that scissors are meant to cut paper, not hair, clothes, or skin. Though decorative scissors don't have very sharp blades, you can still do some damage with them, so remind kids to handle them properly. The same goes for paper trimmers and die cuts, which have sharp blades. It would be best for an adult to closely supervise both of these cutting tools.

## Keep a Neat and Organized Work Area

**Sticky Points**

Safety Tips for Working with Kids:

➤ Use scissors the safe way (children should hold a closed pair of scissors by the blade, and, of course, should never run with them).

➤ Check out one tool at a time to avoid clutter.

➤ Create a safety cutting zone for paper cutters.

➤ Adult supervision is suggested with die cut machines.

As with any craft project, it is important to keep your area picked up so you and the kids won't trip over the punch that fell to the floor or step on that pair of scissors. I let my kids choose one tool at a time to use, and they have to trade that tool in before they can get another one. Designate spots for tools and train kids to use tools and put them back in the right place. The work area will be neater and safer.

## The Least You Need to Know

➤ You and your child will have fun together trying some of the projects in this chapter.

➤ Be patient and teach children the skills—let them create without your interference or "help."

➤ Encourage children to write down their thoughts in their own handwriting.

➤ Ask your local scrapbooking store to offer classes and projects for kids.

➤ Remind kids to use tools and materials safely.

# Chapter 17

# Dress It Up!
# Layout
# Guidelines for
# Great Pages

I like to start my design techniques class by asking the participants why they chose to take the class and what it is that they are struggling with. The answers I hear are that people know how to use all the scrapbooking tools, but have a hard time putting everything together. They have difficulty actually laying out a page, so they ask for ideas and guidelines to keep page after page interesting. Many women complain that their pages are beginning to look the same—"Boring."

Scrapbooking is a kind of at-home crash course in graphic design. Once you know which products are available, and which are your style, you want to know the most interesting ways to lay out your pages.

Some people have a natural eye for decorating and graphic design—they put pictures and embellishments on a page and voilá—it looks terrific! Some of us don't have this intuition, but everyone will find that the design rules in this chapter will make a world of difference in your books. This chapter contains advice for creating a focal point, choosing shapes for your pages, placing embellishments, and adding your own signature touches. Remember, don't be too critical of yourself and enjoy this process!

**Anecdotes from the Archives**

The pioneer in page design is Stacy Julian, the author of *Core Composition*. She has "the eye," and took it one step further to explain to others what works and why. You can see her work regularly in *Creating Keepsakes* magazine as she continues to teach us how to lay out our pages. She has personally taught me her techniques, and it has made a big difference in my pages. For more details on this topic, look for her informative book at your favorite scrapbook store or online site.

# Keep It Simple— Basic Layout Guidelines

Start simple and then go from there.

## *Dive into the Pool*

The first step in creating your layout should be selecting the photos to use. How many you have to select from depends on your "photo pool." If you are a photo fanatic like me, you take as many pictures as possible. I have a father-in-law who prides himself on his picture-taking ability, and he always has great photos for me to add to my collection. I usually end up with a huge selection of photos, which gives me many scrapbooking options. If you aren't as lucky, you'll have to make do with the pictures you have.

People ask me how many pictures of any one event they should use. Guess what I say? That's right, there is no rule. If you want to use all ten rolls of Christmas photos, go ahead! When my sister and I went to Disneyland with my two older sons, we took four rolls of film, and the pictures turned out so great that I created an entire album of our Disneyland trip. You can choose what works best for you, but don't get stuck thinking that you must use every single photo from a given event. Remember, this is your family story, so use the pictures that best tell the story.

**Words for Posterity**

A **photo pool** refers to the selection of pictures you have available to choose from.

**Shortcuts**

For birthdays, try doing three or four double-page layouts showing the day's events, such as breakfast in bed, opening presents, and the kid's party.

196

### Anecdotes from the Archives

Many families go a little crazy snapping shots of their firstborn and get a bit more lax when they have their second. To compensate, take some photos you have of your second (or third or fourth) child and add to them extra embellishments to create pages with different themes (even if the photos are from the same day). I took a roll of film of my second son swinging and playing in the backyard, and I used those pictures to fill in four or five pages with different themes. It's sneaky, but it works!

## Choose a Theme

The next step is choosing a theme for your pictures. That way, you can choose the embellishments and accessories that work best with the photos. If you end up with numerous photos within the theme, you can break the photos down into smaller categories. For instance, if you have a lot of pictures from Christmas 1995, you could divide them into categories such as hanging the stockings, decorating the tree Christmas morning, Christmas dinner, and so on.

## Focus In on the Story

Now choose the focus of the story. Lay out your pictures and decide how you want to tell the story. When I am helping people in a class work on layouts, I ask them to get 6 to 10 pictures of an event and tell me about them. I like to talk with them about what is going on in the pictures, asking questions such as what are you trying to show on these pages, what is your favorite picture, and which picture best tells the story? You can ask yourself these questions at home to help you decide how to present the story.

### Sticky Points

If you find a layout you like in a book, magazine, or other source, go ahead and copy it if you wish, but be sure to personalize it by changing the colors and embellishments to match your photos.

## Pick Colors and Embellishments

When you are sure of your storytelling direction, go to the next step—choosing colors. Colors affect not only the look of your layouts, but the mood. Select colors that reflect the mood of the events you are portraying by experimenting with different colors to get the feeling you want.

Selecting embellishments is my favorite part of scrapbooking. I suggest you choose embellishments that enhance your layout, not distract from it. To do this, keep in mind

## Sticky Points

The embellishment stage is where pictures can tend to get misplaced; for example, if you have the pictures out and can't find any embellishments to use with the photos. If you don't immediately find any embellishment to go with them, be careful that you don't put them away somewhere where you'll never see them again. Put your pictures in the proper place, even if you can't find something to match them right away.

the story you are telling and the mood you have chosen. Pick embellishments that match your color scheme.

There will be times when you'll fall in love with a particular sticker or die cut, place it on your layout, and then realize it is actually distracting. I once put an adorable school bus sticker on one of my son's school pages; the only problem was that my son doesn't ride a bus to school, there was no bus in the photo, and the colors didn't match. Now I try to choose the photos first, then the embellishments. I want my stickers to complement the layout, not control it! There should be a reason each embellishment is there.

# Double the Pages, Double the Fun

When I refer to a spread or a double-page layout, I mean two pages, side by side that go together. Double-page layouts are pleasing to the eye because when a scrapbook is open you see both pages at the same time. Two cohesive pages display your pictures in the best possible way.

*The double-page layout sends a message across with the bright colors and bold lines.*

If you don't have enough pictures to create a double-page layout but don't want to leave the other side blank, try using the same color scheme to give a look of consistency to the pages, even if the photos on the facing page are of a different event or theme. Another option is to use the additional page for journaling—we can always say something more about our photos (each is worth a thousand words, right?).

# What's Your (Focal) Point?

This is the most important composition tool for the scrapbooker. Every design has a focal point, whether it is the fireplace mantle in your living room or the island in a seascape painting. A focal point is something your eye is naturally drawn to, and you can manipulate the elements on your pages to highlight the focal point of your choice just as you would when decorating your living room. How do you do this? It is very simple, really! Emphasize the picture you chose as your favorite by treating it a little different than the rest.

Following are some ways to make your focal point picture stand out.

**Words for Posterity**

A **focal point** is that element (usually a photo) where your eye goes first. Every layout has a focal point—be sure you decide what that focal point should be!

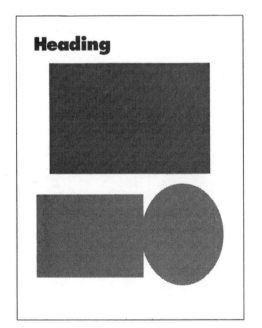

*The large image on top is where the focal point picture is placed—it tells the story.*

➤ Place it on a different angle on the page—If all of the photos in the layout are tilted, place the focal point picture straight and parallel. Try the reverse, too.

*The slight tilt of the photo draws you in.*

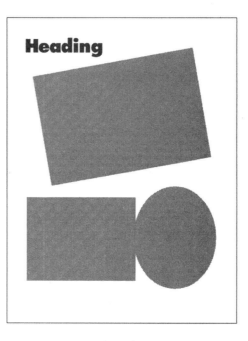

➤ Double-mount the focal photo on an extra color of cardstock while leaving the other pictures single mounted.

*Create an eye-catching focal point by selecting two colors to double-mount your photo on.*

➤ Use decorative scissors to trim around the cardstock the focal photo is mounted on and leave the other photos with straight edges.

*The different edge on the focal point picture gets your attention.*

➤ Try cutting the focal photo into a different shape than the others or placing your main embellishment near it.

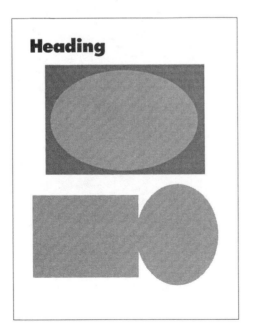

*Look at what using a different shape does to the focal point picture.*

*By placing your main embellishment near your focal point photo you are creating a winning page.*

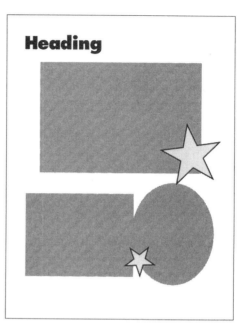

➤ Journal around the focal photo or place the journaling under it to draw the viewer's attention there first.

*Everyone wants to read the story around this focal point picture to figure out what is going on.*

# Shape Up!

Shapes are fun to use in your scrapbook. Using shapes in your books adds variety and interest to your pages. Look around your home and out in nature and see all of the shape variations that surround us. We need the variation in our scrapbooks, as well.

Not only is it great to cut photos into different shapes, you can also add shapes by using embellishments. For example, maybe you have rectangular pictures of you and your friends playing in the snow on a blue-and-white striped paper; to add shape, use embellishments that will contrast with the straight lines, such as snowflakes or a snowman.

Try not to cut too much out of pictures—sometimes the background of a photo has interesting or historical detail. For example, if you have an old picture of your grandparents standing by their car, leave the car in—it's not only interesting to see what they drove, it may help you date what year the photo was taken.

If there is something (or, er, someone) in the photo that you don't like, you can go ahead and cut it out. I recently took a picture of my son playing with our kitten—the kitten is looking right at Justin, and the expression on Justin's face is one of rapt attention. This picture couldn't be cuter, except for the huge pile of dirty laundry in the background! So I trimmed the photo into a circle, eliminating the mess, and put it right into a scrapbook. Trimming the photo not only eliminated an unsightly background, it also helped to focus on the important elements of the photo—the child and the kitten.

**Shortcuts**

You are the storyteller, so use the focal point photo to full advantage and make sure it is the one you want. When doing a Marine World layout, I chose to use a picture of my son with a huge grin on his face instead of the posed one of everyone in our group at the fountain. I did this because it best captured the events of the day.

**Sticky Points**

If you like trimming photos, make sure you only cut photos for which you have a negative or a duplicate.

Although you want variety in your pages, you don't want to get too carried away. Try to achieve a balanced look by using equal amounts of shapes on each page, placing the shapes opposite each other on the pages, or placing similar-shaped photos at the points of a triangle across the layout.

*Shapes add movement to your layouts. Here are the basics.*

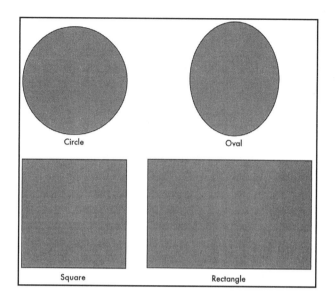

*I had to get rid of that ugly stained couch the kids were sitting on to focus in on the cute kids and kittens.*

# Tips for Placing Embellishments

When working with embellishments, you want to add a certain type of feeling to your pages. Whether it is the close feeling of a family gathering or the elegance of a wedding, embellishments go a long way toward creating a mood.

A few tips for embellishment placement:

➤ Place the embellishments in a triangle shape on your page or pages.

*As in landscaping, interior design elements look good in odd numbers—especially in threes, as illustrated in this layout.*

➤ Group your stickers or punches with a purpose instead of randomly filling up space.

➤ Place the main embellishment near the focal point picture to draw attention to it.

➤ Try out the look before gluing on the page (if you are using stickers, experiment with placement positions before peeling them off their backing).

➤ Use realistically sized embellishments when possible—a little tiny strip of sticker grass under the photo of your niece standing in a meadow with grass up to her knees would seem out of proportion.

**Sticky Points**

Don't feel as if you have to use every sticker on the sheet that you purchased. Use the ones that complement your layout.

Look at the way these stickers are placed on the page. They reinforce the actions of the photo but don't overwhelm it. Notice the stickers are not covering every empty space on the page. Make good use of your negative space.

**Shortcuts**

Empty, or negative, space can serve effectively to highlight an item or allow the eye to absorb all the page elements.

# Negative Space

Another important layout principle is the wise use of negative space—that is, space on your pages that is free of pictures, captions, journaling, embellishments, borders, or any kind of decoration. The eye needs to have time to take everything in, and leaving portions of a layout empty prevents it from being too busy and frenetic. Negative space should be thought of as an embellishment in itself—study layouts that you like and note the use of empty space on the page.

## The Least You Need to Know

➤ The look of your pages will improve drastically by creating a focal point.

➤ Using a variety of shapes on your page can create visual interest. Be careful not to shape or cut a photo with historical interest—never cut a one-of-a-kind photo.

➤ Place embellishments that will complement your layout and help tell your story.

➤ Negative space is a good thing. It leaves places for the eyes to wander and enjoy the images instead of darting all around, trying to take everything in.

# Part 5
# Theme Books and Great Pages

*An old Chinese proverb states that "The journey of a thousand miles begins with a single step." If completing your scrapbooks feels like a thousand-mile journey to you, you have plenty of company. You may have stacks of photos and don't know where to start. My suggestion to you? Theme pages that can be turned into an entire theme book.*

*Theme books are scrapbooks that focus on one specific event or subject, such as weddings or holidays. Theme books are great projects for beginners, because you don't have to buy a lot of different paper and embellishments, and you get a great feeling of completion every time you finish one.*

*To help you along, I've included several new lettering styles, designed especially for this book. Also included are my own suggestions for different ways to use embellishments for each category.*

*This section was designed as a reference guide. Just choose the area of interest to you, and get to work!*

# Chapter 18

# Sunrise, Sunset: Capturing Changes in Your Kids and the Seasons

### In This Chapter

➤ Fresh photo ideas for your children throughout the year

➤ Making a book of your child's favorites

➤ Holiday layouts to get you jumping on finishing up last year's Christmas photos

➤ Making seasonal albums—you can almost smell the pumpkin pie

Parents' desire to capture their children's fleeting childhood is probably the number one reason people begin a scrapbook, but it isn't just parents who make scrapbooks with kids as the focus. I've seen grandmothers lugging in packs and packs of photos of their far-away grandchildren, delighted to show off their photos to anyone who wants to see them. I had a student in my class who had an entire scrapbook of her two adored nieces. If you are running out of creative ideas for those cute snapshots of your favorite sweethearts, read on.

The changing seasons are also a wonderful way to document the passage of a year—all the better if you live in a climate with four of them, but you can do this even if you live in sunny Florida. Of course, you will often make books that combine these two themes together. So many milestones in children's lives coincide with specific seasons that these two are natural co-themes. Think of your kids in swimsuits and then snow-suits (what is cuter than that!), and you'll know what I mean.

*This is a terrific font for seasonal pages.*

## Baby Days

Does anyone know exactly when a baby stops being a baby? One mom I know refers to her 16-year-old daughter as her baby. But babies grow up, and for the sake of this chapter, I will refer to babies as children up to one year old.

My top advice for you is to take tons of pictures during that first year. Babies change so fast that you need a lot of film to document all of it. When my twins were born three years ago, I was in such a daze that I didn't have film in the camera the day they were born! I am lucky enough to have a father-in-law who takes pictures all the time, so he gave some to us. But don't let that happen to you!

Must-have pictures to document baby's first year:

➤ Baby with mom and dad for the first time

➤ Coming home from the hospital

➤ First time in bassinet

➤ First bath

➤ First outing

➤ Baby meeting grandparents and extended family

➤ First solid food

➤ Baby smiling

➤ Baby sleeping

➤ Favorite toy

➤ Baby's special blanket

Pictures that are fun to have:

➤ Photo of mom on the delivery day outside of the hospital (try to capture the weather) with the hospital's sign in the background.

➤ The doctor and nurse who delivered the baby

➤ Mom all worn out after the delivery

➤ The baby on the scale

➤ Baby meeting siblings

➤ Dad asleep in rocking chair with baby

➤ Big brother or sister giving baby a bottle

➤ All the gear you pack into your diaper bag for a one-hour outing

➤ The dishes piled up in the sink

➤ The baby shower

Of course, some embellishments just have to be included in your baby book, such as the bottle, carriage, baby feet and hands, and baby bibs, but don't stop with just these old favorites. Look for some medical embellishments to go along with baby's first trip to the doctor or use some dishes to accent baby's first meal.

**Shortcuts**

Family historians recommend that you take at least one roll a year of black-and-white film. Black and white can pick up details that color can't capture, and you'll be thrilled to look back on these photos.

*This baby page layout uses some creative borders and frames to capture the baby's first year and accomplishments.*

# School Daze

I still have the first attempts my kids made at writing their names. Taylor wrote a *T* and an *O* and that's it. When he started school, his papers, projects, and drawings accumulated so much that I didn't know what to do with them. Now I save the important items in a special school scrapbook. Report cards, school photos, and well-done essays go in there. I sort through my children's art projects at the end of the year and save the best ones, then take them to the copy center to get them bound in a book. My kids like these books because they can look at all the work they've done in previous years; I like them because they are easy to store.

The first year of school, whether it is kindergarten, nursery school, or pre-school, is so exciting for kids (and sentimental for parents) that it is fun to document from beginning to end. Must-have pictures for this book are

➤ First day of school

➤ Shopping for school supplies

➤ Packing lunches

➤ Special programs

➤ Award ceremonies

➤ Sports

➤ First book your child read all by himself

➤ Your child decked out in school colors

➤ Photos of your child's favorite art projects

➤ Child holding an apple for the teacher

**Sticky Points**

Don't forget to document both first and last names of classmates. When your children grow up, they will then be able to find that long-lost kindergarten friend.

Pictures that are fun to have:

➤ Contents of your child's backpack

➤ Child dressed in an outfit she picked out

➤ Your child hopping into the carpool

➤ Child in the cafeteria eating lunch

➤ Your child's friends

➤ Your child with her teacher

➤ Child sitting at his desk

➤ Holding a report card

➤ The doctor's visit for the prekindergarten shots

➤ The last day of school (and kindergarten graduation if there is one)

There are too many school embellishments to name, but here are my favorites: books, crayons, backpacks, apples, pencils, and globes.

*This layout uses special embellishments to tell the story of the first year in school.*

# A Few of Their Favorite Things

My kids love having favorites. Nathan decided yellow was his favorite color when he was just two years old. Jacob loves pink. Any visitors who come to my house are quickly told by these two what their favorites are. I think this gives them a sense of identity and uniqueness, and it's fun to make favorites books for each of my children. A great way to start this is to ask your child all sorts of questions. If you'd like, you can make this an all-day activity by photographing your child next to all of his favorites.

Here are some questions to get you started. Encourage your child to think of more favorites. Remember, you want this to capture your child's unique personality and that may mean including your child's favorite potato chip flavor!

➤ What is your favorite food? Dessert?

➤ My favorite family activity is _____.

➤ My favorite room in the house is _____.

➤ What is your favorite memory?

➤ What is your favorite flower?

➤ My favorite movie is _____.

➤ My favorite vacation is _____.

➤ What is your favorite flavor of ice cream?

Must-have pictures for a favorites book:

➤ Child with best friends

➤ Wearing favorite outfit

➤ Eating favorite cereal

➤ Participating in favorite activity

➤ Playing outside during her favorite season

➤ Singing his favorite song

➤ Drawing with his favorite color crayon

➤ Playing a favorite game

➤ Reading a favorite book

➤ Cooking a favorite meal

When choosing accents for this book, you'll want to use something that reflects your child's interests. If his favorite color is red, focus on that, and if she lists sports as a favorite activity, balls and uniforms would work well. These layouts use a variety.

# Easy as ABC (and 1,2,3)

If you've got duplicates, doubles, or flubbed photos that you don't want to throw out, try an ABC book. These are fun projects for kids to help with, and they're a great way for your child to be the star of a book. Find a photo for each letter of the alphabet. If you like, you can make a theme ABC book, as in "ABC at the Circus," beginning with "A is for acrobat" and going on through to "Z is for zebra." Here is the list I used for my "ABCs in Action" book. Try to be inventive, and you'll come up with a great book.

A: Aunts coming to visit

B: Bouncing on the trampoline

C: Crying over spilt milk

D: Daredevil stunts

E: Eating eggs for breakfast

F: Frosting a cake

G: Giggling

H: Hide and seek

I: Itchy chicken pox

J: Jumping on the bed

K: Kicking the soccer ball

L: Laughing at the movies

M: Making mud pies

N: Nestling under a blanket

O: Opening presents

P: Putting puzzle pieces together

Q: Quitting for the day

R: Running to first base

S: Sliding down the water slides

T: Taking the dog for a walk

U: Using the lawn mower

V: Vandalism cleanup

W: Waking mom up early

X: X-raying a broken bone

Y: Yawning on the bus

Z: Zooming around the schoolyard

The fun thing about these books is you can focus on your children and highlight the items they enjoy. For a simpler task, try doing a number book. You could include pictures of their favorite things they can count (one jelly bean, two stuffed animals, three wooden blocks, and so on). I provide a variety of examples in the following figures.

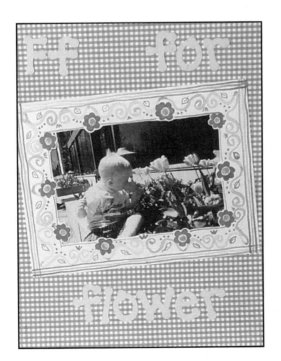

*Now you know your ABCs! There are tons of fun embellishments with numbers and letters.*

*1,2, buckle my shoe.*

## Celebrate Good Times!

In my family, my birthday was the biggest day of the year. When I was a child, a birthday meant breakfast in bed, followed by a day with no chores (I didn't even have to make my bed!), and my mom fixed whatever I wanted for dinner. After that, I had a special cake and, of course, presents. I always felt especially cherished on my birthday, and I try to do the same for my kids. Making a fuss over them on their birthdays makes them feel important, and that's why I like to document these days. The memories are more vivid when there are photos to go along with the story.

I used to take so many birthday pictures that I didn't know what to do with them. I mean, who can resist taking at least three pictures of your child opening each present, five of him blowing out the candles on the cake, and a dozen of him playing with his new toys? If you are in the same predicament, here are my suggestions:

Let's say that your daughter Linda is turning four next week, and you are planning a party with some of her friends. Here is a list of must-have photos:

➤ Linda in her party dress
➤ Linda opening her gifts

➤ The birthday cake with the candles lit

➤ The birthday girl's cheeks filled with air as she gets ready to blow out the candles

➤ The extended family gathered to celebrate Linda's big day

➤ The friends at her party

➤ The stack of unopened presents

➤ Linda greeting her party guests (*that* will be cute!)

➤ The children playing musical chairs, pin the tail on the donkey, and blind man's bluff

➤ Linda unwrapping her gifts

**Shortcuts**

For fun birthday pages, color copy the wrapping paper on the child's presents to use as background paper or mounting paper on your pages. Be sure to include some of the favorite cards along with a list of presents received.

While these are classic photos, be on the lookout for other photo opportunities. It's the details that make each birthday special, so try to record the seemingly mundane scenes, as well as the inevitable mishaps.

➤ Linda holding up four fingers

➤ Linda spilling red punch on her birthday dress

➤ All the party guests gathered around Linda

➤ Linda fighting with her sister over her new toys

➤ Pictures of the apartment after all the kids have left and before you've cleaned up

➤ The birthday girl fidgeting while mom tries to fix her hair for the party

➤ Mailing or delivering party invitations

➤ Linda having a breakdown from all the excitement

➤ Linda's sister poking her finger in the frosting

➤ Finally, after the party, Linda tucked in bed with her new doll in one hand, her crumpled party hat in the other

Although these photo ideas are based on a young child's birthday party, you can easily adapt them for teenagers and adults. Your husband will appreciate the picture of him blowing out fifty candles on his cake!

If you already have pictures but need some fresh ideas on how to display them, remember that many of the classic birthday embellishments span generations. Candles, party hats, presents, and confetti can be used on pages for people from 8 to 80. Since party hats are a favorite birthday accent, I've used them on the layout here.

*Birthday embellishments make this page extra special.*

## A Scrapbook for All Seasons

Another great scrapbook theme is seasons. We measure the passing of life and milestones by noting the seasons, and as each season comes around again, we are reminded of years past and the traditions we participate in. It's important to record these times.

*This versatile lettering can be used with any holiday.*

**218**

# Spring Has Sprung

Spring is my favorite time of year, a time of renewal and possibility, but other than Easter, many of us don't take photos of spring events. Mother's Day, St. Patrick's Day, and Secretary's Day are often neglected, but make great photo opportunities. Spring is also a great opportunity to document nature's changes—no spring scrapbook should be without pictures of daffodils in bloom. How about commemorating the most exciting yearly ritual of all—shoving big winter coats into the back of the closet—yahoo! Spring pictures can turn an ordinary day into something memorable.

These are some must-have photos for spring:

➤ Dressed up in Easter finery

➤ Easter baskets

➤ Egg hunts

➤ Dyeing eggs (and hands and clothes!)

➤ Your child holding the Mother's Day gift he made for you

➤ You and your mom on Mother's Day

➤ Packing up sweaters and scarves until next winter

➤ A green St. Patrick's Day dinner

➤ Bouquet of Secretary's Day flowers

➤ Planting a vegetable garden

➤ Baby birds in their nests

Here are some other fun spring photos:

➤ Splashing in mud puddles

➤ Your dog shaking off the rain inside your living room

➤ The first tulip

➤ Kids holding handfuls of dandelions they brought you

➤ Pushing your kids on swings in the park

➤ Making mud pies

➤ Rainbows

➤ The kids tromping through your freshly planted flower bed

➤ Dad sliding down the slide

Spring is a wonderful time of year, and the photos are usually so full of color they hardly need

**Shortcuts**

When tackling a messy project, such as dyeing eggs or planting a garden, remember to take before and after shots of your project undertaking. These can be very memorable.

embellishments, but there are so many cute ones, it would be a shame to skip them. Here are a few: flowers (especially tulips and daffodils), chicks, bunnies, raindrops, dyed eggs, and baskets.

*Dyeing Easter eggs can make a great page.*

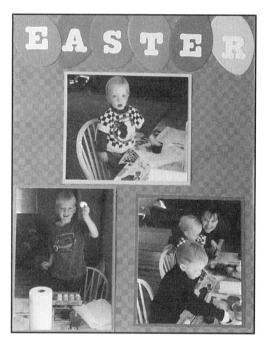

## *Hazy, Lazy, Crazy Days of Summer*

The writer Henry James once said, "Summer afternoon—summer afternoon; to me these have always been the two most beautiful words in the English language." And … ahhh! … I must agree. Summer is a time to take a break from the frantic pace of our busy schedules. Time to sit on the porch and eat watermelon or to lick popsicles while you watch the stars come out. It is a time for laziness, reading books in the backyard while the kids run through the sprinklers, and spraying each other with the hose. Make sure you capture all these fun times as well as the exciting holidays.

Here are some ideas to get you started:

➤ Whether you've got a built-in pool or a teeny inflatable one, snap those swimming shots

➤ Watching the Fourth of July parade

➤ Water fights when the sun is sizzling

➤ Backyard campouts

➤ Family picnics

➤ Wading at the beach

➤ Building sand castles

➤ Roasting marshmallows over a campfire

➤ Trips to the ice cream shop

➤ Playing hopscotch in the backyard

Here are some unusual photos that will make your scrapbook more personal:

➤ Those adorable curbside lemonade stands

➤ Kids with popsicle-stained faces

➤ Fourth of July fireworks

➤ Sunburns (they'll remind you to wear sunscreen next year!)

➤ The towel rack crowded with dripping swimsuits

➤ The ice cream truck stopping by your house

➤ The lawn that got scorched during the heat wave

➤ Your bathtub full of sand after a day at the beach

➤ Another failed attempt at homemade ice cream

Here are some quick tips for photographing fireworks:

1. Have a tripod—this can't be stressed enough—if you don't have one, ignore the rest of this list.

2. Regardless of your film speed (but, yeah, should be at least 400), set your SLR for B (bulb), which will enable you to control how long the shutter stays open.

3. Have a hat or dark piece of paper (or anything wide and dark).

4. Decide how many fireworks you want on one frame.

5. Hit the release button while holding the hat over the lens.

6. Remove the hat when the fireworks are exploding, and leave the hat off for as long as you want the streaks to last on your frame.

7. Either close the shutter or place the hat back over the lens—this way, you control whether you want one to two fireworks on one frame ... or 50! (And you also have control over how long you want the streaks.)

**Sticky Points**

If you are shooting fireworks, use a high-speed film like ASA 800. Set a long exposure to capture several fireworks bursts.

**221**

What to do with these photos? The classic embellishments are always fun—wading pools, water splats, slides, firecrackers, picnics, watermelon, ants, swimming suits, poolside, sunglasses.

*A lazy summer day.*

## Go Jump in the Leaves!

Fall is a wonderful time of year. The temperature drops, leaves fall from the trees, and kids go back to school. There are many photo opportunities in these months, so be sure you have plenty of film. The gorgeous oranges, yellows, reds, and browns of the leaves make for a wonderful backdrop for all your photos.

Must-have fall pictures:

➤ Halloween costumes

➤ Playing in the fall leaves

➤ Thanksgiving feast

➤ Harvesting the vegetables

➤ Pumpkin patch

➤ Carving pumpkins

➤ Carving the Thanksgiving turkey

➤ Raking leaves

➤ Making caramel apples

➤ Going on hay rides

These autumn pictures are fun to have:

➤ School Halloween parade

➤ Putting on the clown make-up

➤ Candy sack filled with candy

➤ You and your friends going off to a costume party

➤ The kitchen before the Thanksgiving dishes are cleaned up

➤ Peeling mounds of apples for the apple pies

➤ Going to the Thanksgiving parade

Here are the must-have embellishments for your fall photos: fall leaves, cornucopia, ghosts, haunted house, pumpkins, waves of wheat, bare trees, jack-o'-lanterns, and acorns.

**Shortcuts**

Save items from your yard and garden and color copy them to put in your scrapbook. My children collected some vibrant leaves and were thrilled when I copied them to put in their scrapbook.

*Use fall borders to hold your little ghosts.*

# Winter Wonderland

I have to admit that I am not a winter person. When December rolls around and those snowflakes are falling, my mood falls, too. I've learned to deal with sun deprivation by finding fun photo opportunities, and winter has a ton of them. Kids making snow angels and pelting each other with snowballs make great pictures. And, of course, there are the holidays. Whatever winter holiday you celebrate, whether it's Christmas, Hanukah, Kwaanza, or some winter solstice ritual, be sure to capture these events on film.

Classic photos:

➤ Family in front of the Christmas tree

➤ Lighting the Menorah

➤ Exchanging gifts

➤ Baking goodies

➤ Frolicking in the snow (no matter how old you are!)

➤ Frosting cookies

➤ Family decked out in holiday finery

➤ A visit to Santa Claus

➤ Holiday meals

➤ Ice skating or sledding

And how about these:

➤ Car covered in snow after the 10th snowstorm

➤ Your kids undecorating the tree

➤ Your two-year-old licking frosting off the cookies

➤ Kitty cat playing with the kitty toys in her stocking

➤ Kids coming in from the snow with red noses

➤ Drinking hot cocoa

➤ Pictures of your favorite gifts and the person who gave them to you

➤ Dad wearing that silly tie the kids gave him

➤ Wrapping paper mess

➤ Baby crying on Santa's lap

➤ Kids asleep with their new toys

Now that you've got the photos, let's dress them up. I love all the holiday accents, such as Christmas trees, stockings, menorah, carolers, ivy, and party hats.

*Building a snowman with the kids.*

---

### The Least You Need to Know

➤ Children grow up, but you can keep them forever young by scrapbooking.

➤ Be sure to photograph the everyday events, as well as special occasions.

➤ There is no such thing as too many baby pictures!

➤ The theme of ABCs and 1,2,3s for children's books provides you with a structure, but gives you lots of room for creativity.

➤ Keep the colors of spring in your scrapbook and capture the dog days of summer by making a seasonal scrapbook.

---

# Chapter 19

# You Must Remember This: Once-in-a-Lifetime Events and Special Memories

---

### In This Chapter

➤ Using duplicates of special documents and photos gives you more scrapbooking confidence

➤ Creating books that commemorate loved ones

➤ Preserve sports clippings and awards in special scrapbooks

---

Last month, a first-time scrapbooker brought in her wedding photos to work on in one of the classes I teach. She was eager to make a scrapbook but was so worried about how they would turn out that she couldn't get up the nerve to start. I told her to work on something else—something she had double prints of!

If you are ready to tackle some of your irreplaceable photos, I have a few suggestions for you. First, make color copies of one-of-a-kind photos, certificates, and documents and use the copies in your scrapbooks so that you've always got a back-up if you aren't satisfied with your work. Store the originals in acid-free envelopes in a safe place, maybe a safe deposit box. Next, if these are professional photos, you probably spent a lot of money on them, so you don't want to obscure them with stickers and embellishments. Last, keep it simple. These are photos that stand on their own, and too many embellishments diminish rather than enhance their impact.

*Use this lettering to add a simple and elegant look to your formal pages.*

Aa Bb Cc Dd
Ee Ff Gg Hh Ii
Jj Kk Ll Mm Nn
Oo Pp Qq Rr Ss
Tt Uu Vv Ww Xx
Yy Zz

# I Do—Wedding Albums

I spent more money on my wedding photographs than the rest of the wedding combined. I didn't mind skimping on the food or even the flowers, but the photographs had to be well done. I have never regretted that. After spending so much money, I wanted my scrapbook to look great.

While your photographer will take many posed and candid shots, be sure to assign some of your friends to take some photographs of the festivities. Some people even distribute disposable cameras among their guests for this purpose.

If you have yet to take photos of a wedding, here are some shots to be sure to get:

➤ Guests eating and enjoying themselves
➤ Children in the wedding party letting loose
➤ The spread of food and cake
➤ The decorations before the people come
➤ People's expressions during the ceremony
➤ Aunt Irene doing the "funky chicken" on the dance floor
➤ The stash of wedding gifts
➤ Bride and groom leaving for their honeymoon
➤ The cutting of the cake
➤ Musical performers

These pictures would be fun to have, too:

➤ The getaway car decorated with shaving cream and tin cans

➤ Parents of the couple dancing together

➤ Flower girl sleeping on her mom's lap

➤ The groom's happy face

➤ The bride sneaking away from the reception line to grab something to eat

➤ The girls fighting to catch the bridal bouquet

➤ The messy reception hall after the guests have left

➤ Father of the bride trying not to cry

The first step with this type of scrapbook is to decide on a theme. While your wedding is the main theme, the style and location of the wedding can determine the look of the scrapbook. If you got married in a garden, for example, floral paper is a natural choice. If your wedding was a black-tie affair complete with a sit-down dinner, you'll probably want to use a more elegant paper, such as embossed, vellum, or handmade. By the same token, make sure the embellishments you use are in keeping with the style of the book. The pictures here will give you a few ideas.

**Sticky Points**

A scrapbooking rule of thumb is never to cut pictures if you don't have the negatives. This is especially important when doing wedding pictures.

*Whether you are doing heritage wedding photos or current, remember to keep the design basic and stick with subtle colors.*

# I Still Do!—Anniversary Albums

Two years ago, my husband's parents celebrated their fortieth wedding anniversary. What a celebration we had! Besides all their children and grandchildren, they had some of the members of their wedding party there, as well as their dear friends. There were many photo opportunities, and I took advantage of them.

While forty years is a big milestone, with the divorce rate as high as it is, each wedding anniversary is a reason for celebration. Make sure you document each anniversary so you can tell your own special love story.

Must-have pictures for an anniversary scrapbook:

➤ Husband and wife in front of the building where they tied the knot

➤ Couple with all their children and grandchildren

➤ Friends of the couple

➤ Officiator who performed the ceremony

➤ The person who introduced the couple (if applicable)

➤ Couple alone

These would be great pictures if you can get them:

➤ Wife holding up wedding gown (or even wearing it, if it still fits!)

➤ Members of the wedding party—bridesmaids, groomsmen, and their families

➤ Friends the couple knew before they married

➤ Friends the couple has met since they married

➤ The couple dancing to their song

➤ The couple enjoying their favorite hobby together

**Shortcuts**

Family members of the couple celebrating a wedding anniversary often like to put together a scrapbook as a gift for the couple. If you are attempting this, give yourself plenty of time and recruit the entire family to help out. Include photos, love letters, and brochures from trips taken together.

The obvious accent choices here are bells, doves, and other wedding items. Bride and groom motifs are appropriate, too, but remember, these people have shared a whole life together since the wedding, and it is important to include designs that reflect that life. You could include embellishments such as golf clubs if the couple enjoys golfing, playing cards if they like bridge, or travel embellishments if that is what they do. Think of things the couple often do and go from there.

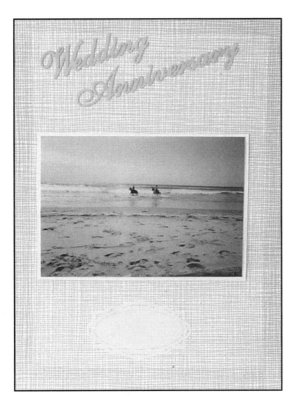

*Your goal here is to portray the feelings of the anniversary. This couple celebrated their tenth anniversary with a trip to the coast. They wanted solitude on their trip to reconnect to one another.*

# Pass It on, Pass It Down

My mom has only about five photos of her childhood. One of them is missing a corner, and another has a crease down the middle. If you are luckier than me and have lots of old family photos to preserve, you'll want to read this section.

### Anecdotes from the Archives

You might want to consider having damaged photos fixed at a photo lab in which the employees are proficient with PhotoShop. This program can make a photo look like it was never damaged.

If you are making a book that uses mostly older photos, keep embellishments to the bare minimum since they often clash with the classic-looking photos. Instead, use muted borders and some journaling to tell the story behind the pictures.

*Old photos are some of the most difficult and rewarding to work with. This layout uses barely any embellishments and classic colors.*

# In Memory Of

We all have hard times in our lives: deaths, major illnesses, auto accidents, and other personal difficulties. If you want to have a scrapbook that documents your life, try to include these in your books. Don't let other people discourage you from this if it is what you want to do; however, you probably don't want photos of these left on the coffee table for any curious visitor to look through.

My friend Jennifer's baby died a few days after he was born, and she was able to hold him once before he died. During the grief, pain, and shock of this time, her mother had the presence of mind to take rolls and rolls of photos of the baby. Jennifer told me that she was happy to have the photos as a reminder of her son and wanted to preserve them in a scrapbook, but the scrapbook took a long time to work on because she felt so deeply about the baby's life and death. The photos are all she had of him, and she wanted to make sure the book looked perfect. I know that I had a similar dilemma compiling a scrapbook about my deceased brother, so I've included some guidelines and tips.

### Shortcuts

Old photos tell so much of the story just by the expressions on people's faces and their backgrounds. Try to avoid the temptation to cut these photos up, as that tends to detract from the classic look. And since most of these pictures are one of a kind, there's no chance of ever getting them back in their original shape.

Include any photos you have in this book. If you have only a handful, use them all. If you have enough photos to pick and choose from, be sure to include as many of the following as possible. Remember, you are trying to preserve a memory of this person, so choose photos that convey his or her personality and that are special to you.

➤ Baby pictures

➤ Important milestones: graduation, wedding, and so on

➤ Person with special friends and relatives

➤ Person doing favorite things: sports, music, and so forth

➤ Pets

➤ Letters, certificates, and awards

➤ Funeral program

➤ Sympathy cards and letters you received, as well as tags that came with flowers

*Soothing colors and design work for this memorial page.*

# Religious Ceremonies

Around the world, people of all cultures celebrate the birth of a baby with a ritual. Here in the United States, many of us christen our baby in church, give the baby a blessing, or hold a bris. Whichever best describes your situation, this is an event that must be photographed!

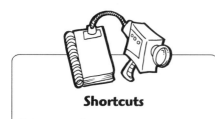

### Shortcuts

Take time after the ceremony to write down what happened, as well as your feelings, what was said, and what you hope it means. Too often, we don't record our feelings soon enough, and we forget.

Other religious ceremonies are held throughout life for people of all ages, from baptisms to first communions to bar mitzvahs. Although you may be prohibited from taking photos during the ceremony, you can still take photos in front of the building where the ceremony is taking place. Make sure you journal the event and include the names of everyone involved.

Here is a list of must-have photos of that event:

➤ Baby with parents and grandparents

➤ Baby in special outfit

➤ Person performing the naming ceremony

➤ Family members

➤ Celebration after the ceremony

➤ Preparation for the event

This is another serious type of activity and should be treated so. For the embellishment, I chose embossed paper.

*Decorative items were chosen to reinforce the significance of the events.*

# Everyday Life

Even the best scrapbookers overlook some topics, but if you want to make a complete history of your life, you need to include some of the less obvious aspects, such as building or renovating a house, playing with your pets, participating in sports, or just hanging around with people you like.

*Use this simple, versatile lettering for anything from your childhood.*

## *Under Construction*

Have you ever built a house or undertaken a big remodeling project? If so, you know what a drawn-out process it can be, but when the project is completed, it is very satisfying. Be sure you photograph the different stages of the construction process so you can look back and see how far you've come!

I know a family who built a cabin by themselves! It took over a year to complete, but all the family members were involved, and they said it was a fun way to spend time together. Of course, they took photos of the cabin's progress. If you've got something like this to work on, let me give you some ideas of photos you must take.

"Before" pictures include

> ➤ Empty lot
> ➤ Old kitchen, bathroom, or whatever you are remodeling
> ➤ Your family standing in the lot
> ➤ Blueprints, magazine pictures, and anything else you used in the decision process

**235**

"During" pictures include

➤ Contractor and other workers.

➤ The mess!

➤ Take pictures at regular intervals, maybe every week or two. That way you can get a real look at the progress.

➤ Choosing paint, linoleum, and other necessities.

### Shortcuts

You will find that this type of scrapbook can be very helpful. Jot down the names of the paint and other details when compiling your pages. You can refer back to them if necessary.

*This was a very significant event at our house— building a fence in the winter. The stickers reinforce the layout.*

"After" pictures include

➤ The construction crew in front of your house

➤ Moving into the new house

➤ Your family standing in front of the new house

➤ Your first picnic in the backyard

➤ Planting a tree

➤ The boxes piled high to the ceiling, waiting to be put away

Lots of fun accents exist for construction projects: houses, tools, hard hats—even bulldozers and dump trucks. I'm going to show you all the things you can do with tools.

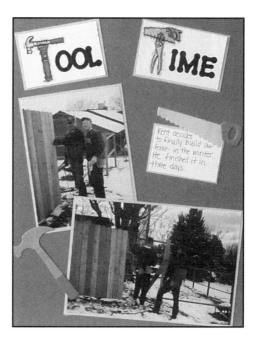

## Man's and Woman's Best Friends

If you are an animal lover, you have at least one pet who is a member of your family. My sister has two cats that she takes everywhere with her. She buys them special food and collars and loves to photograph them in various poses. If you've got pictures of your pet piling up, why not put them in a scrapbook for everyone to enjoy? The kids will love to join in on a pet book, so get them involved.

If you've had your pet for a while, you probably have many snapshots to choose from, but just in case, here are some photo suggestions.

Here are some pictures you must have:

➤ The day you brought your pet home

➤ Your pet at the veterinarian's office

➤ The place your pet sleeps, whether it's in a basket, a box, or your bed

➤ Pet's favorite meal

➤ Pet playing with you and other family members

➤ Going on walks with your pet

➤ Pet riding in your car

➤ Outings with pet—camping, beach, or lake

➤ Pet sitter

➤ Animal friends of your pet

➤ Pet romping in the yard

Don't forget these:

➤ Pet birthday parties

➤ Pet during holiday festivities

➤ Wearing those horrible collars after getting stitches

➤ Pet wearing brand new collar

➤ You and your pet sleeping

➤ Pet wearing sunglasses and hat

➤ Waiting for you to get home

➤ The kids dressing up your pet in doll clothes

You can find all sorts of animal accents, from dogs and cats to farm animals to zoo animals, but since I'm a cat lover, I chose kittens to give you ideas for your books.

*Soft, new kittens.*

## *Play Ball!*

My brother-in-law has an entire file filled with clippings and awards from his high school sports days. When I asked my sister why she hadn't put them in a scrapbook, she told me that the clippings meant a lot to him and that she didn't want to mess them up. If you, your spouse, or children have lots of sports memorabilia, you ought to get them in a scrapbook so you can look at and enjoy them. If you're just getting started on the sports scenes, let me give you a few pointers on taking some must-have photos:

**Shortcuts**

You can always make copies of fragile clippings to include in the book, and color copies of awards and photos of plaques.

➤ First attempts at sports

➤ Wearing oversized jerseys

➤ Practicing basketball in the backyard

➤ Trying out

➤ Athlete buying sports gear

➤ Athlete with teammates

➤ Coach and team decked out in uniform

➤ Competition

➤ Wins and losses

Since there are so many different sports accents out there, I decided to show you how to use balls as an accent on your sports pages.

*To capture the fun of kids' sports, use designs that are meant for kids.*

## The Good Old Days

I consider myself very lucky to have had a wonderful, trouble-free childhood. I want to share that childhood with my kids by preserving those photos in scrapbooks. If you had a less-than-perfect childhood, it's still a good idea to save at least a few of those photos, if only to show how far you've come.

Accents for these are anything that reminds you of your childhood: popsicles, jacks, jump rope, bows, teddy bears, swing sets, or crayons.

**Shortcuts**

Since most of my childhood snapshots have faded over the years, I use muted colors and embellishments so that they don't compete with the photos.

*Can you remember those white zipper boots in the seventies? They're making a comeback.*

---

### The Least You Need to Know

➤ Keep embellishments simple when working with very old photos.

➤ Enjoy your wedding day over and over again through pictures—don't forget to scrapbook those anniversary shots.

➤ Take photos of a construction or remodeling project and make a scrapbook that shows all the steps along the way.

➤ Pet pictures make great scrapbook pages.

➤ Include sports certificates and programs with the sports pictures.

# Chapter 20

# Getting Away and Saving It All: Around the World in Pages

**In This Chapter**

➤ Convey all the color and excitement of a trip in your scrapbook

➤ Designing scrapbook pages that reflect travel adventures

➤ Saving important mementos, from love letters to travel souvenirs

It's human nature to want to get away and explore other places, and travel and vacations are a great escape. They are a naturally colorful topic for scrapbooks, providing exciting visuals, lots of new experiences and people to write about, and great souvenirs you'll certainly want to save. Here you'll see how to make the most of your travel adventures.

This chapter offers tips for saving all kinds of mementos, from the travel brochures collected while you were in Brazil to the playbills you saved from your trip to the London theatres. It is often difficult to find embellishments to accompany travel pages, so use your imagination.

## Into the Woods

Camping is a great vacation. It doesn't cost much, and you can find camping destinations anywhere. My boys love to camp because they can get as dirty as they want and don't have to take baths! I enjoy it because my husband does all the cooking.

*Use these letters to document your travels, from the woods to the sea.*

### Shortcuts

Take advantage of disposable cameras with a flash. You will be able to take photos without risking damage to your real camera.

### Words for Posterity

A brochure details certain events, entertainment, or sightseeing locations. These typically have full-color pictures and a description that will help you remember all about the event or location.

I usually camp in the woods, but you can go to beaches, deserts, mountains—all sorts of places. Wherever you go, make sure to toss a camera in with the rest of your camping gear. This is a time to catch people at their most natural, a must for any scrapbook.

Don't leave without taking at least a few of these photos:

➤ Setting up camp

➤ Everyone gathered around the campfire

➤ Sunrise

➤ Kids exploring around the camp

➤ Eating s'mores or whatever traditional food you enjoy

➤ Cooking breakfast over a camp stove

➤ Fishing by the river

➤ Getting drenched by a cloudburst

➤ All the gorgeous scenery you find on your hikes

If you want to tell the *whole* story, be sure to get a couple of these shots:

➤ Everyone piling into the car to go home, dirty and tired

➤ Fighting while trying to pitch a tent

➤ Burnt breakfast

➤ You bundled up in all the layers of clothes you had to wear to avoid hypothermia

➤ Any animal visitors who come to greet you

➤ The unexpected meadow full of wild flowers

➤ Your campsite after you've set up

➤ The car after your trip—before you wash it

➤ The dirty kids—before you wash them

Because camping is so popular, there are many camping embellishments to choose from: sleeping bags, campfires, starry night, and others.

**Sticky Points**

When traveling, keep your brochures in a separate envelope or a large plastic Ziploc bag to keep them from getting lost and to save them from too much wear and tear. They don't have to be pristine, though—a little wear and tear shows that they were used on your journey.

*Here's a layout that conveys the relaxed camping experience (layout by Susan Johnson).*

# Saving Brochures

Brochures are a great way to document places you've visited or courses you've taken. They are often very professional with beautiful photos, maps, historical information, or just interesting trivia. This includes anything with information on it about your trips.

*I took full advantage of the art on this travel brochure to accompany my pictures.*

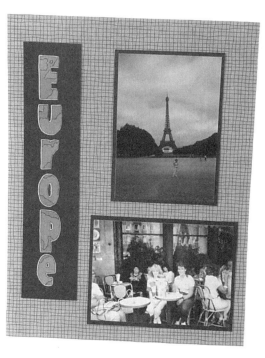

## Shortcuts

Make sure to get some pictures of yourself when you travel. Too often, the photographer gets back from a trip to find that there is not a single photo of them in the bunch! To keep your pictures from being an impersonal travelogue, make sure you ask your travel companions or friendly people on the streets to snap pictures of you.

# Around the World

When traveling around the world, one discovers cultures and landmarks that speak for themselves. Display these photos in scrapbooks to enjoy and treat them as artwork.

Here are some you must have:

➤ Trip preparations

➤ Arrival in different cities

➤ All of the places you visited

➤ Your transportation

➤ Exotic places where you dined

➤ People you met

➤ Landmarks

If you have traveled overseas, you'll most certainly bring back a load of pictures of beautiful and historical landmarks. Some, such as the Eiffel Tower or Buckingham

Palace, are world famous and instantly identify the country you visited. Others, such as the tiny old covered market you happened on in Egypt, are places that are off the beaten path and that you don't ever want to forget. Make sure the embellishments don't detract from the scenery in your photos. Not many embellishments are available for travel, so be selective when choosing designs for your layouts.

Following are a few ideas of items to save and color copy to include as embellishments with your pictures: actual maps, postcards, brochures, foreign menus, currency, flags, playbills, passport stamps, flowers, train passes, hotel matchbooks, coasters … Just don't get sent to jail for taking the guest towels!

**Shortcuts**

Create a title page for your travel scrapbook by marking your journey. Use your travel itinerary or highlight your route on a map. This is a great starting point.

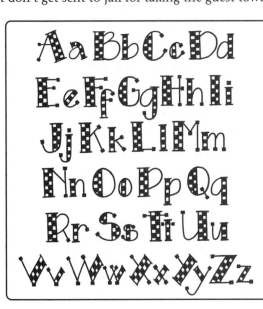

*Find festive travel embellishments to accentuate your layout.*

# Cruisin' Around

Cruise vacations have their own charm—they can be super relaxing (sunning on the deck) and very exciting (dropping the passengers off in interesting and beautiful sites). If you love cruises, like my sister-in-law Linda, a cruise connoisseur, here are some ideas for making a special book about a sailing trip. Whether you've gone on one cruise or a dozen, or are thinking about taking one someday, try to get some photos of the following:

**Shortcuts**

I have seen pages where the letters were made into the background paper. Try this; you will be pleased with the results.

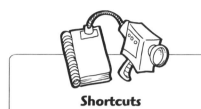

### Shortcuts

Because cruises are famous for their endless cuisine, make sure you take pictures of the food and see if you can take home a copy of the menu to add to your book.

➤ Boarding the boat

➤ Sunning on deck

➤ New friends

➤ Eating at the buffet

➤ Loosening your belt after the buffet

➤ Exciting ports of call

➤ The crew

➤ Your tour of the ship

➤ Your cabin

When I think of cruising, I think of the brilliant blues and greens of the ocean. Emphasize these with a selection of bright colors to use with your photos.

*A lucky friend of mine, happy to be getting away aboard a luxurious liner.*

## Letters, We Get Letters

Letters are a great item to save in your scrapbook because they document your life like nothing else. When my sister and her fiancé spent nine weeks apart before they were married, they wrote plenty of mushy letters back and forth. Fortunately, they thought ahead and used archival ink and paper in their letters so they could save them for posterity. Not only did these letters represent part of their courtship, they also documented her husband's journeys. For Christmas one year, she compiled the letters into a special notebook, a gift that her husband loved!

If you have had relatives who traveled and sent postcards, save them in an album—what fun it will be to look back over them and remember journeys.

Don't forget your kids' letters from camp, letters from your parents dispensing motherly and fatherly advice, and letters from friends who have moved away.

If you have letters that you want to incorporate into your scrapbooks, here are some different techniques. Pocket pages are a great way to contain all of your letters.

### Sticky Points

Even if you are concerned about people reading private letters, you can still preserve them in your scrapbook. Just put them in sealed envelopes, note what is inside, and open it when *you* want to read it, not your nosy cousin!

*If you have a lot of letters, display them closed up, like in this layout.*

### Anecdotes from the Archives

A work of literature that is made up of letters that the characters write is called an "epistolary novel." A few wonderful examples are *84 Charing Cross Road*, by Helen Hanff, and Alice Walker's novel, *The Color Purple*. In one interesting recent book, *Griffin and Sabine: An Extraordinary Correspondence*, the pages were designed to look like a beautiful scrapbook, and the story was told through letters contained in pockets that readers could actually open.

# In Living Color

You can color copy almost anything. Although most people use color copies to duplicate photos, pamphlets, and documents, don't overlook some of the less obvious possibilities, such as your prom dress, the jewelry you saved from your first best friend, or your child's favorite toy.

*My son won a ribbon for his artwork, and here in the layout we see it all— the art, the ribbon, and the artist—thanks to color copies.*

## The Least You Need to Know

➤ Let your vacation photos speak for themselves. Don't overdo the embellishments.

➤ Use colors that bring out the colors of your travel photos.

➤ Take pictures of the people you visit, as well as the landmarks.

➤ Make sure there are some pictures taken of you!

➤ When you travel, save all of your brochures to use as embellishments in your pages.

➤ Including letters in your pages adds a personal, sentimental touch and keeps documentation all together.

# Part 6
# Post-Grad Scrapping

*No matter how many scrapbookers I meet and talk to, they all have one thing in common: they want ideas, ideas, and more ideas. In this part you'll get to explore ways to cure scrapper's block and read some success stories.*

*What about those rubber stamps? Can you use them in your scrapbooks? What about all of those computer programs? These questions will be answered as you read about software available for scrapbooking and what types of ink you can use to stamp in your scrapbook.*

*Now that you have all the supplies to make great scrapbooks, see what else you can do with the supplies you already have on hand in the chapter about extra credit.*

# Chapter 21

# Eureka! Cures for Scrapper's Block

Sometimes, you find time to scrapbook, get everything out, and you can't compile a page. You don't know where to put the pictures, what embellishments to use, or what to use as a heading. You're suffering from Scrapper's Block!

From time to time, all scrappers (myself included) lose some of their enthusiasm, feel creatively challenged, and need a little encouragement to get going again. We all have busy lives, and regardless of how much we enjoy this hobby, it can be time-consuming, and we need new ideas to keep motivated. So next time you hit Scrapper's Block, don't give up—turn to this chapter for some help and a quick cure.

## Flip Through Magazines

Pick up the latest copy of a scrapbooking magazine. Check out all the layouts and note what products they contain that you would like to use. Check out their color combinations and study the pages you love for design tips.

When browsing through the magazine, don't forget to read the articles! They have information about the newest scrapbooking tools and embellishments, as well as new techniques for the old standbys. Browsing an article may be just what you need to perk up your scrapbooking interest.

## Aha!—Tips for Magazine Inspiration

Here are my favorite flipping tips:

Tip 1.   As you are flipping through your new magazine, mark your favorite layouts so you will be able to find them later.

Tip 2.   Take note of the ads. Advertisements often include innovative ways to use their products.

Tip 3.   Look at the graphic design of the magazine itself to see how their magazine pages use borders, pattern paper, and scissors.

Tip 4.   When looking at your favorite layout magazine, list the products used and note any instructions given. Now if you find a layout that you must copy, you can do it with ease!

**Shortcuts**

Some scrapbooking magazines offer special freebies, such as patterns or templates as an added bonus. Don't overlook these when you need a new idea.

**Anecdotes from the Archives**

Would you love to see your favorite scrapbook page in a magazine? Magazines love to showcase their readers' pages. They are always looking for unique pages, so check out the resource guide for addresses to submit your own page. As a bonus, they often give products to those whose pages they publish.

## Sweet Success Story #1—Take Two Die Cuts and Call Me in the Morning

A gal in one of my workshops painstakingly discussed with her friends what colors to use, where to place pictures, and what to write. I could tell that she was beginning to drive her friends crazy, and I knew she needed to develop some confidence, or her scrapbooking days would be over. I decided to show her how to be a scrapbook copy-cat. While I do discourage people from doing this all the time because it is easy to lose your personal look, I knew it was just what the doctor ordered in this case. I pulled her aside, took her scrapbook history, listened to her Scrapper's Block symptoms, and then preceded to write this prescription for her ailment—"Scrapper's Intimidation."

1. Select 6 to 10 pictures that you want to use on a page. Make sure they have a theme, such as birthday, camping, travel, and so on.

2. Look through your collections of magazines and find one with a similar theme that you like or one with a different theme that you can adapt to your theme.

3. Closely examine the layout you have selected to determine what tools they used. Did they use punches, decorative scissors, or die cuts? Do you have the means to duplicate the layout to your liking? For example, I love layouts that use creative lettering, but I don't do creative lettering very well, so I would be setting myself up for failure. The same would be the case if they used punches that you didn't have access to.

4. Select the colors you are going to use. Are they the same in the layout? If not, try to pick a similar type of paper even if it is different colors. If they use the mini-dot paper for pattern paper, select that.

5. Prepare your photos and do the basic layout. After you see your photos on the page, you will have a better idea about your embellishments.

6. Create your embellishments and place them on your page. At first, do this as the layout shows, then move the photos around to see what else you can create.

7. Choose which way you want to lay everything out and adhere. There! You're done. I bet you can come up with your own layout ideas after you have done this a couple of times.

**Shortcuts**

Are you an avid magazine reader? Do you love all of those layouts? Make an idea file for yourself—cut out your favorite layouts and compile them in a small notebook. Try organizing them according to theme for easy reference.

**Shortcuts**

Don't live close to a scrapbook store but still want to learn all of the latest techniques that the stores are teaching? Pick up the latest idea book and learn from it how to layer die cuts, paper dolls, or get journaling ideas.

# That's a Great Idea

There are many idea books on the market that have scrapbook pages and illustrations devoted to displaying ideas that will motivate anybody.

These books are typically devoted to either a certain theme, product, or technique. You will find idea technique books on anything from using circle cutters to making paper dolls.

Need ways to make your pet pages more appealing? Check out an idea book filled with cute pet pages. If stamping is your favorite, why not check out an idea book that gives you new ideas and techniques for stamps?

Idea books are great because they are created by professional, seasoned scrapbookers who have many tips and tricks to share with their readers.

## *Aha!—Tips for Using Idea Books*

Following are some tips for using book ideas:

Tip 1. Flip through the supplies list before you buy. You may not own a circle cutter or have access to the paper doll die cuts. Buying the book without the supplies is more frustrating than rewarding.

**Sticky Points**

Don't be intimidated by the artwork and illustrations featured in the idea books. Remember that they are created by professional artists.

Tip 2. Idea books are great for journaling ideas because they include captions and page headings.

Tip 3. If you are trying a difficult technique, start with the easiest ideas first to minimize frustration.

Tip 4. When shopping for supplies to create layouts featured in the idea books, have the pages marked so that you'll know what supplies you need to purchase.

Tip 5. Adapt the ideas to suit your photos.

## *Sweet Success Story #2—Sudden Inspiration*

My fellow scrapping friend was so tired of her pages looking the same that she stopped scrapping. One day, when she was shopping for stickers for her son's school project, she saw an interesting punch-art book and purchased it. She let the book sit for awhile until, one day, she took it out because she needed some card-making ideas, and, suddenly, the light came back on. She pulled out all of her scrapbooking supplies and started creating pages with different punch designs for her embellishments. The techniques she learned from the punch-art book carried over into her die cuts and templates. She had learned a new skill of layering punches and was able to incorporate it in other ways in her book.

She, too, was cured of her temporary Scrapper's Block.

*By combining punches, look what you can create. (Page by Kathy Hardy)*

# The Hustle and Bustle

When all else fails, go shopping! Seeing the store displays always motivates me. Plus, I like to check out new products and pattern paper. Take a look at the classes being offered and see if you can learn a new technique.

## Aha!—Tips for Using Stores, Classes, and More

I often find it inspiring to be around other scrapbookers as they shop for products.

Tip 1.  Go and check your favorite companies to see if anything new is available. For me,

**Shortcuts**

Wondering when the best time for shopping is to avoid the crowds? Try in the morning or during the dinner hour. During the year, the winter months are the busiest, right after New Year's Day.

anytime I see new stickers, I get a surge of scrapbooking energy. My friend Marcia checks out the stationery and pattern paper for her inspiration.

Tip 2. More and more scrapbooking stores feature contests. They sell discounted kits and see which customer creates the best look with the given supplies. The winning entries are displayed in the store, and the winners receive free products—can't beat that!

Tip 3. Shop your stores for exclusive products, like one-of-a-kind die cuts or original stickers.

*Shop around to see what exclusive items you can find.*

Tip 4. Clerks can be helpful. They can point you in the right direction, as well as help with color selection. It sometimes helps to have a second opinion.

They can also fill you in on any of the cute pages they've seen created by other customers.

Tip 5. Sign up for the store's mailing list. You'll find out in advance about all the new classes and workshops.

### Anecdotes from the Archives

Does it seem like you spend more time shopping at your favorite scrapbook store than you spend at home? Spending all of your extra money purchasing the latest supplies? Perhaps you should see if your local store is hiring. Many people have started working in scrapbook stores this very way. If you have a great idea for a class, take it in with your books to show the store owners or managers. You would be surprised how many people began teaching this way. Either way, you will help pay for your scrapbooking habit, and you might even get a discount on store merchandise.

## Sweet Success Story #3—A Little Time Alone

A while back I was feeling overwhelmed and underappreciated; I needed some time alone, so I hired a baby sitter for the kids and had a great scrapping day. Here's how you can set up a nice scrapping day on your luxurious afternoon alone:

➤ Set up your scrapbook supplies

➤ Select the pictures you want to work on

➤ Sort through the supplies you already have

➤ Take the photos that you don't have supplies for and go shopping

➤ Check out the new products first

➤ Purchasing items for those pictures you are working on

➤ Take everything home (after you've stopped by to rent some videos and buy some treats) and start scrapping

This is definitely my favorite way to scrapbook, and the shopping trip is always motivating.

## No-Fail Packets

When I talk about packets, I am referring to scrapbooking kits that come with everything you need (except adhesive) to re-create a specific page layout. The page idea is usually printed on the front or back of the packet. Packets can be especially helpful when you are just starting out and nervous about selecting compatible products. Packets come in themes, such as baby or travel, and are designed by professionals.

*An idea packet with everything you need.*

# Aha!—Tips for Using Packets

My favorite tips when purchasing and using these idea packets follow.

Tip 1.   Use a packet when you hit Scrapper's Block. Finishing the page will give you the confidence you need to try your own ideas.

Tip 2.   Purchase a packet that will go with pictures you already have. You want to go home and do it right away, not store it until you take appropriate photos.

Tip 3.   Study the packet ideas to discover what it is you like about them. Use the packet ideas as guides for your own pages.

Tip 4.   You don't have to follow the packet layout to the tee; you can adjust it to suit your photos and style.

Tip 5.   All stores have different styles, so shop around to get a taste of everything out there.

**Shortcuts**

Trying to get your friends hooked on scrapbooking? Give them an appropriate packet for a gift along with an adhesive. Before you know it, they will be coming with you to your next scrapbooking class.

# Sweet Success Story #4— Developing a Good Eye

I once met a scrapbooker named Jen who had begun scrapbooking by buying packets and duplicating them. That was the first workshop she had attended, so she was a little timid, and I gave her some suggestions to get started. Before too long, other class attendees were stopping by her table to see the pages she was creating. It was the first time she had tried scrapbooking without a packet, so we tried to figure out why her pages were so successful and eye-catching. She and I concluded that because she started out duplicating packets and did so many of them that she had developed a great eye for design. After duplicating what professional scrappers had put together, she had a great idea of how to put together a pleasing scrapbook page—another great reason to try these no-fail packets.

# Group Therapy

This is by far the most popular way to stay inspired and motivated. Scrapbooking with others takes the form of a crop, workshop, or even a weekly scrapbook get-together. Some people have gone so far as to create scrapbooking clubs that meet on a regular basis and do product swaps and idea exchanges.

Whichever way you choose to do it, you are sure to be encouraged by your fellow scrapbookers.

## Aha!—Tips for Scrapping in a Group

Tip 1. Bring a notebook with you so you can jot down other layout ideas to use later.

Tip 2. If you meet regularly with a group, you may find someone who has a style you love. If this is the case, by all means, ask them questions and observe the way they design their layouts. You can learn a lot!

Tip 3. If you meet in a group to share tools, you know that it can be frustrating to work on a page and not have the particular punch you need. If you are sharing supplies in these groups and your neighbor has that punch that you want to use for your zoo page, look ahead and punch some out while you are there.

Tip 4. Get product reviews from your friends. Ask them what they think of the newest software programs, scissors, or other tools. They can help you decide if the product is worth the money and can show you how they've used the product in their books.

**Sticky Points**

Don't let this happen to you: One time I fell in love with some classic Winnie-the-Pooh paper in a packet, and I thought I would buy the paper separately when I needed to use it. I found the perfect pictures to use with that paper and went to purchase the paper to discover that it wasn't sold separately. It only came in the packet and, of course, the packets were sold out.

**Sticky Points**

One thing to be aware of when you gather with friends is that participants often take up a lot of time chatting and looking at pages. To get the most of your scrapbooking time, save the chatting for in between pages or when you get stuck. You don't want time to go by and have nothing to show for it.

### Anecdotes from the Archives

*Paper Kuts*, a scrapbooking magazine, has a column devoted to showcasing scrapbooking groups. They highlight how these groups got started, some of the pitfalls to watch for, and their best creative suggestions. Check out the column to read what's happening with groups all over the nation.

## Sweet Success Story #5—A Family Who Scraps Together

Although I enjoy scrapbooking alone, I occasionally enjoy scrapping with friends. It is fun to share your hobby and talk about things only scrapbookers are interested in while sharing ideas and tricks. I know a family that has three sisters who love to scrapbook together with their mom. They go shopping together, take classes together, and, of course, create scrapbooks together. The sisters are all married, and some have children—this is their sanity as well as their connection to each other. They can bounce ideas off of one another, trade pictures of the family reunion, and share supplies. The only problem they have is that they stay up too late during their get-togethers and have to pay the price the next morning when it is back to reality! Whether you have family or friends to scrapbook with, try scrapping in a group. It is a great answer to Scrapper's Block.

# Online Inspiration If You Dare (for Those Who Have Online Access)

You will find ideas on many manufacturer's Web sites, as well as a million links to everything from personal page ideas to magazines online. Just be careful to not spend so much time surfing the Net that you have no time left to scrapbook.

## Aha!—Tips for Online Searches

Tip 1.  Be sure to keep track of your favorite sites as you are surfing the Web. I like to start at www.jangle.com for links. Remember to bookmark sites that you particularly enjoy.

Tip 2.  If you are interested in giving your opinion or want to find out how real scrapbookers feel about products, you can participate in product review sites. My favorite review site is www.scrapbookaddict.com.

Tip 3.  Check your favorite product to see if its manufacturer has a Web site. Some of them have contests, surveys, and more. My favorite product site is www.cockadoodledesign.com, which features their Page Toppers product, sneak previews of new products, and page ideas using their products.

Tip 4.  Try visiting www.gracefulbee.com. This site is for beginning scrapbookers and has a great article archive list with some very helpful information for the novice scrapbooker.

Tip 5.  There are so many ideas online, you can find hundreds of layouts. Just start and don't stop until you feel satisfied. Another favorite of mine for layout ideas is www.dmarie.com.

### Shortcuts

If you are alone in your hobby and don't have any friends or family who scrapbook, try looking on the Internet at www.jangle.com. This site has a place where you can look for your twin. Go to the JANGLE Twins message board and post a message.

These are just starting places for you. If you haven't surfed the scrapbooking sites on the Web, you will be truly amazed at what you find.

## Sweet Success Story #6—Finding a Community of Scrappers

At a recent scrapbooking convention, I met a scrapbooker who had her own small Web page dedicated to scrapbooking. She shared her story with me. She wanted to start scrapbooking but had no idea where to start since she lived in a small town in Idaho. Little did she know what awaited her when she got online and typed "scrapbooking" in one of her search engines. She not only found places that taught how to scrapbook, she located stores and online sites where she could purchase products. Now that she has been an avid scrapbooker for over a year, she still turns to the Internet for the latest news about new products, conventions, and, of course, page ideas. One of the nicest developments is that she has found many friends online who scrapbook as well.

### The Least You Need to Know

➤ There are places to turn for help when you just can't come up with another idea. Start with the many magazines for scrapbooking.

➤ Packets are a fail-safe way to get the pages done.

➤ Keep a notebook with you to jot down great layout ideas you discover when you are scrapping in a group.

➤ The Internet is a terrific source for layout ideas, finding out where classes are held, and connecting with other people who like to scrap.

# Chapter 22

# Heading for the Border: Great Border Ideas

---

**In This Chapter**

➤ Why borders work so well in scrapbooking

➤ Festive holiday borders you can use over and over again

➤ Making your own borders from all kinds of materials

➤ Placing borders for the best effects

---

In design, borders define space in useful and decorative way. Borders help keep designs contained and organized. Wallpaper borders are a great example; they are often featured with wallpaper designs because they separate and unite patterns. Borders are appealing and comforting to the eye. Borders are used in scrapbooks to decorate pages, but also to tie patterns and themes together and define space on pages. Borders are simple to create and can give your book a great look. A border can be anything from a solid coordinating color to a combination of journaling, hand-drawn curly cues, or stickers.

Classes that focus on borders are among the most popular scrapbooking classes offered these days. One reason that scrapbookers want to learn about borders is that it is much less intimidating to come up with a creative look for a small space with a border than an entire page. People feel much more competent when they attempt creativity and are successful at it. Read on to discover foolproof ways to create borders in your scrapbook.

# FAQs About Borders

Invariably, I meet women and men who want to begin creating scrapbooks but who don't have the time or money to make each page unique. I suggest to them that after they have decided on an album size, they create borders for the pages and then embellish in these borders as they go, with a few decorative items to dress up the album a little bit. You could place all of your pictures on the pages and add a little something to the borders—quick and inexpensive. Below are questions I hear from students in classes and things you might want to know.

**Q.** When is the best time to use borders in a scrapbook?

**A.** Borders add a finishing touch to your page. It's great to use them on all but the simplest pages. From large 12-by-12 books to mini-books, borders are a way to emphasize your story.

**Q.** Where can you put borders in a book?

**A.** The only rule about borders is that they belong on the edges of your paper. Beyond that, where they go is up to you.

**Shortcuts**

For border ideas, study your favorite stationery to see how it is designed. You can even try to duplicate some of your favorite looks.

**Sticky Points**

To avoid throwing a border in the trash, first use a pencil to trace in the border design to see if you like it before you use a pen to make it permanent.

**Q.** How can borders help me tell my photo story?

**A.** You can use items in the borders that repeat the theme of the page. Try using cloud and plane punches for an airplane trip or spatulas and broken eggs for a cooking class. Borders not only look nice on your pages, they tell a story.

**Q.** What types of borders are available?

**A.** The sky is the limit when it comes to borders because you can do whatever you like. From stickers to die cuts, from scraps to stickers, anything goes!

**Q.** Where can I find ideas for different borders?

**A.** Look for books with border designs in them. Try some of the online sites. Catalogs and magazines are good places to look. Fellow scrappers are another source. Glance through their books to see what they've come up with. You're sure to come away with great ideas.

**Q.** What tools do I need to create borders?

**A.** Templates are a great tool. You can use regular templates that have coordinating borders with them or the special border templates to draw and doodle designs on the edges of your pages. Border rulers are another option. You can use your decorative scissors to create borders. Use small punches to create borders. Mix and match designs to get hundreds of different looks.

# To Border or Not to Border?

Ask yourself these questions:

➤ Do you like the look of coordinating colors?

➤ Do you want the embellishments to reinforce the photo story?

➤ Do you want others to notice the photo story first, instead of all the other cute stuff covering the page?

➤ Do you like to get the most use out of your tools?

➤ Do you like the look of layouts with borders used in them?

If you answered yes to any of these questions, you are a candidate for borders.

## *Border Placement*

Although you can place borders along any page margin, the common placement is along the bottom.

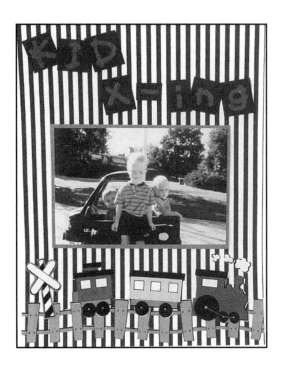

*Here is the most common way to place a border— along the bottom of the page using stickers.*

When you are using larger objects and want a different emphasis, try basing your border design across the corner of your layout.

*Base the border design in the corner of your layout. I like to use larger shapes for this, such as this die cut.*

For fun, especially with the larger albums, create a border around the entire circumference of the layout. This, of course, is most successful when smaller embellishments are used.

You can also go along the sides of your layout—try one or more sides.

*Borders can help reinforce your photo story.*

*Here the border design goes along the side of the layouts.*

One of my favorite tips is to use a border to frame my focal point photo. You can do it around the entire picture or just along the bottom.

The only rule with border placement is to make it work for you. You want to emphasize your photos, not the latest stickers. You can place the borders just about anywhere; try out new ways to see what you can create.

## Creating Your Own Borders

The minute I walk into a scrapbook store, I am immediately drawn to stickers and pattern paper. I know what to do with pattern paper—but stickers can sometimes be more challenging because of their size. My favorite stickers to use in borders are Mrs. Grossman's. Her stickers contain coordinating elements in a particular theme, so they are perfect. Step-by-step suggestions follow for using stickers with your borders:

1. Once you have selected your pictures, select the stickers you want to use to reinforce your photo story.

2. Decide on the placement of your border.

**Shortcuts**

*Creative Memories* is known for introducing and teaching the use of borders in their yearly idea books. Look for these to get some great ideas on different methods to use in creating your borders.

**Shortcuts**

Pencil in boundaries for your border to avoid taking up too much space on the page.

269

*Here the border design goes around the focal point picture using punches to embellish.*

3. Place the stickers where you want them.

4. Connect the sticker designs somehow, either by overlapping the stickers or by connecting them with hand-drawn doodles.

Not only are stickers great for making borders, so are punches. Use up all of those scraps of paper to punch out shapes and then create border after border.

When using punches, keep in mind that the color will be flat so you'll need to add a little more depth with your doodles and drawings. This would be the time to use a few different pen colors and stick with one color for the punch.

**Shortcuts**

If you get a little tired doing all those punches, put your kids to work punching them out for you. Helpful for you, fun for them.

## *"Die"ing for Perfect Die-Cut Borders*

While die cuts tend to be a bit larger, they can be used in borders. In order to make them work, you need to consider the size of the die cut. The larger pages work best with die cuts.

Layer your die cuts for a look that will add dimension to your borders. I prefer to create a corner border when I am using die cuts and continue the design throughout the page. Try placing the die cuts in different corners.

With die cuts, it is easy to get the layered look, and this can create a great look for the bottom of your page. I also like to use die cuts across the top of my page in a border as a title with letters inside the die cuts.

For an elegant border, work with a monochromatic color scheme:

1. Select the color of paper you want to use.

2. Cut dies using a shade of the same color.

3. Mount dies on yet a different tint or shade paper.

You will love the elegant look of this page.

As with any scrapbook project, mixing different embellishments makes your page look great. You may want to use a die cut as the centerpiece of your border and use stickers or punches to go around the design.

# Trace It Once, Trace It Twice

There are numerous templates available for use in borders. Decorative border rulers are available to assist you. Here are some things you can do with tools of the trade when tracing borders onto your pages.

Once you have the starting point, place the tool down and trace lightly with a pencil. If you are brave enough, go ahead and use your marker. After you have checked to make sure it is working, trace the other places. If you traced over in pencil and you are only using one line, go over it with your marker now. If you are planning on doing more than one line, proceed to the next one. Do the same as above with the different design. When it is all complete, erase pencil marks that weren't covered up by the markers. Add any journaling or embellishments that you want to use. See below for some festive border ideas.

**Shortcuts**

Some border templates have pre-drilled holes to be placed in the corner of your pages.

# Running for the Border

Do you have a theme book you are working on where the pictures speak for themselves? If yes, you might want to tone down your embellishments so as not to distract from the photos. My suggestion is to create a continual border, called a *running border*, throughout that entire section of your book. You would create a border and then repeat the same design on each of the following pages. You could stick with the same colors, or choose to change them. Either way, repeating the border will provide great continuity to your book.

*For a long road trip section in a scrapbook, try using a small road border on the bottom of each page. As the trip progresses further, so does the car. Notice the sign.*

Sometimes, when it's hard to come up with another idea for a holiday page, a holiday border is just the ticket. You can add whatever appropriate embellishment you wish to.

*Have yourself a merry little Christmas.*

## The Least You Need to Know

➤ Use borders in your scrapbook to define space and tie together themes.

➤ Use designs in your borders that will reinforce the theme of your page.

➤ Experiment with tracing border designs using different pen tips to see what you can come up with.

➤ Use a continual, or running, border on every page of an album to achieve a consistent look.

➤ Look around to get ideas on creating great borders—try creating your own.

# Scrapper's Delight

As a child, when I was bored in the summer I would wander around the house looking for something to do or create. We didn't have great craft supplies back then, just ordinary scissors, glue, and construction paper, so I used what we had and discovered the neat containers I could make out of cereal boxes. I stored letters, school papers, and magazines in them. This project gave me so much satisfaction. The same can be applied to your scrapbook projects.

Try looking around the house for items you can use to add into your book. Many of us have rubber stamps from the time we thought we would make our own birthday cards and scraps from various craft projects over the years. Read in this chapter how you can use these in your books. What about the wealth of freebies on the Internet? There are numerous sites where you can download free fonts or even try some clip art for fun. Don't forget to read about some of the latest photo software programs. Make notes to yourself in this book about sites you have visited and items you have in your household you could use for free.

## Goin' on a "Stamp"ede

When I was younger, my dad had an address stamp in his desk drawer along with a stamp pad. I liked to play with the stamp and pad, stamping the address on construction paper, magazines, newspapers, or any other unsuspecting scrap paper that I found lying around the house. Now that there are so many stamps on the market, stamping is more fun than ever. Instead of one address stamp, scrappers can choose from thousands of designs, letters, and patterns, as well as ink pads that come in every color of the rainbow.

To get started, you need some stamps and pigment ink. *Pigment ink* is permanent and non-fading. Look for stamps and pads at mass-merchandising stores and educational stores, as well as specialty scrapbooking and craft stores.

# Ink 'Em Up

Start with some versatile stamps, such as stars, hearts, and letters, then add to your collection as your budget allows. Getting together with your stamping friends to trade specialty stamps will help stretch your stamping dollar. Make sure you get basic ink colors, such as black and the primary colors, before you splurge on fuschia or turquoise.

## Applying Stamps

Apply the ink to your stamp by marching your stamp across the inkpad. Move the stamp around a bit to be sure that it is covered with ink. Take care, however, not to press so hard that the ink gets in the crevices of your stamp because this will obscure the image. If the ink pad you are using is smaller than the stamp, turn the stamp over and apply the ink to the stamp, moving it around until the rubber is covered.

Now the fun part—place the stamp on the paper and apply firm, even pressure. Don't rock the stamp back and forth as this will result in an inconsistent ink application. Try out your stamp once or twice on some scratch paper to get a feel for the technique.

## Where to Use Stamps

You can use stamps instead of or in addition to stickers and die cuts. Keep the stamps in scale with your page and each other. If the stamp you are applying is large, use less per page. If you are using small stamps, go ahead and use three or four or create a border. It's easy to go overboard with stamps, so try to resist the temptation to cover your entire page with them.

### Words for Posterity

A **rubber stamp** is a detailed, intricate design cut out of rubber and mounted on wood or foam. An impression is made by applying color to the rubber stamp and imprinting that onto paper.

### Shortcuts

Color Box is one company that makes pigment stamping ink. Their pads are safe for use in your albums.

### Shortcuts

Use a folded baby diaper or paper towels dampened with water to clean your stamps. After stamping on your page, simply march your stamp across the cloth until it no longer leaves an impression.

*Use the stamps just where you would use a die cut.*

## Caring for Stamps

When you are done with the stamp, clean the rubber part. Use a damp towel or stamp-cleaning solutions. Don't worry if you can't get all the ink out of the stamp. The rubber will become discolored overtime; this won't affect the next application.

# Stamp Out Titles

Who could resist a baby page with baby's name stamped in pastel pink letters? Or a beach page with "Sunshine" spelled out in bright yellow letters? Stamp letters make great titles, and the smaller letters make wonderful captions. You can color in the letters with pens that match the mood of the page. "Diggin' in the Dirt," for example, can be colored in with a few different shades of brown to look like real dirt and make a wonderful addition to your construction photos.

You can buy specially designed border stamps, which are great. Many come on a roller and are easy to apply. Simply run them around the edge of your page, and you've got instant border! Color

**Shortcuts**

To get a reverse image, stamp the image on an oversized white eraser and quickly stamp the eraser on your paper.

**Shortcuts**

When you are done using stamps, clean them and store them in a container that is away from sunlight and dirt.

the entire design with your pens or simply fill in a few spots here and there. Floral borders look great when you color in the flowers and leaves. If you find that too time-consuming, simply color in the blossoms and leave the foliage plain.

*Endless heading options with alphabet stamps.*

*Border stamps to create great pages.*

## Masking with Stamps

Some stampers use their stamps to create a mural-like scene on their pages. This is a very artistic look and requires a little extra time employing a technique called *masking*. Masking creates a layered effect; it may sound complicated, but with a little practice, you'll feel like a pro. Try this technique a couple of times on scrap paper first.

1. Select two stamps that you want to use to create a landscape; for example, a tent and trees would be good together. Choose which stamp you want to appear in front—in this case, the tent. The trees will be the background design.

2. Stamp the tent onto your page. On a piece of scratch paper, stamp the tent again. With small scissors, cut this image from the scrap paper completely, paying close attention to detail. This creates a "mask."

3. Position the cut-out tent mask directly on top of the tent on your scrapbook page so as to cover and protect it.

4. Next stamp the trees on your page, stamping over the mask if needed. Remove the mask from the tent, and there you have your landscaped stamped scene.

You can create embossed designs with stamps. There are two ways to do this.

To achieve the beautiful embossed look, follow these steps.

1. Stamp image on paper with slow-drying or embossed ink.

2. Apply embossing powder to image, shake off excess.

3. Heat powder with a special tool for embossing; a blow dryer won't work.

You do have to stick to ink pads for stamping, but you can fill the image in with watercolors, colored pencils, and decorating chalks. Experimenting with different media will produce a variety of wonderful looks. You can use watercolor markers to apply ink to the rubber surface of a stamp.

**Shortcuts**

It is sometimes a good idea to stamp on a separate piece of paper, cut around it, and mount it on your page. This gives your page extra depth and gives you a little more control.

**Words for Posterity**

**Embossing** is the creation of a raised surface by applying heat or pressure. With rubber stamps, you can create elegant embossed images, like the ones you might find on a wedding invitation.

**Sticky Points**

Some inks stain stamps. The best way to avoid this is to clean stamps off as soon as you are done using them. Occasionally, you will discolor the rubber.

*Masking creates beautiful effects.*

# Faking It—Great Lettering, No Pens!

Developing an interesting lettering style can be a big challenge. Some people have a hard time doing it no matter how many classes they take or pens they try out. Thank goodness for sticker letters, page toppers, letter templates, and die cut letters. Computer fonts can also help out the "il-letter-ate."

Search through your scrap bin and use all your scraps by creating great headings for your scrapbook. Die-cut letters and templates make fabulous page headings. You can give your pages a scrapbook look and customize them to your page. Don't forget to use those leftover sticker letters to create great titles.

To use scraps, trace them with a pencil on the back of the paper you want to use. Keep the stencil backward, too. Then cut out. When you are done, the pencil lines will be on the back where no one can see them.

Instead of just using one color for letter headings, try these to dress up your titles:

➤ Use more than one color to create the desired effect, such as red and white for candy cane stripes.

➤ Mount sticker strips on cardstock close together and create great letters that way.

➤ Top your letters. For snow pages, put snow on top of the letters, dripping down, or add paint splats to your letters for those finger-painting pages.

*Letter titles.*

*Going the extra mile with your headings.*

## You'll Have Fonts, Fonts, Fonts

If you have a computer at home you can have your letters for free. Using premade computer fonts is one of the most widely used methods to journal in scrapbooks. They are easy to control, versatile, and convenient, and you have the luxury of selecting the size you want the letters to be. Many people use a large size for a page heading and the smaller size for journaling.

When looking at purchasing software with fonts, make sure your computer is compatible. See if you can find some examples of the fonts before you buy them. Decide if you are looking for fonts only or clip art, too. It is a good idea to have some basic fonts, as well as specialized ones.

*These are just some of the great computer fonts you can use.*

For variety, try printing out the words in different colors. It is amazing what you can do with a computer. You can print your heading directly onto your cardstock—just run a practice sheet through to make sure it is lined up properly. Try printing on small cards for invitations or birth announcements. Many people love to journal inside stationery.

For a real adventure, go online to look for free fonts or for fonts you can purchase. There is an amazing amount of material on the Internet. To make your search a little less overwhelming, start at a scrapbook Web site and connect with the page's links from there. One great site—www. Learn2Scrapbook—has some great fonts and tons of links, including:

**Shortcuts**

If you are trying to print a large heading and it won't fit on your page, try changing the page setup option to "landscape." This will let you print more letters across the page.

➤ www.rover.wiesbaden.netsurf.de/~kikita/ Fontastic

➤ www.e-signature.com/fonts/main.htm True Type Font Home Page

➤ http//members.aol.com/mmqchome/fonts/ fonts.htm Free Font Fiesta

➤ www.crypted.com/Crypted and Sunni

➤ http://webhome.idirect.com/~zarum/ littlestarfonts.html Little Star Seeds

➤ www.fontaddict.com

**Sticky Points**

Set aside a time to look for fonts and download what you want. Don't waste your scrapbooking time looking for fonts.

Download fonts according to your computer capabilities.

Compile a collection of your favorite scrapbook fonts and keep them handy so when it is time to use them, you aren't driving yourself crazy finding everything. I like to keep a hard copy of my favorite scrapbooking fonts on hand so I can refer to them quickly and painlessly.

# Computer Cut 'n Paste

I have a friend who has completed an entire scrapbook for her son without using scissors, adhesives, or even pens! She did it all on the computer using a scanner and scrapbooking software. Since she felt that she was not an arts-and-crafts type of person, she figured she'd rather use the computer to save memories than cut and color. It's definitely an option.

### Shortcuts

Save your computer journaling for when you will be doing more than one page. Make notes first and do the journaling when you are on the computer. This saves lots of time.

If you have a scanner, you can scan your photos into the computer and save them onto a disk or CD-ROM. With a software program like the ones made by a company called Dog Bytes, you can create frames, borders, and captions for your photos, then print up the completed page. The great thing about this type of scrapbook is that you've got it saved on your hard drive, so if two-year-old Tommy gets too rough with his scrapbook—no problem, just print up another copy! It's also a good idea to send a copy of this scrapbook to a family member or friend so in case of fire or flood, you'll still have your precious memories.

*This is how your computer-made page might look.*

## Clip Art

You can find software programs with cute illustrations to add to your scrapbook. These are called clip art and are available in thousands of patterns and styles. You can opt to print in the traditional black and white and then color in the image, or, if possible, you can print the image in color with all of the work done for you.

## Hearing Voices

The latest technological toy is software with recording capability. One, Smile Starters, can record voices along with photos. Years from now, you can hear your baby coo and your kitty meow. Plus, you can send copies to family and friends so they can enjoy what you've created.

## Stop and Crop

Some computer programs even let you crop your digital photos into interesting shapes, such as hearts, clouds, and clovers. You can choose from borders, stationery, and clip-art designs. With technology, you will be able to see what a whole page will look like before you print it out—no more messy adhesives.

# Online Scrapping

Depending on what your needs are, you can find most things on the Internet, from friends to fonts. You can also download free clip art and fonts to use in your scrapbooking.

To find friends, ask questions, or just chat about scrapbooking, check out the hundreds of chat rooms on the Net, or leave a message on the message boards. Some chat boards have places where you can find friends who share your interests or you can enjoy sitting back and seeing what the hot topics of the day are (this is called *lurking*).

Interested in doing a product swap? Go online and find a group of scrapbookers who want to do it with you or try to join somebody else's ongoing swap. Typically, they are very detailed about what

**Sticky Points**

Only laser printers use archival ink. So if you don't have a laser printer, be sure to create a backup copy of your scrapbook on disk. Or you can take your disk to a copy store and have them print it on a laser printer.

**Shortcuts**

Clip art is great because, unlike stickers and stamps, you can adjust its size to fit your pages right on your computer.

**Shortcuts**

Keep in mind what your scrapping software needs are. If you simply want some clip art to perk up your pages, there is no need to buy a program that does everything else, too. If you'll be using your computer for all your scrapbooking needs, however, find a program that does it all.

type of products they want to swap and the amount of money that needs to be spent. This is a fun way to see what other people are doing and build up your supplies.

Another idea is to sign up for a few email news pages that can be sent directly to your email address. You can keep the ones you like and unsubscribe from the others. These news pages are great for finding out what is new and upcoming.

Chat rooms are fun places to give your opinions about what you like and dislike. You can even do it under an anonymous name if you're shy. Many sites ask scrapbookers to review new products and then post the reviews. Not only is this fun to participate in, it is great when you are thinking of purchasing a product.

---

### The Least You Need to Know

➤ Stamps are a fun and easy way to dress up your book. Use them for embellishments and borders.

➤ Some people make entire scrapbook pages using only their computers—try it. You might like it, and there's no mess.

➤ Computer clip art adds a fun touch to your book, and there are thousands of pieces to choose from.

➤ The Internet is the place to look for free fonts and other free supplies.

# Chapter 24

---

# Extra Credit: Using Scrapbook Supplies for Fun Projects

As much as I enjoy scrapbooking, I get a little discouraged from time to time. Scrapbooking is a never-ending project, and I sometimes need a sense of completion. If you're looking for some near-instant gratification, try some of these projects. You can make cards, calendars, and other fun gifts with scrapbooking supplies, and they are sure to please the recipient.

## With Love from Me to You

I have created several gift albums over the years. I made my sister Heather a "nephews book" that had pictures of her and all her nephews. She took it to work to show her friends and now keeps it in her purse in case she gets a chance to brag about them. My mother loved the album of her grandchildren that I created for her. And I know some people who have created vacation books—much more exciting than slides!

Any occasion is a good reason to create a gift album. Here are a few examples.

## Grandparents' Brag Book

Include pictures of each grandchild, along with hand-written letters or drawings. Encourage the child to write their favorite activities to participate in with their grandparents. If your child has received diplomas or recognition awards, display copies in here, too. If babies are included in the book, be sure to include footprints, as well as a picture of the grandparent meeting the grandchild for the first time.

*Something for Grandma and Grandpa to brag about.*

## Teacher Appreciation

Don't you think your child's teacher has enough bottles of perfume and boxes of chocolate? Why not help your child create a one-of-a-kind gift. Be sure to include pictures of your child with his teacher, as well as some special drawings. A map of the classroom, including the child's desk, fish tank, and pencil sharpener. This is a charming way to show the teacher that your child appreciates him or her.

Remember to display photos of class field trips and special projects! If your child is a writer, she can create

a book of interesting facts that she learned during the year, along with illustrations. Don't forget the ABCs. An ABC book could include highlights of different classmates' talents. Starting with A, find one fact or fun thing about each child. For example, Jenny likes to read about alligators; Hannah knows how to read books; Zachary is very creative. You can find something special for each letter (and you better hope that one of the kids can play the xylophone!).

*Your favorite teacher will keep this gift forever.*

## A Gift for Your Sweetheart

Make this for the special someone in your life, listing what you love about him or her, places you have gone together, and places you want to go. Include the words to your songs, love letters exchanged, anything that would express your feelings.

## Tribute Album

This could be made for friends, coworkers, or family and is another way to use your scrapbooking talents to let someone know that you care. List your favorite activities to do together, places to go for lunch, e-mails you have shared, humorous or embarrassing stories, pictures of time spent together, and what makes this person special to you.

A very popular gift album is a tribute album as an anniversary gift for parents or grandparents. I have helped many scrapbookers work on pages for these books and have compiled some of their best ideas to share with you if this is a project you are interested in.

*Glance through this when times are tough to remember how much you love your sweetheart.*

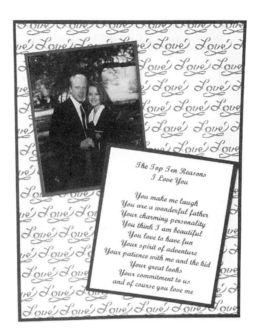

The Top Ten Reasons
I Love You

You make me laugh
You are a wonderful father
Your charming personality
You think I am beautiful
You love to have fun
Your spirit of adventure
Your patience with me and the kid
Your great looks
Your commitment to us
and of course you love me

### Shortcuts

Be sure to journal frequently in these albums, as the notes are as important as the photos for getting the feelings across.

Before you begin, you need to ask yourself these questions to define the parameters of this project:

➤ Who is going to help collect photographs, old letters, and memorabilia?

➤ Who is going to help compile it into an album?

➤ How many albums are you completing—one large one or as many as it takes?

➤ Who and how are you doing the documentation in the album? Maybe you need to conduct oral interviews and transcribe them into words for the album.

➤ Do you have a budget?

➤ What is your target completion date?

➤ What about the design of the book? Do you want to treat each page individually or do you want the entire album to have the same design elements, such as color, embellishments, and fonts?

➤ Where will you work on the project—a central place or in bits and pieces?

*Friends are definitely the spice of life.*

Once you have answered these questions, you are ready to begin the process. The same basic process applies here as with other albums. As a review, here are some guidelines:

1. Gather, gather, gather all the items to go into the scrapbook: photos, love letters, travel brochures, important documents, ticket stubs, dried flowers, anything at all that will help this album be extraordinary. Don't forget to take pictures of important items, such as a wedding dress, homes, collections, defining possessions. These items help the pictures come to life as they add dimension.

2. Organize the items in the order in which they will be put in the album. Use a file folder system to store it if you are including a lot of large documents. If you are dividing up the project, this would be the point to give it to those who are doing certain parts.

3. One important element of this project that is easily overlooked is the documentation and the stories. This is the point where you will gather documentation and stories. As you get

**Shortcuts**

If you are doing an album for someone's birthday, let's say Grandma's 80th, it is a fun idea to give pictures to all of the family and extended family and ask them to do some scrapbook pages with these pictures and pictures they have. Have the families write down their favorite memories of this relative, too.

information, you can add it to the corrsponding section in your file folders. Try interviewing neighbors, close friends, and family members to get a variety of information on certain events. Use a tape recorder or take down notes. If you are dividing this project, it might be a good idea to make each person responsible for documenting their own section, or you can have one central person in charge of this.

4. Now begins the design and compilation of the album. Please remember that you want to showcase the photos and the stories, so use these items as your focal point. Add embellishments that will reinforce the story and add to it.

5. After you have the album pages designed and compiled, add the finishing touches. You can divide the album into sections or time periods using divider pages or title pages. Another suggestion is to customize the cover of the album. Cover it with fabric, put a picture of the couple on the cover—do anything you can to customize it.

One issue for you to consider before you give it away is whether you want to color copy it for you and other family members. You might all enjoy having this priceless gift.

# Beyond Scrapbooks

As I've mentioned, scrapbooking materials can be used to make all sorts of fun craft projects. Here are just a few.

## *Creating Dazzling Posters*

Does being asked to create a poster for the school carnival send you into a frenzy? There's no need to worry. Simply use the basic layout rules and all your scrapbook tools to make it an easy job.

Creating a border is the first step in creating a dazzling poster. Just be sure your border is in scale with your poster. Next, you'll need to write any information that is needed. Do this freehand or with letter templates. Now you get to decorate with large stickers, die cuts, or shapes traced from templates. Keep your creations to three or four colors, and you're set.

**Shortcuts**

There are limited products available for doing pages for old black-and-white photographs. You want to stick with the more classic, subtle colors and limit your embellishments.

**Shortcuts**

If you need large letters for your poster, you can enlarge templates by photocopying them.

**Sticky Points**

When making a poster, it's a good idea to create a preliminary sketch. You don't want to find out halfway through your project that there isn't enough room to write "Mrs. Zimmerman's first-grade class" on one line!

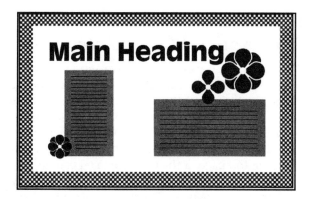

*Use this layout plan to make an eye-catching poster.*

## Wait a Minute, Mr. Postman—Make Your Own Greeting Cards

Why spend money on cards from the store when you can make your own for less? Handmade cards tell people that you care about them. These can be as simple as cardstock with a photo of you and your family adhered to it or as complex as a watercolor, embossed, floral thank-you note. Whatever the occasion, it's worth it to send a handmade card. After you have committed to scrapbooking, you have many of the supplies you'll need.

Decide on the size you want to use and check your envelope selection if you are going to use an envelope to send your card. Then, depending on the occasion, select the type of embellishment you want. Decorate and include an appropriate message. Kids love to make cards, so let them do it with you.

*All of these great cards are made of scrapbook materials.*

## Eight Days a Week— Personalized Calendars

Think how fun it would be to have a calendar with your favorite photos in it instead of the free calendar they give at the bank. Just think, you could glance at *your* puppy doing the macarena while you mark down your dentist appointments. Many copy stores make personalized calendars with your photos by enlarging the photos to fill the top page of the calendar. You can do this or try laying out the scrapbook and having them copy these onto the calendar. There are companies that offer premade kits for these calendars, and some sell blank calendars already bound. You can also print your own blank calendar right on the computer.

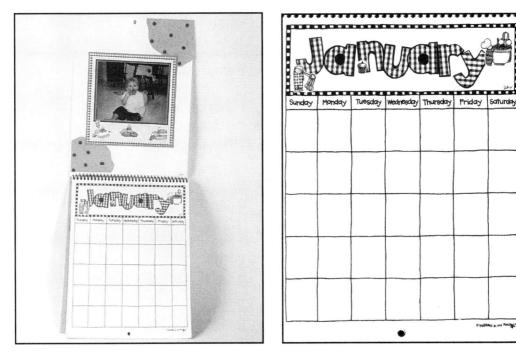

*You could color copy these and give them away as gifts to family members.*

# Cooking Up Something Special—Recipe Books

My mommade homemade macaroni & cheese for us when we were growing up, and I loved it. When I was suffering from morning sickness when I was pregnant with my first child, the only thing that sounded palatable was mom's macaroni & cheese. I called her for the recipe, but she was gone for the day, and my dad didn't have the faintest idea where my mom stashed it. She called me that evening with the recipe, and I cooked it right away. When I tasted it, I felt instantly better. Now that's what I call comfort food!

That incident prompted me to create a collection of favorite recipes. I jotted the recipes in a spiral binder, but the pages got ripped, and the book eventually fell apart. That was the end of that project—until I saw a customer in the store bring in a beautiful family cookbook she had created for her family. In addition to wonderful recipes, her book included photos of the family around the table enjoying meals together.

Some simple steps for you to follow to create your own personalized cookbook:

➤ Collect all the recipes to be included.

➤ Organize them in categories. This could be the obvious ones, such as recipe types (desserts, entrees), or you could do it according to family, time period, or occasion.

➤ Select size for recipe book. Do you want to do an 8$\frac{1}{2}$-by-11 album with protectors and room for pictures and stories, or do you just want to include the recipe with a note or two? If so, select smaller albums.

➤ Decide what extras you are going to add, such as photos or family stories, and put these in order with the recipes.

➤ Decide on how to decorate. Do you want to select decorated recipe cards and leave it at that? Or do you want to treat it like a scrapbook page?

Now that you have everything gathered and a basic idea of how you want to organize, get started and enjoy.

**Shortcuts**

If you have original copies of favorite recipes printed in someone's handwriting, photocopy them and include them in your book.

**Shortcuts**

You may want to consider compiling all of your favorite recipes for family and friends and giving the recipe book to them as a thoughtful surprise gift. It might spur them to compile their own recipes and hand them down or inspire them to cook you something yummy!

Here is the fastest, easiest way to put together a personal cookbook:

➤ Twenty-five great recipes divided into five categories

➤ Five Frame-Ups to use as category dividers

➤ Assortment of embellishments to go with the categories (optional)

➤ Cardstock on which to mount recipes and embellishments

➤ Binding done at a local copy store

**Shortcuts**

Include all favorite recipes, no matter how mundane. If you loved Rice Krispy treats as a child, go ahead and put the recipe in.

Mount recipes onto cardstock the same size as the Frame-Ups. Add embellishments to individual recipes as desired. Combine recipes into categories and place behind Frame-Up dividers. Add a title page. Take to the copy store and have it bound. Give away to see the delicious reaction.

You can take this idea further by including bits of family history in the cookbook along with recipes. This is a great forum for the story about Uncle Ted having his jaw wired shut for six weeks and living off Grandma's cheese soup. Just make sure to keep a copy of this book for yourself—you don't want to get caught without a macaroni and cheese recipe!

*A delicious, simple, and rewarding recipe book.*

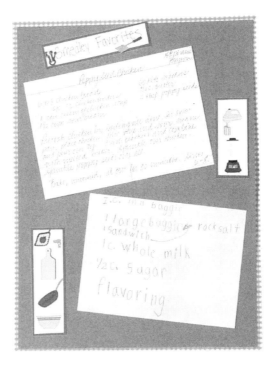

# Fun Motivational Charts for Kids

How many of us need to encourage the children around us to remember to do their jobs? I hate to nag my children and have found that giving them control works much better than constantly nagging them. As grown-ups, we know how frustrating it can be to work for someone who doesn't specify what your job is—every day you are guessing what task you should be completing. It is much better to work in a situation where you know what is expected of you and when it needs to be accomplished. The same goes for children—they prefer knowing what is expected of them and when they are supposed to be done. They also enjoy visual reminders and rewards. I have found that it works best to customize your job chart according to your family's needs. It doesn't have to be fancy, but you can dress it up with scrapbook supplies.

These projects don't have to be limited to job charts. Try creating fun reading charts or a chart that motivates kids to complete difficult tasks. I have a child who had a difficult time sleeping in his own room when he was small. Though we tried everything, we still weren't making any headway. We created a chart for him, and every night that he slept in his bed the entire night, he placed a sticker on his chart. After so many stickers, he got rewards. That worked wonders for us.

Here are a few things to consider when designing your charts:

➤ What are age-appropriate tasks?

➤ What are age-appropriate rewards?

➤ What size chart will you need to put everything on?

➤ Where will you place the chart upon completion?

➤ How will the child mark his accomplishments? Will you use stickers or checkmarks?

➤ If giving rewards to the child, do you want to list the rewards on the same chart?

### Shortcuts

Place job charts somewhere central, such as on the fridge or by the child's bedroom door.

These questions will help direct you in deciding what you are going to need to include. I like to use stickers and embellishments in the place where I list the jobs and chores and then let the kids check in the boxes for the days of the week when they have completed their tasks. At the bottom of the charts, I list different rewards in a unique and fun fashion. The secret to these charts is dressing them up a little bit to make them more fun but not creating a work of art that is only going to be used temporarily.

### Sticky Points

To make sure kids don't rip or color on their chart, laminate it for extra protection. The reward stickers will go right on top of the lamination.

*Scrapbooking products can add flair to your job charts.*

| Jobs | Monday | Tuesday | Wednesday | Thursday | Friday | Saturday | Sunday | |
|------|--------|---------|-----------|----------|--------|----------|--------|--|
| make bed | | | | | | | | |
| pick up toys | | | | | | | | |
| set table | | | | | | | | |
| feed pets | | | | | | | | |
| brush teeth | | | | | | | | |

## The Least You Need to Know

➤ Give yourself plenty of time to organize your supplies for a gift album and delegate tasks to other friends or family members if at all possible.

➤ All you need are blank calendar sheets, fun photos, and a little creativity to create a keepsake calendar.

➤ Don't let those old recipes be forgotten—preserve them for everyone.

➤ Motivate your children to accomplish their jobs with a fun chart to remind them.

# Resource Guide

The following companies, organizations, and Web sites offer scrapbookers products and information.

## Archival Quality Items

**Light Impressions**
439 Monroe Ave.
Rochester, NY 14603-0940
1-800-828-6216
fax 1-800-828-5539

**Restoration Source**
P.O. Box 9384
Salt Lake City, UT 84109-0384
1-801-278-7880
fax 1-801-278-3015

**Archival Mist**
1-800-416-2665

**Creative Memories**
2815 Clearwater Road
P.O. Box 1839
St. Cloud, MN 566302-1839
www.creative-memories.com
1-800-468-9335

## Direct Sales of Scrapbook Supplies

**Creative Xpress!!/Provo Craft retail**
295 West Center
Provo, UT 84601-4430
www.creativexpress.com
1-800-563-8679
fax 1-801-373-1446

**D.O.T.S./I Love Remembering**
Close to My Heart
738 East Quality Drive
American Fork, UT 84003
www.iloveremembering.com
1-800-965-0924
fax 1-801-763-8188

## Direct Sales and Quarterly Magazine

*Keeping Memories Alive*
P.O. Box 728
Spanish Fork, UT 84660-0728
www.scrapbooks.com
1-800-419-4949

## Retail Mail Order

**Pebbles in My Pocket**
P.O. Box 1506
Orem, UT 84059-1506
www.pebblesinmypocket.com
1-800-438-8153

**Memories**
P.O. Box 1188
Centerville, UT 84014
1-800-286-5263
Wholesale/retail catalog
www.memories.com

## Albums

### Hiller Industries
631 North 400 West
Salt Lake City, UT 84103
1-800-492-5179

### Tie Me To The Moon
23011 Moulton Pkwy. #1-8
Laguna Hills, CA 92653
1-888-509-2193
(albums)

### Memories Forever—Westrim Crafts
P.O. Box 3879
Canoga Park, CA 91313
Chatsworth, CA 91311
1-800-727-2727
(albums/scrapbook supplies)

## Magazines

### *Creating Keepsakes Scrapbook*
P.O. Box 1106
Orem, UT 84059-9956
1-888-247-5282
www.creatingkeepsakes.com

### *Memory Makers*
475 W. 115th Ave. #6
Denver, CO 80234
1-800-366-6465
www.memorymakers.com

### *PaperKuts*
P.O. Box 697
Spanish Fork, UT 84660-0697
1-800-320-0633

## Manufacturers

### Apple of Your Eye
P.O. Box 521984
Salt Lake City, UT
84152-1984
(design book)

### Paper Adventures
P.O. Box 04393
Milwaukee, WI 53204-0393
1-800-727-0699
www.paperadventures.com

### In My Mind's Eye
P.O. Box 1012
Bountiful, UT 84011
1-800-665-5116
www.frame-ups.com

### Mrs. Grossman's
P.O. Box 4467
Petaluma, CA 94955
www.mrsgrossmans.com
1-800-429-4549

### EK Success
611 Industrial Rd.
Carlstadt, NJ 07072
1-800-524-1349

### Platte Productions
6660 Sausalito Ave.
West Hills, CA 91307
1-818-992-0529

## Makers of Crop-In Style Bag

### Cropper Hopper
8855 Cypress Woods Drive
Olive Branch, MS 38654
(storage items)

**Stampin' Up**
Kanab, UT
www.stampinup.com
1-800-STAMPUP
(retail stamps)

**Sticker Planet**
10736 Jefferson Boulevard
Sticker Station 503
Culver City, CA 90230
www.stickerplanet.com
1-800-557-8678

**Quick Cuts**
1-714-671-9438
www.puzzlemates.com
(maker of puzzle mates templates)

**Spot Pen**
P.O. Box 1559
Las Cruces, NM 88004
1-505-523-8820
(manufacturer)

**Fiskars Inc.**
7811 W. Stewart Ave.
Wausau, WI 54401
www.fiskars.com
1-800-950-0203
(manufacturer)

**Frances Meyer Inc.**
P.O. Box 3088
Savannah, GA 31402
www.francesmeyer.com
1-800-372-6237
(manufacturer)

**Cock-a-Doodle Designs**
3759 West 2340 South, Suite D
Salt Lake City, UT
1-800-262-9727

## Page Toppers and More

**Amy Wilson Designs**
P.O. Box 123
West Jordan, UT
1-801-280-3227 (Fax)

## Clip Art

**Hot Off The Press**
1250 NW Third
Dept. PK8-99
Canby, OR 97013
1-503-266-9102

## Trade Associations

**International Scrapbook Trade Association (ISTA)**
Hobby Industries Association (HIA)
P.O. Box 348
Elmwood Park, NJ 07407-2712
1-201-797-0657

**The Heartland Paper Co.**
Retail Store
616 West 2600 South
Bountiful, UT 84010
www.theheartlandpaperco.com
(online store)

## Web Sites

**Current Inc.**
www.currentcatalog.com

**Cut 'N Fun**
www.cutnfun.com

**Design Originals**
(craft supplies and books)
www.d-originals.com

**Dogbyte Development**
www.dogbyte.com

**Inspire Graphics**
www.inspiregraphics.com

**Matters Of The Heart**
www.mattersoftheheart.com

**The Paper Web**
www.artpaper.com

**The Scrap Patch**
www.scrappatch.com

**Seems Like Yesterday**
www.angelfire.com/biz2/
SeemsLikeYesterday

**Family Photo Historian**
www.geocities.com/Heartland/2878

**Scrapbook Addict**
http//members.tripod.com/~tln123/
luv2scrap.html

# Suggested Reading

Anderson, Marilyn. *Scrapbook Your Family Memories*. Addison, TX: Sonburn, 1997.

Bearnson, Lisa, and Gayle Humphreys. *Joy of Scrapbooking*. Oxmoor House, Inc., and Leisure Arts, Inc., 1998.

Carroll, Souzzann Y.H. *A Lasting Legacy: Scrapbooks and Photo Albums That Touch the Heart*. Bountiful, UT: Living Vision Press, 1998.

*Design and Layout Ideas for Scrapbook Pages*. St. Cloud, MN: Creative Memories, 1997.

Dixon, Janice. *The Art of Writing Scrapbook Stories*. Mt. Olympus Publishing, 1998.

Eastman Kodak Company, Ed. *The Joy of Photography*. Reading, Massachusetts: Addison-Wesley Publishing Co., 1991.

Greene, Bob, and D.G. Fulford. *To Our Children's Children: Preserving Family Histories for Generations to Come*. New York, NY: Doubleday, 1993.

Hart, Cynthia, Lina Morielli, Ryn Williams, and Ellen Liberles. *Cynthia Hart's Scrapbook Workshop*. Workman Publishing Company, 1998.

Hite, Mary Margaret, Tar Choate, and Katie Hacker, Eds. *The Ultimate Book of Memory Albums*. Leisure Arts, 1997.

Jayes, Kathleen, and the Scrapbook Guild. *The Simple Art of Scrapbooking: Tips, Techniques, and 30 Special Album Ideas for Creating Memories That Last a Lifetime*. Dell Books, 1998.

Julian, Stacy. *Core Composition*. Salt Lake City, UT: Apple of Your Eye, 1997.

Norton, Don. *Composing Your Life Story*. Orem, UT: Don Norton, 1990.

Paulsen, Diedre M., and Jeanne S. English. *Preserving the Precious*. Salt Lake City, Utah: Restoration Source, 1988.

Rinner, Jill A. *Paper Doll Collection*. Pleasant Grove, UT: Red Point Publishing, 1999.

Tyson, Sandy. *Alphabet Soup*. Salt Lake City, UT: Wasatch Mountain Design, 1998.

# Words for Posterity

**acid**   A substance found in most paper that fades photographs.

**adhesive**   Any substance used to make items stick to each other (for example, glue, paste, tape, or reversible adhesives).

**album**   Blank book used to store photographs and scrapbook pages.

**analogous colors**   Colors that are next to each other on the color wheel.

**aperture**   The opening in a camera that lets in light. The aperture opens and closes when the shutter is released.

**archival**   Term used to describe a product or technique used in preserving artifacts, photos, memorabilia, and other items.

**basic templates**   Templates in basic shapes (ovals, circles, and so on).

**blending pencil**   Tool used to blend colored pencils to create shades of a color.

**bold colors**   Bright, high-intensity colors.

**buffered**   Term used to describe products capable of maintaining the basicity of a solution. Buffered paper prevents acid from moving from a photo to paper.

**calligraphy**   Formal, old-fashioned lettering.

**calligraphy pen**   Pen with a slanted tip designed to write calligraphy.

**cardstock**   Thick, sturdy paper available in a variety of weights.

**CK OK**   Creating Keepsakes Okay. Scrapbooking seal of approval; items that have the CK OK are considered safe to use in scrapbooks.

**clip art**   Art purchased in book or software form with pictures that can be applied to scrapbook pages.

**collage**   An artistic composition made of various materials (such as paper, cloth, or wood) and glued onto a surface.

**color wheel**   Shows color relationships and placement.

**complementary colors**   Colors that are opposite each other on a color wheel.

**conservationist**   Someone who studies archival methods and techniques and uses them to preserve artifacts, artworks, or precious documents.

**corner-edger scissors**   Scissors that cut corners. Each pair creates four different types of corners.

**corrugated paper**   Thick, wavy cardstock available in many colors.

**crop**   1. To cut or trim a photo. 2. A scrapbooking party hosted by an expert who shares techniques, products, and information with the group.

**cutouts**   Designs that are meant to be cut out. They don't have perforated edges.

**deacidification spray**   Spray that neutralizes acid in newspaper clippings, certificates, and other documents.

**decorative scissors**   Scissors with a decorative pattern on the blade.

**die-cut designs**   Paper designs cut from die cut machines. Paper is placed on the die and pressure is applied either by rolling or pressing down on the handle.

**double-mount**   To place a photo on two background papers.

**embellishment**   Any scrapbooking extras, such as stickers, die cuts, and punches that enhance scrapbooking pages.

**emboss**   To create a raised surface by applying heat or pressure.

**encapsulation**   A method of displaying three-dimensional memorabilia and protecting nearby items from acid contained in the memorabilia. Items are encased in stable plastics.

**favorites file**   A personal book of ideas and layouts.

**film speed**   Refers to a film's sensitivity to light. Lower-speed films are less sensitive; use these on a bright, sunny day. Higher-speed films are more sensitive; use these in low-light situations.

**fine-tip point pens**   Pens with extremely small tips good for doodling and precise lettering. Pens tips range from .005 mm to .08 mm. Good for journaling and lettering.

**fine and chisel pen**   This pen has a fine tip (0.5 mm) and a chisel tip (6.0 mm). The fine tip is good for lettering, and the chisel tip is very versatile.

**focal point**   The element of a design where lines converge. The eye is naturally drawn to the focal point in an image.

**gel-based rollers**   Pens with pigment ink.

**genealogy**   The study of the descent of a person, family, or group from an ancestor. Many people who wish to create a family tree start by researching their family's genealogy.

**general pattern paper**   Paper with patterns, such as stripes, dots, plaids, that is made to be used for any occasion.

**gift album**   A compilation of photos and mementos created with a person or event in mind.

**handmade paper**   Paper made by hand that is often rough and uneven in texture. There are sometimes flowers or leaves in the paper, which add to the natural look.

**handmade scraps**   Embellishments made from layered-looking die cuts.

**heading**   The caption or title that explains the theme of a layout.

**heritage**   Traditions passed down from generation to generation.

**idea books**   Books usually about one aspect of scrapbooking. Some are written for particular themes, such as wedding, baby, or pets, while others are devoted to a particular product, like stickers, die cuts, or templates.

**intensity**   The strength of a color based on how true it is to the primary color.

**journaling**   Any words you write in your book, from titles and captions to long descriptions, poems, or stories.

**journaling templates**   Templates with space left for writing.

**layout**   The grouping of pages in your scrapbook that go together. Some layouts fit on one page, most fit on two, and some are put on panoramic layouts.

**letter templates**   Templates in the shape of letters of the alphabet.

**light refraction**   Light bent through a prism that shows the colors of the visible light spectrum: red, orange, yellow, green, blue, indigo, and violet.

**lignin**   A naturally occurring acid substance in wood that breaks down over time. Paper with lignin is not suitable for archival projects.

**mass-merchandising store**   Stores that sell a large variety of products from sundries to automotive tools to craft supplies.

**master family album**   Holds pictures of everyone in the family and family documents, typically in chronological order.

**memorabilia**   Certificates, documents, and other items that tell a story. Memorabilia can include souvenirs from trips and mementos from special occasions or historical events.

**monochromatic color scheme**   Employs different values of the same color.

**mount**   To adhere a photo, embellishment, or other item to another piece of paper.

**muted colors**   Subdued tints or shades of colors that tend to be more suitable for backgrounds.

**oval croppers**   Paper trimmers that cut paper and photographs into ovals.

**page protectors**   Plastic sheets that display and protect pages.

**page toppers**   Hand-drawn illustrated phrases in bright colors meant to be used as titles at the top of pages.

**page exchange**   Participants are invited to create a page to share with other scrapbookers. Often, a theme is given, such as Halloween. Each participant brings enough copies of an original page to trade with the others.

**paint pens**   Pens with soft, brush-like tips. The amount of ink dispensed is controlled by the pressure that is applied to the tip.

**paper trimmers**   Paper-cutting tools used by placing paper, lining it up on a grid, and moving down a blade.

**pass the chocolate**   A phrase commonly spoken by members of a scrapbooking club.

**pattern paper**   Paper with designs repeated on the entire page.

**perforated punches**   Shapes that the scrapbooker can use as embellishments on a page by punching out on the perforations.

**pH level**   Measurement that tells a scrapbooker how acidic or basic something is. For scrapbooking, you want to use products with a pH level of seven or above.

**pH testing pen**   Used to test the acidity of paper. The pen mark changes colors, depending on the level of acid present.

**Photo Activity Test (P.A.T.)**   This test, created by the American National Standards Institute, determines if a product will damage photos. If a product passes the P.A.T., it is safe to use with your photos.

**photo corners**   Paper with adhesive on the back used to adhere photos to a page on the corners. Used to adhere photos in scrapbooks and photo albums without applying adhesive directly to the photo.

**photo display album**   A combination of special scrapbook pages along with photos displayed in regular sheet protectors.

**photo pool**   The selection of pictures available to choose from.

**polypropylene, polyethylene, and polyester**   Stable plastics that are safe for photos.

**post-bound albums**   Albums that are held together with metal posts that run through the pages.

**pre-embossed paper**   Paper with a raised design. Some of it is thick, like cardstock, and some is vellum.

**primary colors**   Red, yellow, and blue. These are the base from which all other colors are created.

**product swap**   A scrapbookers' swap meet where the host gathers up duplicates of products or tools that she doesn't use anymore and calls up some friends. They bring their unwanted scrapbooking items to trade. After it's done, you've got a clean closet and tons of new products to put in it.

**punch**   1. A tool used to create small shapes. 2. The shapes created by the punches.

**puzzle templates**   Templates in puzzle shapes.

**PVC (Polyvinyl Chlorides)**   Because this substance is harmful to photos, scrapbookers should avoid it and use products that are composed of polypropylene.

**red-eye pen**   Used to take the "red eye" out of flash photographs.

**reversible adhesive**   An adhesive that can be undone.

**rubber stamp**   A detailed, intricate design cut out of rubber and mounted on wood or foam. A design is made by applying color to the rubber and imprinting that on paper.

**scrapbook**   An artfully arranged collection of photographs, memorabilia, and journaling that's fun to look at.

**scrapbooking club**   A group of scrapbookers that meet regularly to encourage each other and compare books.

**scrapbooking magazine**   A magazine devoted to scrapbooking, featuring layout ideas, product uses, and purchasing information.

**scroll and brush pens**   Pens that have one tip for coloring and one for writing.

**secondary colors**   Colors created by blending primary colors. Orange, green, and violet are the secondary colors created by mixing combination of red, yellow, and blue.

**shade**   A color with black added to it.

**shape cutters**   Tools designed to cut shapes, such as ovals and circles. The cutters can be adjusted to created different sizes of these shapes.

**specialty paper books**   Books that contain information about different papers, both pattern paper and plain. Some may come with extras, such as templates.

**specialty templates**   Cut-out shapes that match a theme.

**specific pattern paper**   Pattern paper with a themed pattern, such as weddings, vacations, or holidays.

**spiral-bound books**   Albums that are secured with a metal or plastic spiral binding running up the side.

**stationery**   Paper with a decorative border that is blank on the inside.

**sticker**   An adhesive decorative accent ranging in size from a few centimeters across to a full page.

**strap-binding albums**   Albums secured with plastic straps that run through a holder directly on the pages and keep the book in place.

**tape roller**   A device that distributes tape on the back of photos and scrapbooking pages.

**template**   A stencil used to trace shapes onto scrapbook pages or photos.

**tertiary colors**   Also called intermediate colors, these are blends of primary and secondary colors. Colors like red-orange and blue-green are tertiary colors.

**theme**   The overall emphasis of a page or scrapbook.

**theme album**   A scrapbook devoted to one idea. Some popular theme albums focus on birthdays, weddings, and school days.

**three-ring binders**   Albums with three metal rings of varying sizes to attach the album covers and hold pages.

**time capsule**   A container holding historical records or objects that represent a culture and that is deposited for preservation.

**tint**   A color that has had white mixed in.

**title sheets**   Pages with a variety of premade titles. They are often used as the starting point for a section in a scrapbook.

**tole painting**   Painting on wood, typically done in a rustic style and depicting country scenes.

**triad**   A group of three colors that form a triangle on the color wheel.

**vellum**   A lightweight, translucent paper.

**velveteen**   An archival paper with a fabric-like, velvety texture.

**vivelle**   An archival paper with a fabric-like texture similar to a terry cloth towel.

**wax, or grease, pencils**   Soft pencils designed for use on photographs.

**wide-edge scissors**   Decorative-edge scissors that make a cut that is five times deeper than normal scissors.

**workshop**   A class usually held at a scrapbooking store and taught by an expert. Participants bring photos and pages to work on and get advice from the instructor.

**xyron machine**   A machine that applies adhesive to pages and can also laminate.

# Index